The Orestes Plays

EURIPIDES

The Orestes Plays

Translated, with Introduction and Notes, by

Cecelia Eaton Luschnig

Hackett Publishing Company, Inc.
Indianapolis/Cambridge

Printed in the United States of America

18 17 16 15 14 13   1 2 3 4 5 6 7

For further information, please address:

Hackett Publishing Company, Inc.
    P.O. Box 44937
    Indianapolis, IN 46244-0937

    www.hackettpublishing.com

For information regarding performance rights, please email us at
Permissions@hackettpublishing.com

The translation of *Electra* featured in this volume first appeared in *The
Electra Plays* (Hackett 2009). Minor revisions have been introduced in
this volume.

Cover design by Brian Rak
Text design by Meera Dash
Composition by William Hartman

Library of Congress Cataloging-in-Publication Data

Euripides.
        [Works. Selections. English]
        The Orestes plays / Euripides ; translated with introduction
    & notes by Cecelia Eaton Luschnig.
            pages. cm.
        Includes bibliographical references.
        ISBN 978-1-60384-932-6 (pbk.) —
        ISBN 978-1-60384-933-3 (cloth)
        1. Euripides—Translations into English. 2. Euripides—
    Criticism and interpretation. 3. Greek drama (Tragedy)—
    Translations into English. I. Luschnig, C. A. E. II. Title.
    PA3975.A2 2013
    882'.01—dc23
                                            2012037634

Contents

For the Finlay women,
my three splendid cousins,
Anne, Leila, and Susan

Introduction

Late Euripidean Plays

Euripides began his career as a tragedian in 455 B.C.E. The plays of his earliest years are now lost. *Alcestis* (produced in 438) is the first of his dramas to survive. The tragedies in this volume, *Electra, Iphigenia among the Tauri,* and *Orestes,* are dated between 422 (at the earliest: *Electra* is variously placed between that date and 413, with a later date favored) and 408. Of these, only *Orestes* is firmly dated (to 408) by external evidence.[1] This date justifies our classifying these three plays as late Euripidean tragedies. They come at a time in the history of Athens when the city was weary of the decades-long Peloponnesian War that had begun in 431 and did not end until 405, the year after the playwright's death. The city was further shaken by a series of political upheavals, the heavy losses sustained in the failed invasion of Sicily (413), followed by oligarchic revolutions resulting in the coup of the Four Hundred, which overthrew the Athenian democracy (in 411). Although Euripides and the other Athenian tragedians rarely made direct reference to contemporary events in their works, as poets and citizens they cannot have escaped being affected by the constant political, social, and human crises. More or less distinct reflections of the outside world are to be seen in the tragedies.

Treatment of Orestes in Homer, Aeschylus, and Sophocles

Because Greek tragedy so often opens a dialogue with the past, a brief look at Orestes in earlier literature will help orient the reader and bring into focus the departures that might have surprised the original audience of Euripides' versions.

---

1. A note in the *scholia,* or ancient commentaries, tells us that it was performed in the archonship of Diocles, known to have been 408 B.C.E. The other two plays are dated relative to one another by a comparison of metrics.

Homer

In Homer's *Odyssey*, the story of the murder of Agamemnon, the usurpation of Aegisthus, and the return of Orestes is told several times with varying amounts of detail. Orestes is an exemplar of heroic behavior to Odysseus' son Telemachus as he wonders what to do about his mother's suitors, who are devouring his father's household.[2] Aegisthus, who usurped the throne after killing Agamemnon, is an example, too, of foolishness on the part of mortals in spite of warning from the gods. At the *Odyssey*'s very first Olympian council, Zeus is troubled by thoughts of Aegisthus' crime and relates how Hermes was sent to Aegisthus:

> To tell him not to kill the man and marry his wife,
> Or Agamemnon's son, Orestes, would pay him back
> When he came of age and wanted his inheritance [that is, his land].
> (*Odyssey* 1.44–46, tr. Lombardo = 39–41)[3]

This story is referred to several times: at 3.193 ff. by Nestor, who emphasizes the importance of a man leaving a son to carry out his interests; at 3.232 ff. by Athena, who first brings Clytemnestra into the plot (Agamemnon died "by the treachery of Aegisthus and of his own wife"); at 4.92 by Menelaus, who also mentions Clytemnestra; and at 11.410 by Agamemnon's ghost, who relates the tale to Odysseus in the Underworld. Nestor speaks of Orestes' return in the most detail:

> Having killed the son of Atreus
> And subdued the people, he reigned
> For seven years in gold-crusted Mycenae.
> In the eighth year, though, he met his doom
> In the person of Orestes, come back from Athens.
> Orestes killed his father's murderer,
> The treacherous Aegisthus, and, having killed him,
> Invited all the Argives to a funeral feast
> For his hateful mother and her craven lover.

---

2. In Euripides' *Orestes*, by contrast, Orestes uses Telemachus as a comparison (588–90): Telemachus did not have to kill his mother because she remained faithful to her husband.

3. The quotations from the *Odyssey* are from Stanley Lombardo's translation.

On that very day Menelaus arrived,
Bearing all the treasure his ships could hold.
(3.337–47, tr. Lombardo = 304–12)

The details of Aegisthus' seven-year rule and Orestes' exile (in
Athens, according to Homer, though the tragedians place him in
Phocis at the home of Strophius, Pylades' father), and of Menelaus'
absence, noted earlier in the same speech (285–302), and his
arrival in Argos too late to save his brother or prevent the matricide (311–12) come up in the tragedies. It is not clear in this or any
of the Homeric passages how Clytemnestra died. Aegisthus is the
murderer of Agamemnon; Clytemnestra is at most an accomplice.
Quite different from the setting in Aeschylus and Euripides (where
Agamemnon is killed in his bath), the scene of Agamemnon's murder in Homer is a feast (4.534–35, 11.410–11; cf. Sophocles, *Electra*
204) to which Aegisthus invited him:

So he brought Agamemnon up to the palace
Unaware of his doom and slaughtered him
The way an ox is slaughtered at the stall.
(4.561–63, tr. Lombardo = 534–35)

Between Homer and tragedy, two poems of the epic cycle, *Cypria*
and *Nostoi* (of the mid-eighth century B.C.E.) that survive mainly
in a summary by Proclus (a philosopher of the fifth century C.E.),
Stesichorus' *Oresteia* (sixth century B.C.E.), of which only a few
fragments survive, and a victory ode by Pindar (c. 522–443) are
our sources for the development of the legend of Agamemnon's
homecoming and its aftermath. The *Cypria*, which narrates the
events leading up to the Trojan War, includes Agamemnon's sacrifice of Iphigenia (not mentioned by Homer). The *Nostoi* in its
account of the heroes' returns mentions the fact that Agamemnon
brought Cassandra, the last of his concubines, home with him.
Both of these actions add to Clytemnestra's motivation for killing her husband in some of the tragedies. Stesichorus' poem
mentions Clytemnestra's guilty dream (which comes up again in
Aeschylus' *Libation Bearers* and Sophocles' *Electra*) and names
Electra, a major character in tragedy, who is not even included in
Homer's list of the daughters of Agamemnon (see Gregory 2009,
pp. xii–xiii). Pindar's eleventh *Pythian* ode alludes briefly to the
Orestes legend, but packs a lot of detail into a few lines (11.15–25):

Orestes' friendship with Pylades, the saving of Orestes by his nurse (named there Arsinoe), Clytemnestra's guilt in the murders of both Cassandra and Agamemnon, and alternative motives for the murder (the slaughter of Iphigenia or Clytemnestra's sexual desire). Pindar also explicitly makes Orestes the killer of both his mother and Aegisthus (11.36–37).

Aeschylus

Aeschylus' *Oresteia,* the only surviving connected trilogy (three plays on the same legend produced together) from the fifth-century Athenian theater, was first staged in 458 and probably revived in the 420s not long before the productions of the *Electra* plays of Sophocles and Euripides. The *Oresteia* consists of *Agamemnon, The Libation Bearers,* and *The Furies (Eumenides).* I will not attempt to describe the magnificence of Aeschylus' masterpiece here, but only to catalogue various plot features pertinent to a discussion of Euripides' Orestes plays.

The Story

1. Agamemnon returns victorious from Troy. He is killed by his wife and her lover, Aegisthus.
2. Orestes returns from exile. He kills Aegisthus and his mother.
3. Orestes reaches Delphi, pursued by the Furies. A trial is arranged in Athens by Athena. Orestes is acquitted.

Some Details

Agamemnon takes place in front of the palace of Atreus in Mycenae. The play begins with the news that Troy has fallen. Midway through, Agamemnon returns and is welcomed by his wife. After enticing her husband inside to the bath she has prepared for him, abetted by Aegisthus, she kills him and his lover Cassandra. His cries are heard as Clytemnestra strikes him twice (1343, 1345 of the Greek); she strikes him a third time after he is dead (1386). The motives she herself gives for her action are his sacrifice of their daughter (1415–18); the fact that she hated him (1375) and loved Aegisthus (1435–56); her resentment of his many infidelities (1438–43). Her lust for power is strongly implied as a motive by the way she dominates the stage and intimidates the chorus. The chorus is made up of male citizens, giving it an explicit political role. The drama ends with the chorus showing its antipathy to Aegisthus and predicting the return of Orestes (1646–47, 1667).

Libation Bearers opens with the return of Orestes to the land and palace of his ancestors. At his father's tomb he offers a lock of his hair, a symbol of mourning, before catching sight of women (Electra with the chorus) coming out of the palace. He and Pylades withdraw from view, setting the scene for Electra to find the lock of hair and his footprint, tokens of recognition (which Euripides' Electra will mock in *Electra*). Orestes steps forward and the two siblings are reunited, the recognition confirmed by a weaving Electra had made for him. Orestes has come to avenge his father's death, relying on the oracle of Apollo (269–305). Brother and sister with the chorus now sing a long and violent song of mourning (the *kommos*) in which they invoke their father's spirit. Orestes learns that Electra and the chorus are bringing offerings from the palace (hence the play's title) to Agamemnon's tomb. They have been sent by Clytemnestra, who has been terrified by a dream that she suckled a snake that drew her blood. Orestes accepts the dream as referring to himself. Electra is sent inside. She has no further part in this drama. The plan for vengeance is simple (554): Orestes and Pylades will approach the palace as strangers and, once inside, kill Aegisthus. They are greeted by Clytemnestra. They tell her the false story that Orestes is dead. They are invited inside, but Aegisthus must be summoned from his estates. Upon his return he is quickly dispatched. His cry is heard from within (869). Orestes and his mother face each other. For a moment he hesitates (899–902, Meineck's translation):

ORESTES:
    Pylades, what should I do? How can I kill my own mother?

PYLADES:
    And then what becomes of the Oracles of Apollo
    declared at Delphi, or the unbreakable oaths we took?
    Better to be hated by every man on earth than hated by the gods.

Until this moment, Pylades had been silent. In the two *Electra* plays by Euripides and Sophocles, Pylades has a nonspeaking role, though in *Orestes* and *Iphigenia among the Tauri* he has plenty to say. With this encouragement, Orestes forces Clytemnestra into the palace and kills her. Orestes has little time to celebrate his equivocal victory. The Furies, whom he alone can see (1061), swarm at once to hound him and he is driven off the stage.

ORESTES:
> Lord Apollo! They are coming! Closing in!
> I can see their eyes dripping with blood!
>   (1057–58, tr. Meineck)

The Furies (*Eumenides*) opens at Apollo's temple in Delphi where
Orestes, already ritually purified, has come as a suppliant to beg
Apollo to save him from the Furies. Apollo sends him to Athens,
where he is to undergo a trial. The Furies, who form the chorus,
have been sleeping in the orchestra, an area of the theater for both
dancing and acting, and are now roused to their pursuit by the
ghost of Clytemnestra. Orestes reaches Athens, where Athena sets
up the first court for homicide. The jurors are Athenian citizens.
The case is prosecuted by the Furies and defended by Apollo on
behalf of Orestes. The result is a tie and Athena, presiding over
the court, casts the tie-breaking vote. Orestes departs to return to
his kingdom of Argos (777). The Furies, maintaining their role in
deterring the shedding of kindred blood, become the Eumenides
("Kindly Ones," a title used euphemistically by mortals to avoid
naming the dread goddesses) and enter a cleft in the earth (805)
where they are to be honored in cult. The play ends with a joyous
celebration of Athenian civilization.

Sophocles

Sophocles' *Electra* places Electra at the center of the action. She is
the one who waits at the scene of the murder of her father for the
avenger to come, living with his murderers. Like Aeschylus' version,
Sophocles' *Electra* is acted in front of the palace of Atreus, and
the murder of Clytemnestra is perpetrated inside. The play opens
with the return of Orestes to Argos with Pylades and the old slave
who raised him—*paidagogos*, "child-minder." (This character is
often called Tutor in English translations, though, despite its ety-
mological meaning, "tutor" has ceased to mean "guardian" in the
spoken tongue.) This Orestes is ready for vengeance and has a fully
worked out plan including an elaborate false report of his death.
After hearing a cry from within (which is the opening of Electra's
lament), he leaves the acting area to make libation at his father's
grave, which is to be imagined not far out of our view. Electra
now enters to begin her daily song of suffering in which she is
joined by the sympathetic chorus of women. Electra dominates the
scene from now until the end of the play. Her sister, Chrysothemis,

comes out with offerings for Agamemnon's tomb from her mother, who has been disturbed by a dream that Agamemnon has returned and planted his scepter, which in turn sprang to life. This gives Chrysothemis the opportunity to depart for the tomb, where she will find the offerings made by Orestes. In the meantime, however, during a bitter scene between Clytemnestra and her daughter, the old man from the prologue arrives and reports in detail the demise of Orestes (in a chariot race). Clytemnestra reacts ambiguously. Electra is devastated. When Chrysothemis returns with what she believes is good news—proof that Orestes has returned—her testimony is dismissed by Electra, who has heard the all-too-believable report of her brother's death. Electra tries and fails to persuade her sister to join her in the killing of Aegisthus. Before she can carry out her reckless plan, Orestes arrives carrying an urn that purports to contain his ashes. Her grief overcomes his scruples to remain incognito and he reveals himself, offering proof by showing her their father's signet ring. Their reunion is cut short by the need to perform the deed for which he has come. Electra stands outside the door, to filter the noises that are heard from inside. Clytemnestra cries out when she sees them, and when she is struck she shrieks the same words Aeschylus' Agamemnon used when Clytemnestra killed him (*Agamemnon* 1343, 1345; Sophocles, *Electra* 1415, 1416). Between Clytemnestra's two cries, Electra shouts:

> Hit her again! Make it twice if you're strong enough.
>
> (1415, tr. Woodruff)

Aegisthus returns (he is always away from the palace when Orestes arrives). Clytemnestra's body is revealed to him and he is finally forced into the palace to be killed. There is no explicit mention of Orestes being haunted by the Furies or of his having to undergo a criminal trial of any kind.

It is unknown which of the Electra plays, that of Sophocles or that of Euripides, was produced first. Good arguments can be made on either side (see, for example, Gregory 2009, pp. xxi–xxii; Roisman 2010, pp. 28–32). Both plays make abundant allusion to Aeschylus' *Oresteia*, but only one can allude to the other. The early nineteenth-century German poet and scholar August Wilhelm Schlegel proposed the idea that Euripides wrote his *Electra* in order to reject Aeschylus' optimistic interpretation, that Sophocles then wrote *his Electra* to bring the story back in line with its Homeric roots, and that Euripides wrote *Orestes* in answer to Sophocles. I do not see Schlegel's argument as persuasive: in my own opinion, the order of composition is likelier to have been: Sophocles' *Electra,* followed by Euripides' *Electra,* followed by Euripides' *Orestes.*

Unique Treatments of the Traditional Material in Euripides' Orestes Plays

In Euripides' *Electra* the setting is changed from the palace of Agamemnon to a poor farmer's small house in the Argive countryside. This has the effect of disorienting the audience and uncoupling the story from its heroic façade. Murder committed in a shack is just murder, a fact underscored by the adolescent snobbism of Orestes and Electra's ambivalence. In *Iphigenia among the Tauri,* Orestes' journey to the land of the Tauri and the escape of the siblings with the image of Artemis, which is not treated in any other extant tragedy, is probably an invention of Euripides. The audience would not know where the story is heading at first and is later deliberately misdirected. *Orestes* is full of incidents and characters that must have surprised the audience. The presence of Helen and Hermione, the plots on their lives, the large and vocal role of Pylades, not to mention the roles of Tyndareos and Helen's Phrygian slave, are unknown in other versions of Orestes' story.

Electra

In Euripides' *Electra,* Orestes returns to Argos, after growing up in exile, to avenge his father's murder. He kills Aegisthus under the guidance of an aged family retainer, and kills his mother with the help of his sister. This is not very far from what happens in Aeschylus' *Libation Bearers* or the *Electra* of Sophocles, though the order of the murders is reversed in the latter play. The difference is in the details. The drastic change in setting is accompanied by equally great changes in the characters. Except for the Farmer (a character from rural life, new to the legend and rare in Greek tragedy), they have the same names as their Aeschylean and Sophoclean counterparts. Without the nametags and the genealogies that go with them, however, they would be barely recognizable.

Electra, etymologically "the unwed," has been married off to a poor Argive farmer, hardly a type expected to be heard from in a tragedy. She has moved to center stage and is no longer the hesitant girl she had been in Aeschylus, where she was relegated back to the women's chambers after her part in the evocation of Agamemnon's ghost. On the other hand, though she does her share of complaining, Euripides' Electra is not the monomaniacal figure Sophocles turns her into, but a victim of jealousy toward her mother, both financial and sexual. She feels as sorry for herself as she does for her father and her brother, and bullies her reluctant brother into committing matricide. Understandably so: Electra is a young woman whose royal expectations have been cruelly disappointed. She has been deprived of her home and her brother, father, and mother. Her mother's lover gave her in marriage to a good man, who feels that his poverty makes him unworthy of his royal bride. He will not touch his wife, leaving her childless and without a place in society either as a marriageable girl or a married woman. Removed from the palace, she is left to mourn without even the satisfaction of being seen by her mother or Aegisthus (something Sophocles' more histrionic Electra glories in). The little generosity of spirit that she has left she shows to her husband, in sincerely desiring to make his life better by helping around the house (73–76), even if her motives are mixed, and in defending his honor (253, 261).

Sophocles' Orestes is single-minded. Euripides' Orestes is a complex mixture of hesitancy and resolution. He is often criticized for being a snobbish youth, uncertain of his identity, undecided about his mission, too cowardly to enter Argos and face his father's killers, in need of his sister's help and stronger personality to egg him on to act. In his first speech in the play, however, he speaks of his decision to take vengeance on his father's murderers (89). That decision does not change. But unlike the Orestes of Aeschylus or Sophocles, Euripides' Orestes has returned to Argive territory without a plan for how to take his revenge (614) and he is, in fact, looking for his sister (98) as helper and co-conspirator (100). That he remains incognito for so long may be understood as a sign of reluctance to do the deed and to take up the identity that must be his as soon as he is recognized. In forming a plan he needs the help of others, as he acknowledged at the beginning, but once the plan to kill Aegisthus is made, he does not hesitate, but sets out at once to confront his victim (669). Before killing his mother he shows the same reluctance as Aeschylus' Orestes (*Libation Bearers* 899–902) and in fact questions the oracle (*Electra* 962–81), something his Aeschylean counterpart is dissuaded from doing by Pylades in *Libation Bearers*.

The characters in Euripides' *Electra,* both major and minor, are shown in new roles and new settings that take away some of the respectability the story has acquired from being a traditional tale from the heroic past. Clytemnestra, for example, is not the figure of awe and authority who controls the stage in Aeschylus' *Agamemnon,* nor the cruel Sophoclean harridan. It was Clytemnestra who prevented Aegisthus from killing Electra (28). In her one scene, she seems genuinely concerned for her daughter's sorry state (1107–8), and even shows some contrition for her own past misdeeds (1105–6, 1109–11). Aegisthus, for all the paranoia attributed to him by the Farmer and Electra, is a generous host, so unwary that he invites his killer to the feast and even provides him with the murder weapon (779, 784–87, 817, 836–37; see Luschnig, in Luschnig and Woodruff 2011, pp. xiii–xv.) After the murder the perpetrators come to the stark realization of the horror they have committed and regret the action that has consumed their consciousness for years.

Iphigenia among the Tauri

Iphigenia is a familiar figure in the tragic tradition: her death at Aulis, a sacrifice by her father Agamemnon to appease Artemis and calm the winds so that the fleet can sail to Troy, is described with pathos in the parodos (choral entrance song) of Aeschylus' *Agamemnon* (184–257; also 1412–21, 1555–59). It is brought up in Sophocles, *Electra* 530–76, and in Euripides, *Andromache* 624–25, *Electra* 1018–29, *Trojan Women* 370–72, and *Orestes* 658–59. Euripides' *Iphigenia at Aulis* is devoted to the dramatization of her sacrifice and the decision to perform it. In the tragedians the sacrifice of Iphigenia becomes a major motive for Clytemnestra's later murder of her husband. Iphigenia is not mentioned by Homer, but she figures in the summary of the *Cypria* (a poem from the epic cycle that narrates the events leading up to the Trojan War) made by Proclus (a philosopher of the fifth century C.E.): following Agamemnon's killing of a stag and boasting that he surpassed Artemis in skill at the hunt, the goddess sent adverse winds that kept the Greek armada from sailing against Troy. According to Proclus, at the instigation of the seer Calchas, Iphigenia is brought to Aulis for sacrifice under the familiar ruse that she is to be married to Achilles. The Greeks try to sacrifice her, but "Artemis snatched her away, transported her to the Tauri, and made her immortal; she placed a stag on the altar in the girl's stead" (*Cypria* fragment 1 in Proclus, *Chrestomathia* 1) Pausanias in his *Description of Greece* (of the second century C.E.) claims that in Hesiod's *Catalogue of Women*, "Iphigenia does not die, but becomes Hecate, by the will of Artemis," which may explain what the author of *Cypria* meant by "made her immortal" (1.43.1). Herodotus discusses the Tauri in the section of his *Histories* that describes the coastal region of Scythia (4.99–103). Of the Tauric cult to Artemis he writes:

> [The Tauri] sacrifice to the maiden shipwrecked sailors and any Greeks they capture on the high seas in the following way: after an initial rite, they strike the head with a club. Some say they shove the body down from a precipice (the temple is built on this precipice) and impale the head; others agree about the head, but say the body is not shoved from a precipice, but is buried in the earth. The Tauri themselves claim that this deity to whom they sacrifice is Iphigenia, daughter of Agamemnon (4.103).

In Herodotus' version, then, Iphigenia is not the priestess, but the goddess: in fact she probably started out as a goddess but faded into an aspect of Artemis (Cropp 2000, pp. 43–49).

The myth as enacted in *Iphigenia among the Tauri,* which involves Orestes' journey to the land of the Tauri and the escape of the siblings with the image of Artemis, is not treated in any other extant ancient Greek tragedy and may very well be Euripides' invention or a "new combination of pre-existing mythical elements" (as Wright suggests, 2005, p. 113). The motivation given for Artemis' demand for the sacrifice (that Agamemnon had failed to fulfill a vow to sacrifice the most beautiful creature born in a certain year) is also unknown in other sources of this myth (Kyriakou 2006, pp. 19–29). Clytemnestra's motivation for killing Agamemnon is glossed over: both before and after the recognition, Iphigenia questions Orestes about her family, why the son killed his mother (557, 924, 926), and why the wife killed her husband, but Orestes refuses to talk about it (554, 925, 927). While the motivation is not entirely suppressed, only the circumstance of Iphigenia's death, which (in the world of the play) was universally believed by the Greeks to have taken place, suggests it may have been a factor, as it had been in other works about both the run-up to the Trojan War and the homecoming of Agamemnon. (See Wright 2005, pp. 156–57 for a fuller and more ambitious treatment of the myth.)

Orestes

Orestes includes incidents unknown in other treatments and takes the story in new directions before coming back to something close to the known version. Martin West suggests, "The new story does not replace existing stories of what became of Orestes, it is interpolated into them as an extra episode" (1987, p. 30). The action takes place in the traditional setting, the palace of Atreus in Argos, but even this famous site[4] is in danger of being burnt to the ground before the play's end. Orestes lies sick, tormented by his mother's Furies, an invalid in his sister's care. A striking departure from other versions is that the Argive assembly has convened before the play opens and has voted to isolate the mother-killers, both Orestes and Electra, from the community. The existence of an Argive assembly is in itself a novelty, anachronistically recalling democratized monarchies found in some tragedies (such as Aeschylus' *Suppliants*), but not associated with Mycenae, and, perhaps, parodying the ineffectual assembly in the *Odyssey* that has not met for the twenty years of Odysseus' absence. A second vote will be taken today on whether or not to put the two perpetrators to death. The arrival of Menelaus and Helen, soon after the matricide, is announced at the close of Euripides' *Electra,* but in no other extant Orestes play are they actually among the dramatis personae. Orestes' grandfather Tyndareos, also in the cast, suggests that Orestes and his sister ought to be convicted and put to death by stoning even though he disapproves of Clytemnestra's actions. His conclusion that Menelaus was wrong to undertake the Trojan War in pursuit of Helen is untraditional, in view of the well-known oath that bears his name in which he obliged the suitors for his daughter's hand to defend militarily whichever one of them became her husband. Most surprising and disturbing are the plots proposed and carried out by Pylades, Electra, and Orestes to murder additional members of the family, first Helen and then Hermione, who is abducted and held hostage with a blade to her throat. These unexpected incidents, following as they do in rapid succession, give the play a hectic or even chaotic feel. Its plot is only brought back to something like the myth as we know it by the appearance of Apollo on high. Wright (2008, p. 23) writes: "Euripides himself often seems to be deliberately exploiting

---

4. The citadel of Mycenae is, in fact, a UNESCO-designated World Heritage site.

the fact that the mythical tradition was full of inconsistencies and alternatives, and suggesting that no one could ever really have accurate knowledge of all (or any) of the details."

The Epilogue Gods

All the Euripidean Orestes plays close with a divine epiphany: Castor and Polydeuces in *Electra;* Athena in *Iphigenia among the Tauri;* and Apollo with Helen in *Orestes* (and in *Andromache,* a much earlier play in which Orestes appears, Thetis makes an epiphany at the end). Not every appearance of a god in a Greek tragedy is a deus ex machina, a god whose appearance is facilitated by the use of a crane. A god sometimes simply speaks from the roof of the scene building (or standing on a special raised area of the roof called the *theologeion* or god-platform). In Aeschylus' *Furies* (*Eumenides*), the gods Apollo and Athena walk on stage, using the same level as the human characters. In our three plays, on the other hand, there are reasons to believe that the *mēchanē* (*machina*, the flying machine, or crane) was used. In *Electra* the chorus chants that the approach of the Dioscuri is in an otherworldly manner (1231–37), and near the end of their appearance Castor says that they must fly away through the sky to rescue sailors (1347–49), suggesting entrance and exit on the crane. In *Iphigenia among the Tauri* neither Athena's sudden appearance (at 1435) nor her words make the use of the *mēchanē* absolutely certain, but the fulfillment of her parting announcement that she will accompany her sister's image to Athens onboard Orestes' ship would be greatly expedited and rendered theatrically more credible by a flying machine, with its suggestion of flight, to get her to the harbor swiftly. The rooftop of the palace of Agamemnon in *Orestes* is already crowded with the human characters Orestes, Pylades, and Hermione (the latter two played by nonspeaking extras) before the arrival of the divinities Apollo and Helen. The use of the *mēchanē* would set them apart from the other actors and extras, make the scene less confusing visually, and allow the two deities to arrive together, rather than having Helen follow Apollo onto the *theologeion.*

The use of the *deus ex*—if indeed it was used—is also different in each play. Only in *Orestes* can it be said that the god comes to solve a hopelessly complex plot and restore a known ending. In doing so, he also saves the life of an innocent girl and prevents the utter destruction not only of the palace of Atreus but of its inhabitants.

The Dioscuri in *Electra* appear in order to comfort their niece and nephew and send them on their way with directions for their future: marriage for Electra and Pylades, the trial in Athens, and permanent exile for Orestes (a departure from Aeschylus' version). They assert that not Helen, but a phantom in her likeness sent by Zeus to cause the deaths of humans, went to Troy, and so undercut the mythological framework of the tragedy we have witnessed. In *Iphigenia among the Tauri* Euripides creates an unnecessary crisis in the escape plot at the last minute for added excitement and suspense in order to have Athena appear and give her aetiologies, as if to give a mythological and traditional framework to what is essentially an invented story. One effect of all these divine interventions is to reinforce for the audience the understanding that what they thought they knew, whether about the myths or the world in general, they did not know. The use of the gods ties in with Euripides' choice of less well-known versions of the myths that may include invented incidents as well as obscure ones. The appearances of these gods lead us to ask more questions than they answer (see Wright 2008, p. 71). They do not mitigate the misery of the human participants—guilt, separation, exile, loneliness—nor do they take away the years of suffering that went before.

Questions of Genre

Throughout the twentieth and into the twenty-first centuries, the three Orestes plays along with some other late Euripidean dramas (such as *Helen* and *Ion*) have been subject to debate regarding the genre (or genres) by which they can be classified. Because of the complexity of its intrigue plot and its supposed happy ending and light touch (elements it shares with *Helen*), *Iphigenia among the Tauri* has been labeled romance, romantic tragedy, romantic thriller, melodrama, comedy (in the manner of new rather than old comedy), and tragicomedy (see Wright 2005, pp. 4–5, 6–43 for the history of and a refutation of this relabeling).

Euripides' *Electra* is so full of everyday objects like household utensils, agricultural tools, implements for sacrifice, food, domestic animals, and clothing—from the rags of Electra and the Old Servant to the dazzling royal garb of Clytemnestra and her slaves—that some critics are tempted to describe the play as somehow less than tragic (Gellie 1981, pp. 1–12; Gregory 2000, pp. 59–74; Jones 1962, pp. 239–60; Michelini 1987, pp. 182–230; see also Marshall

2000, pp. 325–41; Pucci 1967, pp. 365–71). The poverty and sim-
plicity of the setting, as well as the recognition of Orestes (after
what seems to many an untragic parody of Aeschylus' recognition scene) by means of a scar, are reminiscent of scenes from the
Odyssey (14; 19.390–475; see Hammond 1984, pp. 373–87; Goff
1991, pp. 259–67) which some critics (though not Aristotle) take
as a prototype of comedy.

On the other hand, the genre problem might really be a "non-
problem" (Wright 2008, p. 20). Many recent critics (Cropp 2000;
Wright 2005; Kyriakou 2006, for example) with good reason recognize these plays as fully tragic, for their serious themes, tragic
diction and construction, the fact of their production for the tragic
festival, and because of the anachronism of trying to define them
in terms of genres that did not exist in the fifth century.[5] Euripides
experimented with and even stretched the limits of tragic style and
content, but elements that might be called "comic" are also found in
Aeschylus and Sophocles. Think only of Orestes' former wet nurse
in *Libation Bearers* with her earthy talk of changing his diapers or
the guard in Sophocles' *Antigone*, who talks so forthrightly about
saving his own skin.

On the surface, *Iphigenia among the Tauri* appears to be one
of those tragedies in which the characters' fortune goes from bad
to good (Aristotle, *Poetics* 1451a14), though some recent critics
would dispute even this (for example, Wright 2005, pp. 36–38;
Tzanetou 2000, pp. 204–9) because of the suffering that has gone
before and brought on the denouement, and because Iphigenia must
remain isolated and childless even after her return to her homeland.
Similarly, of *Electra*, it can be said that the myth loses its glamour
when displaced to the countryside, but in the suffering, loss, and
separation of the characters and in their recognition of their own
wrongdoing and failure, it remains tragic (de Jong 1990, pp. 1–21;
Lloyd 1986, pp. 2–19; Roisman and Luschnig 2010, pp. 241–46).
Orestes, likewise, because of its episodic nature, "happy" denouement, and some bizarre scenes has been called "rather comic" (by

---

5. Most often they are said to resemble New Comedy, a genre rather
like our situation comedies or romantic comedies, which did not exist
in the fifth century. Comedy at that time was Old Comedy, which is
characterized by fantastical plots, blue humor, satire of contemporary
society and political figures, and constant topical reference to persons
and events of the world the audience was living in.

the play's Hypothesis, an ancient summary found in some of the manuscripts) or even compared to satyr play (Burnett 1971, p. 222). Its cheesy characters have been the subject of critical disdain since ancient times: the Hypothesis of Aristophanes Grammaticus characterizes all the personae except Pylades as *phauloi*, "bad," and in the *Poetics* Aristotle singles out Menelaus as an example of "unnecessary badness of character" (1454a29, 1461b21). On the other hand, Orestes and his friends are only reacting to a world in which there is nothing they can count on, nothing stable, neither family nor fellow citizens. West believes it to be "first-rate theatre, a rattling good play that deserves the attention of everyone interested in ancient drama" (1987, p. 28). Porter, stressing the ideas rather than the dramaturgy, writes, "*Orestes* is best regarded as a study of betrayal, frustration and outrage and as a portrayal of the extremes to which individuals can be driven when faced with the injustice of a corrupt and seemingly malevolent world" (1994, p. 53; see also Wright 2008, pp. 32–33), just what we might expect from tragedy in the late fifth century. Finally, to Aristotle, both the *Iliad* and the *Odyssey* were prototypes for tragedy (*Poetics* 1449a1), encouraging us to accept a broad definition of the ancient tragic genre, broad enough to include *Orestes, Electra,* and *Iphigenia among the Tauri.*

The Trial of Orestes and What Happens Next

Central to either the plot or backstory of all post-matricide Orestes plays is his trial and ultimate acquittal. The exception is Sophocles' *Electra,* which does not explicitly refer to the haunting by the Furies or the trial but ends with Aegisthus being forced into the house to his death and the completion of Orestes' revenge. It has been argued that Furies are implicit in that play; it has also been argued that matricide is underplayed and that Sophocles' aim was to restore Orestes to the heroic status that he attained in Homer. In the other tragedies, the haunting of Orestes by the Furies makes visible and visceral the horror of matricide and the extreme nature of Orestes' position—that in avenging his father, he must kill his mother. In Aeschylus, Orestes undergoes a series of steps that ultimately reintegrate him into society: he receives ritual purification; he is pursued by the Furies but is accepted into people's homes; finally, the trial pits two ways of seeing the world against each other. The old chthonian gods oppose the new Olympian deities; the old way of revenge killing is set against the more civilized modern system of trial by jury. In a brilliant stroke the older playwright makes this dilemma insoluble by either gods or humans; only together can they create a better, more just society. Nor are the old gods banished. The Furies represent something necessary for the social good, a taboo against shedding the blood of the members of one's group, extended in the *Oresteia* from the family to the whole citizenry.

Electra

In *Electra* the trial and haunting by the Furies are foretold as part of the divine dispensations given by Castor from the machine.

> CASTOR: (*Speaking to Orestes*)
> And you—leave Argos. You are not permitted
> to walk in the city after killing your mother.
> The terrible fates, the dog-faced goddesses,
> will drive you wandering in madness.
> When you reach Athens, embrace the holy statue
> of Pallas Athena. As they swarm you with their hissing snakes,
> she will keep them off, so they cannot touch you,
> raising over your head the circle of the Gorgon's face.
> There is the Rock of Ares where the gods first sat
> to pass judgment in a case of murder
> when brutal Ares killed Halirrhothius
> son of the lord of the sea in anger
> over his daughter's ungodly coupling, where a vote
> most sacred in the eyes of the gods is secure from that time.
> There you must risk trial for murder.
> Equal votes cast will save you from
> the penalty of death. Loxias will take the blame
> upon himself for commanding the murder of your mother.
> And this law will be established for all time
> that the defendant always wins when the votes are equal.
> And the dreaded goddesses overcome by this distress
> will go down into a cleft of the earth right beside the hill,
> which will be a solemn holy oracle for humankind.
> You must go to live in a city of the Arcadians
> by the streams of Alpheus near the sacred Lycian precinct;
> the city will be named after you.
>
> (1250–75)

In its general outline, this outcome follows the Aeschylean version but without the notion that a better world has come about from all the human suffering. The guilt and grief of the human actors persists. In *The Furies* (*Eumenides*), the rehabilitated Orestes leaves Athens so that he can return to rule over Argos. In Euripides' *Electra*, the line of the house of Atreus as rulers of their homeland is broken. The gods' part, furthermore, relies on coercion rather than cooperation in the later play.

Iphigenia among the Tauri

Orestes explains to his just-recognized sister what brought him to the distant land of the Tauri.

> Then when I came to the Hill of Ares, I stood trial,
> taking my seat on one side of the court, and the eldest
> of the Furies on the other. The arguments were made
> concerning the shedding of my mother's blood.
> Phoebus testified on my behalf and saved my life,
> as Pallas, presiding, counted out the equal votes
> and I walked away, acquitted of the charge of murder.
> Those of the Furies who were persuaded by the trial
> marked off a holy sanctuary to keep beside the court;
> but those who were not persuaded by the verdict
> pursued me ceaselessly with homeless wandering . . . .
>   (961–71)

In Aeschylus the trial ended the torment of Orestes and he returned home acquitted and free of pollution. In Euripides this is not enough: some of the Furies do not accept the judgment of the court and Athena's persuasion. Throughout the play, the old endings are not the final word (see Goff 1999, pp. 116–19): Iphigenia is sacrificed but does not die; Orestes is tried and acquitted, but his persecution by the Furies does not end; the well-planned escape does not succeed, but needs another try. The final actions of liberating the image of Artemis and—now that he knows she is in his presence and alive—rescuing his sister will bring Orestes release. Iphigenia, Orestes, and Pylades are seen by many readers to participate in and deserve their change in fortune and the rehabilitation of the family because of their love and loyalty and unselfish actions toward each other, as if they are being given a second trial and another chance (see, for example, Cropp 2000, pp. 38–39; Kyriakou 2006, pp. 9–13; Burnett 1971, pp. 47–48; O'Brien 1988, pp. 101–15).

Orestes

Orestes treats us to two trials. The Argive assembly, as anticipated by the characters and reported by the messenger, meets six days after the murder of Clytemnestra and Aegisthus and decides the fate of Orestes and Electra. It has apparently already met and fixed this date for the final sentencing before the play opens. Alternative punishments are not listed. The assembly will vote on whether Orestes and his sister are to be put to death by stoning or (presumably) not be put to death (in the event, an argument is made for exile rather than death). The debate, described in detail by the Messenger (884–946), shows the court to be already corrupted by political factions, but its very existence undermines the mythological basis of the story: blood for blood is obsolete. There was no need for Orestes to take vengeance for his father's death because a legal system was already in place (see 500–502).

From the machine Apollo foretells a more traditional trial to take place in Athens as in Aeschylus, but with significant differences:

> Orestes, now, you must
> travel beyond the borders of this country
> and live on the Parrhasian plain for a year's cycle.
> It will be called by the Azanes and Arcadians
> Oresteion, named after your year of exile.
> From there set out for the city of Athenians
> to undergo a trial for your murdered mother's blood
> by the three Eumenides. The gods, judges of the trial,
> will each give a most sacred vote on Ares' Hill:
> it is preordained that you will be acquitted.
> (1643–52)

Later in the same speech, Apollo tells Menelaus to cede to Orestes his claim to Argos (1660), bringing the future of Orestes and Argos back in line with Aeschylus' version. In this, the strangest of the Orestes plays, the result—though it may seem somewhat forced—is most traditional, with Orestes returning to rule Argos (as in Homer, Aeschylus, and Sophocles). The judges, however, are not Athenian citizens as in Aeschylus, but the gods, removing a significant feature of the Aeschylean trial, that justice and an end to blood vengeance are achieved by humans and gods working together.

Some Common Themes in the Orestes Plays

Philia

Friendship and fellow feeling are the most positive themes in all of Euripides' Orestes plays. In *Iphigenia among the Tauri*, the three friends are willing to give up their lives for each other. Iphigenia offers to save Orestes (not yet knowing who he is) if he will deliver a letter to her family in Argos for her, but he insists that Pylades be the one to return safely home (597–608). Pylades, not as practical as his friend, but displaying equal affection and loyalty, argues that he should die with his companion (674–86), but Orestes refuses this generous offer. After the recognition scene, Iphigenia is willing to die to ensure her brother's homecoming (1002–5, though earlier in her recitation of the letter she had threatened to become a curse on him and his house if he failed to rescue her from the land of the Tauri, 778–79). Pylades, furthermore, promises eternal loyalty to Orestes, alive and dead (716–18). He has already been described by the Herdsman as a loving and caring friend, wiping Orestes' mouth after his fit and protecting him with his own body (310–14). To Iphigenia's question concerning the two captives, "Are you brothers, born of the same mother?" Orestes says of Pylades, "In affection, yes, but we are not brothers by blood" (497–98). *Philia* can include kinship, and in *Iphigenia among the Tauri* the lead characters are both blood relatives and loyal, loving friends. Orestes acknowledges that Pylades is his cousin, but also his only true friend (919; cf. Euripides, *Electra* 82–83) and the preserver of his life (923). Even before the recognition, brother and sister show fellow feeling toward each other. Iphigenia's intention had been to show the prisoners no mercy (344–53), but as soon as she sees them she expresses the most humane feelings toward them, even putting herself in the place of their imagined sister (472–75). When Orestes refuses to be saved, she compares him to her brother (609–13) and offers to tend his body as a sister would (630–35). Though reluctant to give his name (which would have been a plot spoiler), Orestes is otherwise generous with information and even shows pity (619) to the woman whose duty is to initiate his sacrifice (as had, admittedly, an earlier victim who wrote the letter for her in case she should ever be able to give it to someone to take home, 585–87).

All the characters in *Orestes* are "bad" (or "rotten," *phauloi*), according to the play's Hypothesis—except for Pylades. "Why not

Pylades?" some modern critics have asked (for example, Wright 2008, p. 57). He was, after all, a co-conspirator with Orestes and Electra in the killing of Clytemnestra and Aegisthus (33, 1089–91, 1158). It is he who devises the plot to murder Helen and manages to justify it (1105, 1131–51). What he has in his favor is his unfailing and unflinching loyalty to Orestes, which is much appreciated by his friend (804–6; cf. 1155–61) and, apparently, by the hypothesist:

> This is what it means to have friends, not just family.
> Even an outsider, who yokes his ways with your own,
> is a friend more worth having than a thousand close kin.
>
> (*Orestes* 804–6)

The theme of *philia* is not without its paradoxes: Hermione, brought up almost as another sister, and sympathetic to the friends' cause, does not count, in their eyes, and her life is expendable until Apollo awards her to Orestes as his bride. What, we may ask, is *her* reward for her love and loyalty? A cynic might answer that she is, at least, free of her father and not much different from any bride, given to a husband at the whim of an elder male member of the household. Others who should be "friends" do not meet the requirements: Menelaus, for example, chooses discretion over family feeling when he neglects to stand up for Orestes. The three friends carry loyalty to a criminal extreme. I remember a paper delivered by Charles Rowan Beye some years ago in which he suggested that in Euripides' *Orestes,* the closest modern analogy for Orestes and Pylades was a motorcycle gang.

Likewise, in *Electra* the theme of friendship is problematic. Electra counts the husband whom Aegisthus arranged for her to marry as a friend equal to the gods (67), but does not consider him worthy of her (247). The brother and sister have been apart so long that they do not recognize each other and yet their future separation is devastating to them (1308–10, 1321–26). The Dioscuri are conflicted, unable to prevent the murder and the pollution of their kin, unable also—despite their own story of brotherly love and sacrifice—to quite understand the pain Orestes and Electra are experiencing (1311–13, 1319–20, though they may come close at 1327–30). Electra is awarded as bride to Pylades: it is clear that she admires him, at least (886–89), and with good cause.

Soteria (Salvation or Self-Preservation)

In *Electra*, a revenge drama, salvation is a minor theme, but it plays a more important part in the other two plays. Orestes had been rescued from Aegisthus as a baby by his father's old attendant and, again, after the killing of Aegisthus, his life is saved by another old family servant who happened to be in the royal retinue and was able to recognize Orestes before Aegisthus' bodyguard set upon him. The dispensations of the Dioscuri, though somewhat insensitive to the human pain of Orestes and Electra, are salvific, at least as far as the siblings are concerned. Electra is saved from an unwanted perpetual virginity by being married off to Pylades; Orestes is eventually to be saved from the Furies through Athena's intervention (1249–75). A function of the Dioscuri is to save ships in trouble on the sea and they report that they have just now come from putting down a storm (1241–42). In spite of their salvific role, Fate and Apollo's commands prevented their saving their sister (1301–2). Menelaus, too, has just now sailed home from his wanderings, safe at last but too late to save any of his kin (1278–79).

In *Iphigenia among the Tauri*, an escape play, and *Orestes*, a suppliant drama of sorts, salvation is not only the culmination of the plots, but runs through the dramas from beginning to end. A mere listing of examples in *Iphigenia among the Tauri* is impressive: Iphigenia, though sacrificed to Artemis before the eyes of the whole Greek army, was actually rescued by Artemis. Orestes has come to the land of the Tauri to "rescue" (or steal) the cult figure of Artemis. The chorus longs for rescue and return home. Orestes is undertaking this quest in order to be rescued from the pursuit of Furies. At his trial he has already been rescued once by Athena. Iphigenia offers to rescue one of the prisoners. She herself is sending the letter in order to be rescued by her brother. After the recognition, the three friends unite in saving each other and "liberating" the statue. They manage their escape but need to be rescued once more, by Athena with Poseidon's help. For good measure the chorus, too, is promised rescue and return home. It is said by some critics that salvation and the rehabilitation of the family is deserved because these members of the house of Atreus have proven themselves uncorrupted (Burnett 1971, p. 47; Kyriakou 2006, p. 22; O'Brien 1988, pp. 105–15) and now, at last, break the cycle of violence that has plagued their family for generations. Not all is sweetness and light, however. Brother and sister share a hatred for Helen

(521–26). Iphigenia shows a sophisticated suspicion of Menelaus (930) and wishes that he and his wife would be shipwrecked on the Tauric shore so that she could take her revenge by killing them (354–59). Orestes—to his sister's horror—suggests killing King Thoas to effect their escape but refuses to have any more kindred blood on his hands when Iphigenia suggests that he save himself at her expense (1020, 1007–8). Their salvation is achieved, furthermore, by deception and temple robbery.

The first half of the last play in this group, *Orestes,* is a suppliant drama and focuses, therefore, on self-preservation. After her tales of woe (1–51), Electra expresses hope in the arrival of Menelaus, finally home from Troy with Helen (52–70). She is waiting for Menelaus who, she believes, can save her brother and herself. With her, the audience expects Menelaus to enter next, but Helen comes on first, disappointing expectation. It turns out—when Menelaus, against custom and our generic expectations (suppliants are usually respected in drama) refuses the suppliants—that Helen is to be used in an attempt to bring about a reversal of their fortunes. Orestes tries to rely on his own resources by pleading his case in front of the Argive assembly, but fails to win the debate.

At Orestes' moments of greatest despair, Pylades comes through. His is one of the more surprising roles. Following the lukewarm response from Menelaus to Orestes' plea, Pylades arrives out of the blue, rushing on stage like a messenger, not as much to bring news but to hear it and declare his loyalty and support. After the debate in the assembly and the actual messenger's narrative, Pylades postpones the imminent demise of his friend and of Electra, his own bride-to-be, by proposing the harebrained scheme of murdering Helen and burning down the house. He introduces this new revenge plot in the hope that they will get even with Menelaus for his disloyalty and that he and Orestes will be greeted as heroes for killing the evil woman who caused so much suffering (1134–42)—never mind that they are in fact universally despised for their murder of Clytemnestra. Electra improves on the escape plan by adding the plot to take Hermione hostage and threaten to kill her if Menelaus will not lend his support (1189–1203). Finally, Apollo from the machine rescues Electra and Orestes, as well as Hermione and Pylades, and saves the house of Atreus for one more generation.

Deception

Another theme common to Euripides' Orestes plays is deception (common, as Hartigan demonstrates for all Euripides' plays that feature Apollo or Artemis, 1991: passim). In *Electra*, Orestes hides his identity for nearly half the play, but he does not go as far as his Sophoclean counterpart, who deceives even his sister into believing that he has died: he comes, in fact, with the news that Orestes is alive. Euripides' Electra, however, uses the most ironic and pathetic device to deceive her mother and lure her to her death: the false announcement of the birth of a baby boy, using her mother's better nature to trap and kill her. All the main characters are victims of self-deception as well, imagining themselves and each other not as they are but as they best fit the mythical world each has invented (see Hartigan 1991, pp. 107–26). The real world that we see in the drama's many details of everyday life, harnessing the oxen, fetching water, bringing provender for a feast, is overwhelmed by a life-denying imagined world of heroes, villains, and interfering gods.

Hartigan remarks of *Iphigenia among the Tauri*, "Deception is its main action" (1991, p. 94). Iphigenia was lured to Aulis on the pretext that she was to be married to Achilles (24–25). All the Greeks believe that she died there (564). Orestes has been sent to seize the statue of Artemis by trickery (89). This is the background. For the escape plan, much as her mother had done in Aeschylus' *Agamemnon*, Iphigenia uses truth in the service of deception to trick King Thoas into letting them escape with the statue (1031–35). In *Agamemnon*, Clytemnestra had used Agamemnon's vanity to lure him to his death. Iphigenia uses Thoas' piety to get him to participate in the theft of his precious cult image and the escape of his respected priestess. Iphigenia and the audience are deceived in multiple ways by the dream Iphigenia describes in the prologue: she believes her brother is dead, but the audience is teased by the thought that she will participate in the sacrifice of her own brother (see Trieschnigg 2008, pp. 461–71; Goff 1999, p. 118).

In *Orestes*, until Orestes and his friends take over the plot, the main deception is that of Apollo, whose commands caused Orestes to kill his mother and then left him a victim of the Furies, his callous kin, and the citizens of Argos. Once the situation turns from the suppliant plot, Orestes begging for his life first from Menelaus and then from the assembly, to a drama of desperation and ongoing revenge, the deception becomes more personal: Pylades schemes to trap Helen by pretending to supplicate her (extending the suppliant plot) and Electra similarly tricks Hermione by asking for her help. The younger generation has been betrayed by their false and self-serving elders and by the corrupt institutions both religious and civil, epitomized by the Delphic Apollo and the political factions of the citizen assembly, who have left them in a world without values. Even the house of Atreus and the people's loyalty to Agamemnon—on which every other Orestes could rely—fail them. Menelaus, for whom Agamemnon sacrificed his daughter and led the expedition to Troy, is unwilling to repay the favor to his brother's children. There is in evidence no citizens' antipathy to the hated tyranny of the usurper, who murdered the good king Agamemnon, to give justification to their own regicide. The three friends are simply on their own. This world resembles the factionalized political scene in Athens with its series of oligarchic coups in the last years of the fifth century, in which the members of political gangs were bound together by their complicity in crime (see Wright 2008, pp. 101–14; West 1987, p. 36; Porter 1994, pp. 96–97, 329; Hartigan 1991, p. 156; Lloyd 1992, p. 118). A less desperate Orestes and his friends, including Hermione, who grew up with them and sympathizes with their cause, in a modern production could almost be portrayed as part of the "Occupy" movement, young people dismayed by their elders' greed and incompetence and brave enough to stand up to it.

Divine–Human Interactions

What of the gods? In *Electra*, they are almost absent until the end. They are little on the lips of the characters. Orestes speaks of the oracle in only the vaguest of terms (87, 399–400), referring to "sacred rites" and saying on first entering his sister's house, "the oracles of Loxias are certain"—perhaps to him, but not to anyone else in the cast or audience, except possibly the taciturn Pylades. At last, just before he enters the house to commit matricide, the horror of what he has been directed to do leads him to question the god (979, 981) only to be rebuked by Electra, relying on the authority of Apollo's sacred tripod (980). The Dioscuri give the final word: the oracle was not wise (1302), but out of deference to the higher god, they cannot question it (1244–46). The act of matricide is thus morally repudiated on the divine level (1244). Apollo seems as ignorant as the rest of us. Perhaps, like the playwright, he was just following the story. The physical presence of the twin sons of Zeus counterbalances the absence of Apollo, but even they are remote, poised above the action, unable to do anything (1301–2), even understand or comfort the tragic siblings, their own sister's children. Athena still will preside over the matricide trial and protect Orestes with the dreaded Gorgon's head (1257) rather than her sublimely persuasive powers, as in *The Furies* (*Eumenides*). Apollo's role is reduced and Orestes is not even to visit his oracle for succor after the matricide; he will go instead to the sanctuary of Zeus near Olympia (1273–74; see Roisman and Luschnig 2011, pp. 249–53). Zeus and Fate are the cause of all that has happened (1248, 1282, 1301–2). Helen did not go to Troy, as Castor tells us; Zeus brought on the Trojan War "to cause strife and death among mortals" (1282). Wars, as it turns out, are waged not out of motives of fear, honor, or self-interest (*pace* Thucydides, *The Peloponnesian War* 1.76), but simply to give human beings the opportunity to kill each other (see also *Orestes* 1640–42).

Three gods are prominently involved in the plot of *Iphigenia among the Tauri*: Artemis, who demanded the sacrifice of Iphigenia but rescued her at the last minute and now demands that the victim preside over human sacrifice; Apollo, whose oracle encouraged Orestes to kill his mother and who has sent him on this quest to steal the statue of his sister Artemis; and Athena, who helped Orestes at his trial and now with the help of Poseidon (who may or may not have caused the turbulence of the sea in the first escape attempt, 1444–45; cf. 1414–19) saves the ship from adverse seas. Still the will of the gods remains inscrutable to mortals. Orestes assumes that Phoebus has set a trap for him (77) and has been a false prophet (710–15). Pylades' only assurance is that the oracle has not yet brought his friend's death (719–20). Iphigenia, despite her role as priestess, questions whether the goddess really requires human sacrifice (385–91), but there is nothing else in the play to indicate that Artemis opposes the gruesome ceremonies done in her name. Iphigenia's doubt is half-hearted, coming after her indictment of the goddess' hypocrisy (380–84). Apollo's oracle has instigated matricide and sent Orestes on a temple-robbing foray in a far-off land and left him there. Neither Apollo nor Artemis remains involved enough to help the mortals who have suffered from divine intervention in their lives (Kyriakou 2006, pp. 13–16; Hartigan 1991, pp. 89–96). The mortals are left to their own devices and their own morals. Iphigenia uses the goddess to help with the escape by attributing to the divine image the abhorrence she herself feels at the matricide. We are left with the feeling that the gods' role is ambiguous and their will is unknowable (Goff 1999, pp. 111–19; Hartigan 1991, pp. 100–103; Kyriakou 2006, p. 452). A theme of the play is the limitation of human understanding of the way things work, of the gods, of the universe, of pretty much everything (Wright 2005, pp. 362–84; Trieschnigg 2008, p. 467). This does not, however, mean that there is a divine plan. Everything the gods do may be seen as ad hoc. The human actors must plan and rely on luck (*tyche*), which is taken very seriously in *Iphigenia among the Tauri* (Whitman 1974, pp. 6–7, 24; Burnett 1971, pp. 67–68; cf. Wright 2005, pp. 374–79), and their own devices and desires.

Finally the play is full of aetiologies of cult practices such as the feast of Choes and the rites at Brauron and Halae, and many recent critics have concentrated on this aspect of the drama (Tzanetou 2000; Wolff 1992; Goff 1999; Cropp 2000, pp. 43–56; Kyriakou 2006, pp. 19–29; cf. Wright 2005, p. 2). Aetiological reference to known cults is often thought to form a bridge between the mythical world of heroes and the known world of contemporary cultic practices, but even in this *Iphigenia among the Tauri* is equivocal: the actual cults do not match what we are told in the play (either by Orestes or Athena; see Kyriakou 2006, pp. 24–27). As Goff points out (1999, pp. 116–19), *Iphigenia among the Tauri* represents the old stories left unfinished at their old endings: Apollo does not acquire the oracle at Delphi once and for all, but a second round is needed in which Zeus banishes dreams (even though dreams are still used to interpret the future); the Clashing Rocks did not stay open after the *Argo* sailed through (421–22); Iphigenia is sacrificed, but here she is, alive; Orestes underwent a trial for matricide, but some of the Furies continue to torment him to madness; the escape from the land of the Tauri succeeds on the human level but is thwarted by nature or the gods and needs a second go. With so many uncertain endings, it is hard for the audience to achieve a sense of closure of the kind Aeschylus provides with the grand finale of the *Oresteia*.

Orestes is Euripides' last full treatment of the revenge of Orestes and Electra.[6] Apollo is prominent as an excuse and as the one to

---

6. In Euripides' last play, *Iphigenia at Aulis*, Clytemnestra (who has, in all innocence, brought the baby Orestes to Aulis to bring her husband the joy of seeing his son before his departure for war) believes that her

blame (28, 75, 165, 191, 260, 269–70, 276, 285, 330, 416, 419–20, 591, 955, 1389). At 1625 Apollo appears ex machina and with Helen. Are the gods working together under the auspices of Zeus (Wright 2008, p. 67), or is this just a facile wrap-up, almost, but not quite, bringing the play back to the known legend?

> The exodos fittingly concludes this exceedingly agitated and innovative play, providing the appropriate climax to Orestes' growing frustration and outrage, while building to a similar crisis the sense of a world that has gone disastrously and irrevocably awry. Betrayed on all sides, his expectations repeatedly frustrated by a world where the old rules no longer seem to apply, Orestes threatens the destruction of his ancestral palace and, with it, the entire mythical tradition associated with the house of Atreus. (Porter 1994, p. 289)

Apollo's pronouncements from on high can hardly be expected to bring closure to such a crisis. Or is Euripides suggesting that "only a god could save the Athenian state from its contemporary madness" (Hartigan 1991, p. 156)? It did not happen, as we know from the history of the Peloponnesian War.

---

other children would side with her in avenging Iphigenia. We know they will not, because we know the legend and the play is full of references to earlier versions of it.

About the Translations

I begin with the Greek and translate line by line. That does not always make for a very speakable or even readable version. I read that draft through without the Greek several times and rewrite it, striving to make the lines fit English rhythms and usage. And then I go back to the Greek. I aim for a translation that is idiomatic but not too pedestrian, that reflects the Greek but not slavishly, and that comes trippingly on the actor's tongue, unless bombast is called for as in Tyndareos' speech in *Orestes*. To maintain the prissiness of Menelaus' speech in the same play, I have kept it impersonal by frequent use of the pronoun "one." Also in *Orestes*, I have tried to make the Phrygian slave's part sound foreign but not like gibberish. On the other hand, keeping as close as reasonably possible to the lines of the Greek text makes the translation more useful in the classroom.

The notes address difficulties in the text and fill in background that might not be obvious to readers who are not professional classical scholars. Sometimes the notes suggest other possible interpretations or alternative wording or speculations about staging.

One of the courses I offered regularly at the University of Idaho was Greek Tragedy in Context. I used to query the students regularly, asking them to submit anonymous questions and comments. One of the most eye-opening questions from a student was, "Do these plays have anything to say to us?" This was astounding, because, believing I had already bridged the gap, I could no longer even imagine that there might be a problem. This question was both disturbing and inspiring. My intention in the notes and Introduction, as well as in choices of words in the translation, is to say "yes." Even after my retirement, the student's sincere question continues to haunt me. The tragedies are enactments of stories about people on the edge, universal stories that bear repeating again and again. Tragedy offers other ways of seeing the world, of living in society, of seeing humanity in relation to the divine, of recognizing what it means to be human.

In the politics of the plays we can, unfortunately, see ourselves: these plays were written during the decades-long Peloponnesian

War at a time in Athens that the democracy was being undermined by political factionalism and people arguing for the good of their particular ideology rather than the good of the whole (see especially *Orestes* 866–956).

The plays show us truths about family relationships, not only at their worst, but at their best:

> "You see, strangers, I am not without a brother;" says Iphigenia to her brother, "it's just that I do not ever get to see him in the flesh" (*Iphigenia among the Tauri* 612–13). For nearly twenty years she has been separated from her home and all she loves in the world.

> "May I not take your blessed hand?" Electra asks of the mother she hates, not long before she joins her brother in murdering her (*Electra* 1006). Even at this late time in her story, she still longs for her mother's touch.

> Orestes, sick with the hounding of zombie-like Furies, depends on his sister's care and tries to protect her from exhaustion, "For if you fail me and by your constant care you suffer any setback, we are lost" (*Orestes* 304–5).

More than anything else, I believe, they help us recognize and come to terms with wrong we have done:

> Asked by his uncle what is making him sick, Orestes answers, "Awareness—I am aware of what awful things I have done" (*Orestes* 396).

> Even Clytemnestra, seeing her daughter living in poverty, can say, "I'm not really very happy with what I did" (*Electra* 1105–6).

> When his sister offers to give up her life if that will help Orestes escape, he says, "I could not be your murderer as well as my mother's; her blood is enough" (*Iphigenia among the Tauri* 1007–8).

My hope in working on these translations has been to make the plays more accessible and less alien, less like historical artifacts and more timeless and immediate. In language I hope they are speakable, whether in classroom readings or on the stage.

I would like to thank the anonymous student mentioned above and her classmates for their insightful questions and answers; Hannah Etherton and Jesse Thomas, interlibrary loan librarians at the University of Idaho, for their speed, expertise, and kindness; and my husband Lance Luschnig for joining me in dramatic readings of the translations.

House of Atreus Family Tree
According to Euripides

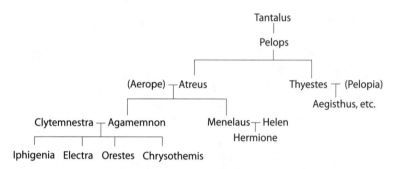

Leda had children by both Tyndareos and Zeus: Two sons, Castor and Polydeuces (called the Dioscuri), and two daughters, Helen and Clytemnestra. Of the Dioscuri, the mortal Castor is commonly said to be the son of Tyndareos and the immortal Polydeuces the son of Zeus. Helen is Zeus' daughter and Clytemnestra the daughter of Tyndareos. Tyndareos, however, is often referred to as father of all the children and both sons are attributed to Zeus (hence Dioscuri, "Zeus' boys").

Clytemnestra and Aegisthus produced unnamed children (Sophocles, *Electra* 588–90; Euripides, *Electra* 62–63)

EURIPIDES

Electra

Cast of Characters

FARMER (unnamed)	Electra's husband
ELECTRA	
ORESTES	
CHORUS	of young Mycenaean women
The CHORUS LEADER	speaks for the group in the dialogue sections
OLD MAN	former personal slave of Agamemnon
MESSENGER	slave of Orestes
CLYTEMNESTRA	
DIOSCURI	Castor [and Polydeuces, nonspeaking] ex machina

Nonspeaking Roles

PYLADES	Orestes' companion

Several extras serve as Orestes' entourage and as male and female attendants to Clytemnestra.

Euripides' *Electra* was first produced for the Greater Dionysia between 422 and 413, possibly around 415 B.C.E.

Electra

SCENE: *The Mycenaean countryside in front of the poor
farmhouse of Electra's husband. The time is just
before dawn. It is about seven years after the end
of the Trojan War. The two side entrances represent
routes to the country (stage right) and the highway
(stage left).*

Prologue

(Enter Farmer through the central doors.)

FARMER:
Earth's timeless soil, Inachus' streams,[1]
here once King Agamemnon deployed the forces of war
and with a thousand ships sailed to the land of Troy.
On Trojan ground he killed old Priam, their king,
sacked the famous city Dardanus[2] built,   5
and came home to Argos.[3] On the high temples
he dedicated the lion's share of foreign spoils.[4]
Over there he had success, but at home

---

1. *1:* Inachus—the main river of the land of Argos. Like most rivers, he is a god.

2. *5:* Dardanus—the son of Zeus and Atlas' daughter Electra. He built the citadel of Troy and ruled over the Troad (Troy and the area around it). He was the ancestor of the kings of Troy down to Priam. Line 5 sets together the first and last of the kings of Troy. This is a favorite device in Greek poetry: at the end of a story, the poet takes us back to the beginning.

3. *6:* Argos and Mycenae are used interchangeably.

4. *6–7:* Spoils, in particular, refers to the armor stripped from dead enemies (see also 1000). Returning warriors nailed the armor to the temples. See Homer, *Iliad* 7.81–84; Herodotus, *The Histories* 5.95.1; Aeschylus, *Agamemnon* 577–79.

3

he was killed by the treachery of his wife Clytemnestra[5]
10 and the hand of Thyestes' son Aegisthus.
He left behind the age-old scepter of Tantalus[6]
when he died. Aegisthus is now king of the country[7]
and keeps for himself Tyndareos' daughter, the late king's wife.
But *he* left his children at home when he sailed to Troy,
15 his son Orestes and a young daughter Electra—
the father's aged minder absconded with the boy
after Aegisthus resolved to kill him,
and gave him to Strophius to raise in the land of the Phocians.[8]
But the girl Electra stayed behind in her father's halls,
20 until she ripened into a young woman, and suitors,
prominent men from all over Greece, came to court her.
In terror that she would marry well and bear a child
to avenge Agamemnon, Aegisthus kept her
in the house and would not let her marry any of them.[9]

---

5. *9:* Clytemnestra—The original spelling was "Clytæmestra" (without the "n"). The name means "renowned schemer" rather than "famously courted," which applies more aptly to her sister Helen.

6. *11:* "Age-old scepter"—The long history of Agamemnon's scepter is told in Homer's *Iliad* 2.102–9: It was made by Hephaestus and given by him to Zeus, who passed it on to Hermes, who gave it to Pelops. From Pelops it passed to his sons, first Atreus and then Thyestes, and finally to Atreus' son Agamemnon. Tantalus was Pelops' father, but the Homeric scepter was never in his hands and is projected backward here. Agamemnon's scepter figures in Clytemnestra's dream in Sophocles' *Electra* (420). The Farmer takes a long view, showing interest in the generations of the people he mentions.

7. *12:* According to Homer, Aegisthus ruled for seven years until Orestes came back and slew his father's murderer (*Odyssey* 3.305–8). Exactly how Clytemnestra died is unclear in the *Odyssey*.

8. *18:* Strophius was married to Agamemnon's sister Anaxibia. He was king of Phocis (in central Greece), where the Delphic sanctuary was located. Pylades was Strophius' son and Orestes' cousin. The two grew up together and were inseparable. Pylades is a presence in all three of the *Electra* plays, but has a speaking part (of three lines) only in Aeschylus' *Libation Bearers* (900–902). He has speaking parts in Euripides' *Orestes* and *Iphigenia among the Tauri*.

9. *22–24:* Aegisthus acted as Electra's *kurios* (guardian): women, as a rule, did not act on their own in contractual matters (though Clytemnestra and Helen made second marital choices for themselves). Aegisthus clearly

When even that strategy failed to ease his fear   25
that she might have children by a secret liaison with some
    noble,
he planned to kill her, but her mother, bloodthirsty
as she was, saved her from Aegisthus' hands.
For her husband's death she made an excuse, but she was
    afraid
the murder of her own child would cause an outcry.   30
Aegisthus had a brainstorm then—
he put a price on the head
of Agamemnon's son, already in exile,
and *to me*[10] he gave Electra to be my lawful
wedded wife. My people are Mycenaean;   35
there's no fault to be found on that score—
we are respectable but poor—
so much for good breeding! By giving her
to a poor man, he hoped to quell his fears.
If a man of rank had married her,   40
he would rouse the sleeping murder of Agamemnon
and at last Aegisthus would have gotten his just deserts.
I have never touched her—Aphrodite be my witness—
I could not shame her. Yes, Electra is still a virgin.
I was ashamed to lay rough hands on the daughter   45
of a wealthy family, being a working man myself.
I feel for poor Orestes, in name my kinsman,
if he ever comes home to Argos and sees
the miserable marriage they made for his sister.
And if anyone says I'm a fool to take a young   50
virgin into my home and not touch her,
he should know that he is measuring
right and wrong by false standards. He's the fool.

---

does not have Electra's best interest—nor that of her side of the family—
at heart, and the farmer who receives Electra as his wife does not view
Aegisthus as having the authority to give her in marriage.

10. *33:* "He gave Electra"—Up to this point the audience would be
wondering who the Farmer is. He is not a mythological figure, not part of
the traditional story, but an outsider, a person from contemporary society.
This is an absolutely extraordinary fact.

*(Enter Electra through the central doors,
carrying a* hydria *[water vessel].)*[11]

ELECTRA:
Black night, nurse of golden stars,
I go now to the running stream
55   with this jug balanced on my head,
not that I need to do such menial tasks,
but I want to show before the gods Aegisthus' insult
and let my laments for Father fly to heaven.
60   Tyndareos' daughter, my mother, damn her to hell,
threw me out of my home to please her husband.
Now she bears Aegisthus a new brood
and makes Orestes and me unwanted stepchildren.

FARMER:
Poor thing, why are you slaving away for my sake
65   and taking on chores, unsuited to the life you used to live,
and why don't you stop, even when I ask you to?

ELECTRA:
You are my true friend. I put you on a par with the gods
for not adding abuse to my troubles.
It's a great stroke of good fortune to find
70   relief from bad luck as I have found in you.
I must then, with whatever strength I can muster, without your
     asking,
try to lighten your load, so you can handle it more easily,
and to share your toils with you. You have enough work
outside. The household chores should be mine
75   to take care of. When a working man comes home
it is nice to find things inside in good order.[12]

*(Exit Electra, as she concludes this
speech, stage right to the country.)*

---

11. *Enter Electra:* The characters are introduced in successive scenes of the
prologue. Fetching water from the stream or springhouse is a traditional
task for women.
12. *75–76:* This is the traditional division of labor in Greek society:
women work mainly inside the house, men outside.

FARMER:
Go on, then, if you want to. It's not so far
from the house to the spring. But with the break of day[13]
I must drive my oxen to my lands and sow my fields.
A lazy lout with the gods on his lips   80
cannot eke out a living except by working hard.

(Exit Farmer stage right to the country.)

*(Enter Orestes stage left from the highway with Pylades;
two servants carry their baggage. Orestes is dressed
in a fine traveler's cloak and a broad-brimmed hat.)*

ORESTES:
Pylades, in my eyes you are first and foremost
my dearest, most loyal friend and host.
You alone of friends continue to respect Orestes
in my current situation, horrors brought on by Aegisthus   85
who killed my father with the help of that damnable woman,
my mother. I have come from the god's sacred rites[14]
here to Argive land, in secret
to repay my father's murderers with death.
During the night just past I went to Father's grave,   90
shed tears, made an offering of my hair,
and slaughtered a sheep on the altar
in secret from the masters of this country.
I will not set foot inside the city-walls,
but have come to the country's borders   95
with two possibilities in mind: to leave
for another place if their spies get wind of me

---

13. *78:* This line (see also 102) gives the time of day (daybreak) for the play's opening.

14. *87:* "The god's sacred rites"—The oracle at Delphi is central to Orestes' revenge plot, but in this play Apollo seems less involved. In Aeschylus' *Libation Bearers* (269–96), Apollo is most graphic in his pronouncements of what will happen to Orestes if he fails to avenge his father: physical torments, social ostracism, and visitation by the Furies. In Sophocles' *Electra*, Apollo's part is full but not clear. Orestes is told by the oracle to use deceit. Euripides' Orestes is vague about the content of the oracle.

and to look for my sister. I hear that she has been joined
in marriage and is no longer a virgin.
100   My plan is to find her and make her my accomplice in revenge
and thus gain knowledge about affairs inside the city.
Now that dawn is raising its white face,
let's get out of the road
in case some farmer or serving woman
105   shows up, so we can find out
if my sister lives anywhere nearby.
Look, I see a slave woman coming this way

(*Electra comes into view and is heard singing.*)

carrying a heavy water jug on her shaved
head.[15] Let's crouch down and listen
110   to this servant in case we can learn anything
about what we have come here for, Pylades.

(*They hide behind the altar in the
center of the orchestra.*)

Electra's Monody

(*Enter Electra stage right from the country, alone
with the water jug on her head, singing.*)

[Strophe 1]

ELECTRA:
Hurry along—the time has come—
go on, go on in tears.
Ah, ah me.
115   I am Agamemnon's child,
and Tyndareos' loathsome daughter Clytemnestra
gave birth to me.
Down in the city, people
call me unhappy Electra.
120   Ah, ah for my never-ending toils
and hated life.

---

15. *108–9:* "Shaved head"—See note on 147–50.

Father, you lie dead and gone,
slaughtered by your wife
and Aegisthus, O Agamemnon, my father.

Move on, waken the same refrain of sorrow,   125
raise high the pleasure that comes with mourning.

[Antistrophe 1]

Hurry along—the time has come—
go on, go on in tears,
Ah, ah me.
In what city, in what house,   130
my poor brother, do you wander[16]
leaving your sister
to the bitterest sorrows
in Father's chambers, mourning?
Come, release me from my life of misery,   135
from these toils.
Zeus, Zeus, bring ashore to Argos
the wanderer, the avenger
of Father's hideous bloodshed.

[Strophe 2]

Take this vessel from my head and put it[17]   140
on the ground. O Father, I cry out
in nightly keening.
A shrill wail, a song of death,
Father, I call to you, a song of death
down deep in the earth
with cries of grief I pass my days   145
forever, tearing at my neck,
dragging down my nails,

---

16. *131:* "Do you wander"—"Are you a slave?" is another reading for
this question.
17. *140:* "Take this vessel"—Does Electra have a slave, as some scholars
believe, to whom she addresses these second-person imperatives, or does
she speak to herself? In either case, she needs to have her hands free for
the gestures of mourning.

and beating my hands on
my head close-cropped for your death.[18]

150   Aiai. Tear the head,
         like a droning swan[19]
         beside running streams
         that calls its own dear father
         killed by the cunning snares
155   of nets, so I cry for you,
         poor Father.

                                    [Antistrophe 2]

         The last bath, your deathbed[20]
         bathed in blood—
         ah me, ah me,
160   the bitter axe blow,[21]

---

18. *147–50:* Electra catalogs the rituals of mourning: her hair is shorn, she strikes her head, and she tears her skin with her nails.

19. *151:* "Like a droning swan"—Birds, especially swans, were admired by the Greeks for their filial piety. The swan was thought to sing in mourning and even in sorrow for its own impending death. Electra thinks of her father as snared by his wife, caught in deadly cloths (see Aeschylus, *Agamemnon* 1382–83).

20. *157:* "The last bath, your deathbed"—In Homer (*Odyssey* 4.534–35; 11.410–11) and Sophocles (*Electra* 203–7, 269), Agamemnon is killed at a banquet. Euripides' *Electra* (1148–49) follows Aeschylus' *Agamemnon* (1107–35).

21. *160, 165:* The axe is associated with Clytemnestra (in Aeschylus' *Libation Bearers* she calls for one when she realizes Orestes has returned, 889). In Homer, Agamemnon dies by the sword of Aegisthus (*Odyssey* 11.424). What weapon Clytemnestra used is not so clear in *Agamemnon*. In art, Aegisthus is usually depicted wielding a sword; Clytemnestra sometimes is shown with a sword and sometimes with an axe (Prag, Pl. 11c). In Sophocles, the instrument used by both Clytemnestra and Aegisthus is an axe (*Electra* 98–100, 193–96, 485). In Euripides, Clytemnestra uses an axe (160, 279, 1160), but Aegisthus wields a sword (165). It is possible that Clytemnestra killed him with an axe and Aegisthus mutilated him with the sword. The use of the axe, an instrument for killing an animal or felling a tree, dehumanizes the victim more than the sword, a weapon of war. On the mutilation, see Aeschylus, *Libation Bearers* (439); Sophocles, *Electra* (445–46); Euripides, *Electra* (164, *lōban*, "outrage").

the bitter plot
you came home from Troy
your wife welcomed you
not with wreaths, not with crowns
but with merciless outrage she handed you over
to Aegisthus, his two-edged sword   165
and took the traitor as her lover.

*(Enter the chorus along the side
entrances, from both directions.)*

Parodos[22]

[Strophe]

CHORUS:
Daughter of Agamemnon, Electra, I have come
to your rustic farmyard.
A stranger is here; a milk-drinking[23]
mountain-roaming man has come from Mycenae.   170
He brings news that two days from now
the Argives will proclaim a public sacrifice
and all the girls will march
in a procession of honor for Hera.[24]

ELECTRA:
No, not for parties, my dear friends,   175
and not for golden rings
does my poor heart
take wing and I will not lead dances
with the Argive brides

---

22. *167–212:* Parodos—the entrance song of the chorus.

23. *169:* "A stranger is here"—The man who brings the news of the festival
is a herdsman, drinker of milk rather than wine. His life is so remote and
he so poor that he lives off what his flock produces. Wine is the drink
of the civilized. In Homer's *Odyssey*, the Cyclops is so uncivilized that
Odysseus is able to overcome him with wine. (See Euripides, *Bacchae*
272–85 on the gifts of grain and grape.)

24. *174:* The *Heraia* (festival to Hera), which celebrates Hera's marriage to
Zeus, was a major festival in Argos. The procession the chorus mentions
is for unmarried girls.

180 or beat my whirling feet.
 I spend the night in tears,
 and mourning becomes me
 in my daytime misery.
 Look at my matted hair
185 and my dress in rags.
 Are they fit for Agamemnon's
 royal daughter
 and for Troy, the city that can never forget
 it was laid waste by my father?

[Antistrophe]

CHORUS:
190 Hera is a great god. Come, now,
 and borrow from me a fancy
 dress to put on
 and golden ornaments to grace its beauty.
 Do you think if you do not honor the gods
 you will defeat your enemies with your tears?
195 No, it's not with laments
 but with prayers revering the gods
 that you will reach your happy day, dear girl.

ELECTRA:
 None of the gods hears the voice
 of the unlucky, none cares about the ancient
200 butchery done to my father.
 I cry for the one dead and gone
 and for the living, the vagabond,
 who lives somewhere in another land,
 unhappy wanderer
205 at the drudges' hearth,
 son of a proud father.
 And here in a poor man's hovel
 I live, wasting away my life
 banished from my father's house,
210 along these mountain crags,
 while my mother lives in criminal marriage
 with another husband.

First Episode

CHORUS LEADER:
So many troubles for all Greeks and for your own house
were brought on by your mother's sister Helen.[25]

*(Orestes and Pylades and their attendants
get up from behind the altar.)*

ELECTRA:
Oh my god! Women, I must break off these laments.   215
Some strangers are here near the house, lurking
behind the altar, and now they are getting up from their
     ambush;
run—you go back along the road and I'll head for the house—
we must try to escape from these outlaws.

ORESTES:
Wait, poor woman. Don't be afraid of me.   220

ELECTRA:
Phoebus Apollo, I beg you for my life.

ORESTES:
There are others I might kill, more my enemies than you.

ELECTRA:
Go away. Do not touch what you should not.

ORESTES:
There is no one I have more right to touch.

ELECTRA:
Why are you hiding there with a sword in your hand?   225

ORESTES:
Stay and listen. You'll be glad you did.

---

25. *214:* The reference to Helen may seem irrelevant, but the end of the
play will reveal that assumptions about her guilt have been made for a
purpose.

ELECTRA:
I'll stay. I'm in your power. You're stronger than me.

ORESTES:
I have come here with news from your brother.

ELECTRA:
My dear friend. Is he alive or dead?

ORESTES:
230   Alive. I'm happy to give the good news first.

ELECTRA:
Bless you. Thank you for this most welcome message.

ORESTES:
It is something we both share.

ELECTRA:
Where in the world is he living his dreary life of exile?

ORESTES:
He doesn't keep to one place but moves from city to city.

ELECTRA:
235   Does he have enough for his daily needs?

ORESTES:
That much he has, but a homeless man carries no weight.

ELECTRA:
What word of him do you bring?

ORESTES:
He wants to know if you are alive and if so in what condition.

ELECTRA:
First of all, do you see how drawn my skin is?

ORESTES:
240   Worn by your cares—it makes me want to cry.

ELECTRA:
And my head with the hair shaved off.[26]

ORESTES:
You must miss your brother and your dead father.

ELECTRA:
Ah me, there is no one dearer to me than they.

ORESTES:
Ah![27] And your brother: don't you think he feels the same?

ELECTRA:
But he is away and not here with us.   245

ORESTES:
Why do you live out here so far from town?

ELECTRA:
I am married, stranger,[28] a lethal match.

ORESTES:
I am sorry for your brother. Who is your husband?

ELECTRA:
Not a man my father expected to choose for me.

ORESTES:
Tell me so I can report it to your brother.   250

---

26. *241:* "With the hair shaved off"—in Greek, *eskythismenon,* "scalped with a razor" (like a victim of the Scythians; see Herodotus, *The Histories* 4.64.2–3).

27. *244:* "Ah!"—In Greek, *pheu* is a cry of dismay or surprise, amounting almost to a gasp. Orestes utters exometric *pheu* after 261, 281, 366, and 968.

28. *247:* The word for "stranger" (*xenos*) means "friend in a foreign country, guest, host," so that Electra's term of address to her brother could also be translated as "my friend," but the irony of her having to call her brother "stranger" is maintained in the translation. At 83 Orestes calls Pylades both "friend" (*philos,* "loved one, family member") and "host" or "stranger" (*xenos*).

ELECTRA:
This is where I live, here at the border, in his house.

ORESTES:
Some dirt farmer or cowhand would live here.

ELECTRA:
My husband is poor but decent and respectful to me.

ORESTES:
What form does your husband's respect take?

ELECTRA:
255   He has never taken advantage of me.

ORESTES:
Is it some sort of religious abstention or doesn't he care for
you?

ELECTRA:
He did not think it right to insult my parents.

ORESTES:
And why didn't he count his blessings in making such a match?

ELECTRA:
He didn't think the man who gave me to him had authority,
stranger.

ORESTES:
260   I understand. So he would not suffer Orestes' retribution.

ELECTRA:
He is aware of that, but he is also a decent man.

ORESTES:
Well, then,[29] he must be one of nature's gentlemen. He
deserves a good turn.

---

29. *262:* "Well, then"—This is another of Orestes' *pheus*; see note on 244.

ELECTRA:
Yes, of course, if my missing brother ever comes home.

ORESTES:
Your own mother: did she put up with this?

ELECTRA:
Women's affections belong to their husbands, not their
children, stranger. 265

ORESTES:
Why has Aegisthus insulted you in this way?

ELECTRA:
By marrying me to such a man, he hoped I would have
powerless children.

ORESTES:
So your children would not be able to take vengeance?

ELECTRA:
That was his ploy. I pray he will pay for it.

ORESTES:
Does your mother's husband know you are still a virgin? 270

ELECTRA:
No, he doesn't. We are keeping it a secret from him.

ORESTES:
And these women who are listening, are they friends?

ELECTRA:
Yes. They will keep their lips sealed.

ORESTES:
What, then, is Orestes' part in this if he comes to Argos?

ELECTRA:
You ask that! Shame on you. Isn't now the time for action? 275

ORESTES:
Then suppose he does come: how can he kill your father's
murderers?

ELECTRA:
By doing to his enemies what they did to Father.

ORESTES:
Would you really have the heart to help him kill your mother?

ELECTRA:
With the same axe that killed my father.

ORESTES:
280   Should I tell him this, and that he can count on you?

ELECTRA:
Let me die once I have shed my mother's blood.

ORESTES:
Ah, if only Orestes were nearby to hear this.

ELECTRA:
But, you know, I wouldn't recognize him if I saw him.

ORESTES:
I'm not surprised. You were both very young when you were
separated.

ELECTRA:
285   Only one person I know would recognize him.

ORESTES:
The one they say saved him from being murdered?

ELECTRA:
Yes: my father's old childhood slave.

ORESTES:
Did your father get a decent burial when he died?

ELECTRA:
He got what he got, flung out as he was from the house.

ORESTES:
What a story! Even strangers' troubles   290
can actually make a person feel pain.
Go on with your tale so I can tell your brother
the news, unwelcome, but he needs to hear it.
Pity is not found in boorish ignorance,
but in men of finer feelings; and even for the sensitive,
too much sensitivity has to have its price.   295

CHORUS LEADER:
I have the same longing in my heart too.
We live far from town and do not know
the troubles in the city, but want to learn them now.

ELECTRA:
I'll tell—or should I?—yes, you are a friend so I must tell   300
the heavy fortune that has struck me and my father.
Since you press me to tell the tale, stranger, I beg you,
bring news to Orestes of my troubles and his own.
First, look at the rags I am kept in, here in this stable,
how much grime I am weighed down with, under what roof   305
I live after my home in the royal palace.
I have to toil at weaving my own clothes
or else go naked and do without
and I carry water from the spring myself.
I live in privation, without sacred festivals and dances,   310
and shrink from the company of women because I'm still a
     virgin,
and I am ashamed to face Castor, my kinsman
to whom I was betrothed before he went up to the gods.[30]

---

30. 312–13: The betrothal of Electra to her uncle (a degree of consanguinity
allowed by Athenian marriage practice) may be an invention of Euripides.
Castor and Polydeuces (Pollux) were the twin sons of Zeus and Leda
(Dioscuri; in Latin, Gemini), one mortal, one divine. When Castor died,
they were allowed to share immortality as stars and protectors of sailors.

But my mother, decked out with the spoils of Phrygia,[31]
315 sits on her throne, and beside her are stationed
slave women, my father's captives,
in Trojan gowns fastened with golden pins.
While in my home Father's blood is still
putrefied to black and his murderer
320 goes driving in the same chariot Father used,
and the scepter with which Father commanded the Greek
armies,
he swaggers around holding it in his blood-drenched hands.
And Agamemnon's burial mound lies dishonored
and never received libations or boughs of myrtle[32]
325 and his altar stands neglected, without offerings.
Meanwhile the rumor is that mother's splendid husband
gets drunk, leaps on his grave, and throws rocks at Father's
headstone[33]
and has the gall to utter these words to mock us:
330 "Where is your boy Orestes? Is he here to protect your tomb
like a good son?" This is how he is insulted because he's not
here.
But, stranger, please, bring him this report.
Its senders are many and I speak for them,
my hands, my lips, my broken heart;
335 my shorn head and his own father.
It is a disgrace if Father wiped out the Trojans,
but *he*, one on one, cannot kill this man,
though he is young and born of a nobler father.

CHORUS LEADER:
I see him, your husband, I mean.
340 He has left his work and is heading home.

---

31. *314–17:* Phrygia and Phrygians are metonymies for Troy and Trojans, respectively.

32. *324:* Myrtle is an aromatic evergreen shrub (genus *Myrtus*), native to the Mediterranean region, and is a favorite plant for various kinds of ceremonial decoration.

33. *326–31:* Electra's description of Aegisthus at the tomb mocking her father is based on rumor, as she admits (327 lit., "so they say"), and contrasts strongly with the gracious Aegisthus we meet in the reported scene.

(Enter Farmer stage right from the country.)

FARMER:[34]

What's this? Who are these strangers I see in front of my door?
Why have they come out here to my house in the country?
Are they looking for me? It's not proper, you know,
for a woman to be in the company of young men.[35]

ELECTRA:

Oh no, dear, do not be suspicious of me.   345
Let me tell you what their story is. These strangers
have come from Orestes to bring me news of him.

(To Orestes and Pylades.)

Please, excuse what he just said.

FARMER:

What do they have to say? Is he alive?

ELECTRA:

Yes, at least that's what they say and I have no reason to
distrust them.   350

FARMER:

And does he keep in mind what was done to his father and
you?

ELECTRA:

That's what I hope. But a man in exile is powerless.

FARMER:

What news have they brought of Orestes?

---

34. *341–400:* The Farmer and Orestes do not engage with each other.
The Farmer addresses Orestes, but Orestes does not answer him directly,
showing a class distinction.

35. *344:* In Athenian society, women were secluded. It was the man's job
to negotiate with strangers. The social norms are defied in tragic action,
which takes place at the gates of the scene building and thus requires that
the female characters be outside.

ELECTRA:
He sent them to observe my troubles.

FARMER:
355   Well, some they can see. The rest, I imagine, you told them.

ELECTRA:
Yes, they know. They have no deficiency on that score.

FARMER:
Why haven't we opened our doors to them by now?
Please, go into the house. For your welcome news
you will receive whatever hospitality my house can offer.

(To Orestes' attendants.)

360   Go on and take the baggage inside my house.

(To Orestes.)

And don't say no. You come as friends
from a friend. Even if I am a poor man,
I will not show a mean spirit.

ORESTES:
My god, is this the man who helps you mask
365   your marriage, to spare Orestes' good name?

ELECTRA:
He is called unhappy Electra's husband.

ORESTES:
Ah, there are no easy answers in the matter of a man's worth.
Human nature is beyond comprehension.
In the past I've seen the son of a noble father
amount to nothing and outstanding children born of worthless
370   men.
I've seen the poverty of a rich man's mind
and a keen intellect in a poor man's body.
[How is anyone to make a correct distinction?
According to wealth? Then he'll be relying on a corrupt judge.
375   By lack, then? But poverty carries its own disease:

it leads a man to crime because of need.
But should I use military prowess? Can anyone face a spear
and bear witness to another's valor?
No, it's best to leave these things to fall as they may.]³⁶
This man is nobody of importance in Argos;   380
he can claim no distinction of family.
He may be common as dirt, but he's a man of quality.
Why not be sensible, instead of deceiving ourselves
with empty speculations, and judge people
by associating with them and knowing their character?   385
[This is the kind of man who could manage a city or home
well. But empty muscle men without a brain
are only good for statues in the public square. The strong arm
does not hold out against the spear any better than the weak
but it is a matter of a man's nature and his mettle.]   390
Well, Agamemnon's son, who sent us,
deserves this, whether he is here or not,
so let us enjoy the hospitality of this house.

 (To his servants.)

You may go
into the house. I'll take a poor but considerate man   395
as my host over a rich one.

 (Exeunt servants into the house with baggage.)

I accept the invitation into this man's house,
but I would prefer to have your brother
receive me into a prosperous home in happier circumstances.
Maybe he will come. The oracles of Loxias³⁷
are certain. Though for human fortune-telling I have no use.   400

 *(Exeunt Orestes and Pylades through
 the central doors into the house.)*

---

36. *373–79:* Brackets [ ] around lines in the translation indicate sections
of doubtful authenticity, especially those scholars suspect of being
interpolations made for later productions, as this one is (see Page 1934,
pp. 74–75), or editors' notes that crept into the text from the margins.
37. *399:* Loxias—Apollo in his role as prophet.

CHORUS:
Now more than before, Electra, my heart is warming
with joy. Maybe now at last
your fortune is looking up and will turn out well.

ELECTRA: (To her husband.)
You fool, you know how poor we are. How could you invite
405   these guests who are so much better off than you?

FARMER:
What's this? If they are as well-bred as they seem,
won't they be just as content with the meager as the plentiful?

ELECTRA:
Meager is what you have! But since you have made this
blunder,
go to my father's dear old childhood slave
410   who was cast out of the city and keeps sheep for company
near the Tanaus River where it forms the border
between Argive and Spartan territory.
Tell him that guests have come and he should bring
something for the strangers' dinner.

            (Farmer starts to object.)

415   Oh, he'll be glad, I assure you, and he'll thank the gods
when he hears the infant he saved all those years ago is still
alive.
We would get nothing out of our ancestral home
from Mother. It's bitter news we would bring her
if that awful woman learned that Orestes is alive.

FARMER:
420   Well, if you think so, I'll take the news
to the old man. But hurry on in
and get things ready inside.

            (Exit Electra into the house.)

                        If she wants to, a woman
can find plenty to serve for a meal.
There is still enough in my house

to fill their bellies for a day.   425
When my mind falls to thinking this way
I consider what great power money has—
to give to strangers and when you fall ill
to pay for medicines. To sustain yourself
day to day doesn't cost a lot. Everybody,   430
rich or poor, can only hold so much.

(Exit Farmer stage left to the highway.)

First Stasimon

CHORUS:

[Strophe 1]

Famous ships that sailed once to Troy
with oars too many to count,
escorting the chorus of Nereid nymphs.[38]
To the music of the pipe a dolphin leapt alongside them   435
whirling around the dark prows
bringing the son of Thetis,
swift Achilles, nimble of foot,
to accompany Agamemnon   440
to the banks of Simois in Troy.

[Antistrophe 1]

Nereids leaving Euboean headlands
carried the armorers' toils from the anvils
of Hephaestus—golden armor[39]
up Pelion's slopes,[40] up through the woodlands of Ossa   445
searching for high lookouts of nymphs
where the Centaur Chiron like a father

---

38. *434:* Nereids are sea nymphs, daughters of Nereus, sisters of Achilles' mother Thetis.

39. *444:* In Homer, the set of body armor made by Hephaestus (*Iliad* 18) is very different from that described here and is brought to Achilles in Troy by his mother after his first set was worn into battle by Patroclus and stripped from his fallen body.

40. *445:* Pelion—the site of the wedding of Achilles' parents, Peleus and Thetis, and the home of Chiron, the Centaur who reared and educated Achilles and other heroes.

raised a bright light for Hellas,
450   the sea goddess Thetis' swift-footed
son, for the sons of Atreus.

[Strophe 2]

I heard from someone in the port, back from Troy
who had come to Nauplia,
how in the circle of your famous shield,
455   son of Thetis,
these icons were forged,
terrors for the Phrygians:
around the surface of the rim
Perseus above the sea on winged sandals
460   holds the Gorgon's severed head
in the company of Hermes, Zeus' messenger,
the rustic son of Maia.[41]

[Antistrophe 2]

Shining in the middle of the shield there glinted
465   the sun's orb
mounted on heavenly horses
and the ethereal choreographies of stars:
Pleiades and Hyades, causing
Hector to turn away his eyes;
470   and on the helmet made of gold
Sphinxes bearing in their talons
their deadly song's prey[42]
and on the breastplate's rounded form, breathing fire
the Chimera raced on her lion's claws
475   peering up at Pegasus, the flying colt of Peirene.[43]

---

41. *460–63:* A direct look at the Gorgon, Medusa, turned people into
stone. Perseus used mirrors to see her face, slew her, and carried her head
around. Later he gave the head to Athena.

42. *471–75:* A Sphinx is a bird-woman who brings death. The Theban
Sphinx sang a riddle and seized and devoured men who could not solve it,
until Oedipus guessed it right.

43. *474:* Chimera is a compound female monster made up of lioness, goat,
and snake who breathes fire. She was killed by Bellerophon with the help of

[Epode]

On the stabbing sword galloped
four-footed horses, black dust swirling over their backs.
The king of those great men in arms
your marriage killed,
evil-minded daughter of Tyndareos.   480
For that, one day, the gods in heaven
will dispatch you to death. Truly one day
to come I will see the blood of murder
pouring out beneath your neck   485
gashed by the sword.

Second Episode

*(Enter Old Man, pulling a sheep and carrying
provisions, stage left from the highway.)*

OLD MAN:
Where is she? Where is my young lady, my mistress,
daughter of Agamemnon, him that I brought up myself?
What a steep climb she has up to her house
for a shriveled old man like me to get to on foot.   490
Still, she is dear to me and on my wobbly knees
I must drag along this hunched back.
Hello, daughter, now I see you there in front of the house.
I'm here to bring you a young lamb
from my flock—here it is, the one I picked   495
and wreaths and some cheese from the press
and this precious vintage wine full of aroma,
just a drop, but something sweet to add,
a cup or so, to a weaker drink.
Someone go and bring this to the guests inside.   500
I have to lift my ragged cloak and wipe
my eyes that are drenched with tears.

ELECTRA:
Why are your eyes dripping with tears, old man?
Does my situation remind you of your troubles after all this time?

Pegasus, the colt of Peirene, the winged horse that sprang from the Gorgon
(Medusa) when Perseus beheaded her.

505   Or do you weep over Orestes' hard exile
        and my father you once held in your arms
        and cared for, in vain for yourself and those you love?

OLD MAN:
        In vain, that's right. Still I did not hold back.
        I took a detour to visit his tomb,
510   and I knelt down and wept at seeing it deserted;
        then I opened the wineskin I'm carrying for your guests
        and poured a libation and I covered his mound with myrtle.
        There on the altar I saw a sacrificed sheep,
        a black one for the dead, and blood spilled not long ago.
515   There were locks of hair cut in mourning.[44]
        I was amazed, my girl, to think who in the world dared
        to visit the tomb. No Argive would have, that's for sure.
        Look here, maybe your brother has come in secret
        and paid respect to his father's neglected grave.
520   Go look at the hair. Put it next to your own
        to see if the color is the same as yours.
        It often happens that people with the same father
        have many physical traits in common.

ELECTRA:
        What you are saying makes you sound stupid, old man,
525   if you think my brave brother has come
        to the country in secret out of fear of Aegisthus.
        Will two locks of hair be alike,
        one from the head of a noble youth raised in the wrestling
              schools,
        the other a woman's and well-combed? It's absurd.
530   Besides, many people have hair the same color
        who do not share the same blood, old man.

OLD MAN:
        Well then, why don't you go to where I saw his footprint
        and see if it's the same size as your own, child?

---

44. 515–46: The cut lock of hair, the footprint, and the weaving are the
tokens of recognition in Aeschylus' Libation Bearers (167–234).

ELECTRA:
  How could his feet leave an impression
  in the rocky ground? And even if there is,   535
  the feet of brother and sister, a man and a woman,
  would not be alike. The man's are bigger.

OLD MAN:
  If your brother has entered the country, is there any way
  you could recognize him by some weaving from your loom
  in which once long ago I stole him away from imminent death?   540

ELECTRA:
  Don't you know that I was a child when Orestes
  went into exile? And even if I was already weaving cloth,
  he was only a baby then. How could he still be wearing
  the same clothes, unless they grew to keep up with him?
  But either some stranger took pity on the grave   545
  and cut his hair or they[45] were sent to spy out the land.

OLD MAN:
  Where are the strangers? I want to see them
  and ask them about your brother.

ELECTRA:
  Here they are, coming out of the house with quick steps.

OLD MAN:
  They look well-born, but there's no telling from looks.   550
  Many well-born men are worthless.
  Still, I bid the visitors good day.

ORESTES:
  Greetings, old man. Really, Electra, this antique relic
  of a man, who in the world is he?

ELECTRA:
  This, stranger, is the man who tended my father.   555

---

45. 546: Textual problems make it uncertain what Euripides wrote here
or what exactly "they" refers to.

ORESTES:
What? Is he the one who spirited away your brother?

ELECTRA:
Yes, he is the one who saved him, if he is still alive.

ORESTES:
Ah, why is he staring at me as if he is examining
the shiny imprint on a coin? Do I remind him of someone?

ELECTRA:
560   Maybe he is happy to see someone Orestes' age.

ORESTES:
Well, Orestes is a friend of mine. Why is he walking around
     me?

ELECTRA:
I'm wondering about that, too, stranger.

OLD MAN:
My lady, dear daughter, Electra, praise the gods.

ELECTRA:
Why? What for, of all that is possible in the world?

OLD MAN:
565   For the thing you most desire, which god is revealing.

ELECTRA: *(Electra gestures, raises arms in prayer.)*
There, I call on the gods. Or what do you mean, old man?

OLD MAN:
Look at this man, my child, the man closest to you.

ELECTRA:
I have been looking at him for quite a while. Are you all right?

OLD MAN:
Of course I'm all right. I am looking at your brother.

ELECTRA:
What do you mean, old man, by this astonishing statement? 570

OLD MAN:
That I see Orestes right here: Agamemnon's son.

ELECTRA:
What sign do you see that I can trust?

OLD MAN:
See that scar over his eyebrow? He got that in your father's
house
one day when he fell and bloodied it, while you two were
chasing a deer.[46]

ELECTRA:
What are you saying? Yes, I do see a scar from an accident. 575

OLD MAN:
Do you hesitate to embrace your dearest brother?

ELECTRA:
Not anymore, old man. I am convinced in my heart
by your token of recognition. *(Embracing Orestes.)* I hold you
at last, against all hope.

ORESTES:
                    And at last you are in my arms.

ELECTRA:
Never expected.

ORESTES:
                    I dared not hope. 580

ELECTRA:
Are you he?

---

46. *573–74:* In Homer's *Odyssey* (19.390–475), Odysseus' old nurse
recognizes him because of a scar. Odysseus in turn uses it to identify
himself to his herdsmen (21.217–19).

ORESTES:
> Yes, your only ally.
> If I pull in the catch I am going after . . . and I am confident.
> Or else we should stop believing in the gods,
> if wrong triumphs over right in the end.

Choral Interlude

CHORUS:
585   You have come, you have come, long-awaited day,
> you have shone down, you have revealed to the city
> a beacon in blazing light, who in long exile
> from his father's house
> was wandering in misery.
590   Now some god, yes, a god brings us
> victory, my dear.
> Raise up your hands, raise your voice in prayers
> lifted to the gods that your brother
595   will enter the city in good fortune.

Second Episode: Continued

ORESTES:
> Well. I have enjoyed the sweet pleasure
> of your embraces and in time we will share them again.
> But, you, old man, you have arrived in good time.
> Tell me, what should I do to take revenge on Father's murderer
600   and my mother, his partner in unholy marriage?
> Are there any in Argos kindly disposed toward me,
> or, like my luck, am I completely bankrupt?
> Who are my allies? Should I act at night or in the daylight?
> What road can we take against our enemies?

OLD MAN:
605   Son, you have no friends when your luck runs out.
> It is a rare find, you know, if you have someone
> to share in common both good times and bad.
> In the eyes of your friends you are totally ruined
> and have left them no hope. But listen to me:
610   you hold in your own hands and in fortune everything
> you need to recover your estate and your city.

ORESTES:
What must I do to reach this goal?

OLD MAN:
Kill Thyestes' son and your mother.

ORESTES:
This is the crown I have come here for, but how do I get it?

OLD MAN:
Even if you wanted to, *not* by going inside the city walls.   615

ORESTES:
Is he surrounded by a garrison and bodyguards?

OLD MAN:
That's right. He lives in fear and does not sleep soundly.

ORESTES:
Good. Old man, you plan the next step.

OLD MAN:
Wait. Listen. I just remembered something.

ORESTES:
Tell me some good news. I would be happy to hear it.   620

OLD MAN:
I saw Aegisthus on my way here.

ORESTES:
I'm very glad to hear this. Where was he?

OLD MAN:
Where he pastures his horses, not far from this farm.

ORESTES:
What was he doing? I see hope coming out of my helplessness.

OLD MAN:

625   I think he was preparing a festival to the Nymphs.[47]

ORESTES:

For bringing up a child or a coming birth?

OLD MAN:

I don't know, but he came prepared to slaughter a bull.

ORESTES:

How big was their party or did he just have his household slaves?

OLD MAN:

No Argive citizens were there, just a bunch of his slaves.

ORESTES:

I don't suppose there's anybody who will recognize me, old
630   man.

OLD MAN:

They are slaves who've never seen you.

ORESTES:

Would they be disposed toward us if we succeed?

OLD MAN:

That's the character of slaves, and a bonus for you.

ORESTES:

So how can I get close to him?

OLD MAN:

635   Go where he'll see you as he is sacrificing.

ORESTES:

It looks like he has his lands right off the road?

---

47. *625:* Mountain Nymphs are divinities of springs and are worshiped
at specific locations. They are associated with fertility, childbirth, and
good health ("nymph" means "bride"). Line 626 hints that Clytemnestra
might be pregnant.

OLD MAN:
Yes, and when he sees you there, he'll invite you to join the
feast.

ORESTES:
A distasteful dinner guest, god willing.

OLD MAN:
From there you must look to the throw of the dice.

ORESTES:
Good. Thank you. But my mother—where is she?   640

OLD MAN:
In Argos; but she will join her husband for the sacrifice.

ORESTES:
Why didn't she set out with Aegisthus?

OLD MAN:
She stayed behind out of fear of public censure.

ORESTES:
Of course. She must know she is an object of suspicion in
town.

OLD MAN:
That's so. Everybody detests an immoral woman.   645

ORESTES:
How will I kill her and him with one blow?

ELECTRA:
I will take care of the murder of my mother.

ORESTES:
With him so close, luck is surely on my side.

ELECTRA: *(Pointing to Old Man.)*
Let him be assistant to both of us

OLD MAN:

I'll do that. What manner of death do you have in mind for
650   your mother?

ELECTRA:

Old man, go tell this story to Clytemnestra:
bring her news that I have just given birth to a baby boy.

OLD MAN:

Was the birth a while ago or just now?

ELECTRA:

Ten days ago, the time it takes for a new mother to be
purified.[48]

OLD MAN:
655   And how exactly does this bring about your mother's death?

ELECTRA:

She will come when she hears I am indisposed from the birth.

OLD MAN:

Why do you think she cares about you, dear child?

ELECTRA:

She does. And she will shed real tears over the baby's status.

OLD MAN:

Maybe so, but bring your story back to the goal.

ELECTRA:
660   When she gets here, obviously, she dies.

OLD MAN:

She will come right to the doors of your house.

ELECTRA:

And from there it is just a small step to Hell.

---

48. *654*: A woman was considered ritually unclean through the labor,
during the birth, and for ten days after the birth. On the tenth day, the
baby was named and acknowledged as a member of the family.

OLD MAN:
Once I have seen this I'll die a happy man.

ELECTRA:
First, old man, show him the way.

OLD MAN:
Where Aegisthus is sacrificing to the gods?   665

ELECTRA:
Yes—then go find my mother and tell her my news.

OLD MAN:
She will think she is hearing it from your own lips.

ELECTRA: (To Orestes.)
It's your work now. You have drawn the first killing.

ORESTES:
I'm off, if he will guide me there.

OLD MAN:
Yes, I am happy to show you the way.   670

ORESTES:
Zeus of my ancestors, defend me against my enemies.

ELECTRA:
Pity us; our suffering makes us worthy of your pity.

OLD MAN:
Pity your descendants.

ELECTRA:
And Hera, you have power over Mycenae's altars.

ORESTES:
Grant us victory, if what we ask is right.   675

OLD MAN:
Grant justice in requital for their father's death.

ORESTES:
And you, Father, foully murdered, living down below in the
  earth . . .

ELECTRA:
And Earth, queen of all, I strike with my hands.

OLD MAN:
Defend these dear, dear children, defend them.

ORESTES:
680   Come now, bring armies of the dead as our allies.

ELECTRA:
Those who with you annihilated the Phrygians in war.

OLD MAN:
All who abhor the unholy polluters.

ORESTES:
Do you hear, Father, you who suffered outrage from Mother?

OLD MAN:
Your father hears all this. Time now to go.

ELECTRA:
685   And so I declare to you: Aegisthus must die.
           Since if you go down, pinned in a fatal fall,[49]
           I'm dead, too; don't speak of me as being alive,
           for I shall stab myself in the heart with a two-edged sword.[50]
           I am going inside to get ready[51]

---

49. *686:* "Pinned in a fatal fall"—a metaphor from wrestling. See
Aeschylus, *Agamemnon* 171–72.

50. *688:* For "heart" the manuscripts have "head," which has been emended to either "liver" or "heart." This is a masculine manner of suicide, but
women sometimes threaten to use it; in ancient Greek literature, a woman's
favored method of suicide was hanging (see Loraux 1987, pp. 14, 54).

51. *689–93:* Some scholars suspect that these lines, seen as bathetic rather
than pathetic, are interpolations by actors or producers (Page 1934, pp.
75–76).

so that if good news of you comes the whole house   690
will lift its voice in songs of thanksgiving, but if it is news
of your death, the opposite. This is what I had to say to you.

ORESTES:
I know all I need to know.

ELECTRA:
                    For this, you must be a man.

*(Exeunt Orestes with Old Man, accompanied
by Pylades and the servants, stage left.)*

Women, you light a beacon to blast
news of this contest. I will stand watch,   695
holding a sword ready in my hand,
and never, if I am overwhelmed by my enemies,
I will *never* allow them the satisfaction of abusing me while
    I'm alive.

(Exit Electra through the central doors into the house.)

Second Stasimon

CHORUS:
                    [Strophe 1]

This myth is told in shadowy rumors
that once in the Argive
mountains Pan,[52] steward of fields,   700
blowing sweet music
on well-pitched pipes,
brought a lamb with
gorgeous golden fleece from its tender mother.   705
And standing on the stone steps
the herald cried,
"To the square, to the square,
Mycenaeans, come all, to see
the marvel, the blessed kings'   710

---

52. *700–706:* Pan—the god of fields and forests who pipes to his flocks
on the panpipes, a rustic instrument of graduated reeds.

portent." With dances they celebrated
the houses of the sons of Atreus.

[Antistrophe 1]

Fire-pans worked with gold were spread
up and down the town—fires gleamed
715   on the altars of the Argives.
The lotus reed, servant of the Muses,
piped in melodious voice.
Sweet songs swelled
celebrating the golden lamb. A new ending
for Thyestes' story:[53] in a secret liaison
720   he had seduced the dear wife
of Atreus and brought the marvel
home. Walking then
among the assembled people he proclaims
that he has in his house
725   the horned sheep with golden wool.

[Strophe 2][54]

Then, it was then that Zeus changed
the shining orbits of the stars
and the fire of the sun
730   and the pale face of dawn,
and he harried the western expanses
with hot god-fanned flame;
in the north, rain-filled clouds,
but the arid ground of Ammon Ra[55]
735   withers without moisture,
deprived of beautiful rains from Zeus.

---

53. *718–19:* "A new ending for Thyestes' story"—The meaning of the
word *epilogoi* in the manuscripts is doubtful. Emendations include "then
came Thyestes' trick"; "in praise of the golden lamb"; "Thyestes had the
luck."

54. *726–36:* The sun used to set in the east, but Zeus changed its course
in outrage at Thyestes' crime. See Plato, *Statesman (Politicus)* 268e–269a.

55. *734:* Ammon Ra—the oracle of Ammon (Amun) at the oasis of Siwa
in the desert of Libya.

[Antistrophe 2]

So it is told, but in my eyes
it carries little credence
that the golden-faced sun   740
reversed course and moved
the torrid zone
to afflict the mortal race
for the sake of human justice.
Frightening myths are a blessing
for humankind and advance the gods' service.
Forgetful of them, you killed   745
your husband, sister of celebrated brothers.[56]

Third Episode

(Loud shouting is heard in the distance.)

CHORUS LEADER:
What's that?
Friends, did you hear a shout—or has a false impression
come over me? Like Zeus' rumbling from under the ground.[57]
Listen, these rising winds must mean something.
Electra, come out of the house, dear lady.   750

ELECTRA:
Friends, what is it? How have we come out in the contest?

CHORUS LEADER:
All I know is that I just heard a scream of murder.

ELECTRA:
I heard it too, but from far away.

CHORUS LEADER:
The sound comes a long way, but still it is sharp.

---

56. *746:* "Sister of celebrated brothers"—This probably refers to
Clytemnestra as sister of the Dioscuri (Castor and Polydeuces).
57. *748:* "Zeus' rumbling"—Earthquakes are caused by Poseidon, but
here the sound of an earthquake (subterranean or seismic rumblings) is
compared to thunder, which comes from Zeus.

ELECTRA:
755   Is the cry Argive or from those I love?

CHORUS LEADER:
    I cannot tell. It's just noise. The words are all mixed up.

ELECTRA:
    You announce my death. Why delay?

CHORUS LEADER:
    Wait until you learn your fate more clearly.

ELECTRA:
    No. We are defeated. Where are the messengers?[58]

CHORUS LEADER:
760   They will be here. It's no trivial matter to kill a king.

(Enter Messenger stage left.)

MESSENGER:
    Women of Mycenae, happy in victory,
    I bring news of Orestes' triumph to all who love him:
    Agamemnon's murderer, Aegisthus, lies dead
    on the ground. Let us praise the gods.

ELECTRA:
765   Who are you? Why should I believe what you are telling me?[59]

MESSENGER:
    Don't you recognize your brother's servant when you see him?

---

58. *759:* The choral ode covers an indeterminate passage of time during
which Aegisthus is killed while the chorus sings of the crime of his father
Thyestes that started the interfilial feud. Messengers often seem to arrive
at the end of an ode, too soon after an event. This question may be a
metatheatrical allusion to the stage convention or an indication of Electra's
impatience or anxiety.
59. *765:* Of the twenty-six messengers in Greek tragedy, this is the only
one whose truthfulness is questioned.

ELECTRA:
Dear, dear man. I was so terrified that I could not recognize
your face. Now I know who you are. What are you saying?
Is he really and truly dead, the hated murderer of my father?

MESSENGER:
He is dead. A second time I tell you what you want to hear.   770

ELECTRA:
O gods and Justice that sees all, at last you have come!
Tell me the manner and order of events
in which he killed Thyestes' son. I want to hear it.

MESSENGER:
When we left this house
we walked along a rutted wagon trail   775
to where the "illustrious" king of the Mycenaeans was.
In fact he had gone into a well-watered garden
and was cutting sprays of young myrtle for his head.
When he saw us, he called out, "Hello, strangers, who are you?
Where are you traveling from? What country do you call
    home?"   780
And Orestes answered, "We are Thessalians. We are going
to the Alpheus River to sacrifice to Olympian Zeus."
When he heard that, Aegisthus continued,
"Now you must join us here at our hearth
and share the sacrifice with me. I am slaughtering a bullock   785
to the Nymphs. At dawn after a good night's sleep
you can start out from here refreshed. Come, let's go in."
And just as he was saying this, he took us by the hand
and led us off the road with the words, "You cannot say no."
When we were inside, he went on, saying to his servants,   790
"Hurry, one of you, and bring water for the strangers' hands
so they can stand at the altar beside the lustral bowl."[60]

---

60. *791–837:* This is a fairly complete documentation of the ritual of
sacrifice: the ritual washing, the carrying in of the implements for sacrifice,
the throwing of barley from the basket onto the altar, the cutting of hair
from the victim, the raising of the animal (if it is small enough) and the
cutting of its throat, the butchering, the inspection of the liver (at this
point, the sacrifice is cut short) for omens, roasting, libations of wine, and
the sharing of the meat (see Burkert 1985, pp. 56–59, 112–13).

But Orestes broke in, "We washed just now
in pure water from a flowing river.
795   If strangers are permitted to join in sacrifice with citizens,
King Aegisthus, we are ready and will not say no."
This conversation took place in the midst of the company.
Setting aside their spears, their master's defense,
all the servants set their hands to the task:
800   some brought bowls for the blood, others lifted the baskets,
others lit the fire, and around the sacrificial altars
some were setting up basins. The whole building was abuzz.
Then your mother's bed-mate picked up barley
and threw it on the altars with these words,
805   "Nymphs of the rocks, I pray that with my wife,
the daughter of Tyndareos, I may continue to sacrifice,
in prosperity as I do now, but for my enemies nothing of the
      sort,"
meaning Orestes and you. My master, of course,
without speaking the words out loud, prayed the opposite,
to recover his father's house. Aegisthus took a straight-bladed
810   knife
out of the basket and cut a tuft of the calf's hair
and placed it on the fire with his right hand,
and he cut its throat while servants hoisted the beast up
on their shoulders. Then he said to your brother,
815   "The Thessalians boast that it is a sign
of merit, if anyone excels at butchering a bull
or at breaking in horses. Here, stranger, take the sword
and show us that the legend about Thessaly's men is true."
Orestes took the well-made Dorian sword,
820   threw off his fine traveling cloak,
and, taking Pylades as his assistant in the work,
he made the servants stand aside. Grabbing hold of the calf's
      hoof,
he reached out, bared the white flesh,
and skinned off the hide quicker
825   than a racer on horseback completes a double track.
Then he loosened the flanks. Aegisthus took the sacred parts
in his hands and examined them. The lobe of the liver
was missing. The portal vein and gallbladder next to it

revealed to his inspection the onset of disaster.
His face clouded over, and my master asked him,   830
"Is something troubling you?" "Stranger, I am in terror
of some treachery from outside. Agamemnon's son
is my worst enemy, and he is at war with my house."
To this Orestes said, "Do you really fear the treachery of an
      exile,
and you king of the city? Let's get ready for the feast—   835
will somebody bring us a Phthian cleaver[61]
instead of this Dorian so I can break open the breastbone?"
He lifted it and struck. Aegisthus held the guts,
trying to sort them out. As he was nodding[62]
over them, your brother, standing on tiptoe,   840
struck his vertebrae and smashed the joints
of his back. His whole body convulsed up and down
and he bellowed in the throes of a horrific death.
When they saw what was happening, the slaves rushed to
      arms,
a lot of them for two to fight against. With a show of courage   845
Pylades and Orestes took their stand, brandishing weapons
in the face of the mob. And he said, "I have not come
as an enemy to the city or my former comrades.
I have avenged myself on my father's killer.
I am the misused Orestes. Do not kill me.   850
You were my father's servants in days past." Hearing his
      words,
they stayed their spears. And he was recognized
by an old man from the household.
They started at once to crown your brother's head,
rejoicing and raising a happy cry. He is coming now,   855
bringing not the Gorgon's head to show you,
but Aegisthus whom you hate. Blood has now been shed
in bitter repayment for the blood of the dead man.

      (Exit Messenger stage left)

---

61. *836:* "Phthian cleaver"—a butcher knife.

62. *839:* "As he was nodding"—At a sacrifice the victim is made to nod as
if assenting to its death by being given a bowl of water to drink or having
its head pushed down so that it seems to be bowed.

Choral Dance

CHORUS:

[Strophe]

Set your feet to dancing, dear,
860   like a fawn skipping up
in a joyful leap high in the air.
Your brother wins the crown,
a victory surpassing those on the banks
of Alpheus.[63] But sing
865   a song of victory while I dance.

ELECTRA:

Daylight, gleam of the sun's chariot,
Earth and Night, which I saw before,
now my eyes are free to open wide
since Father's killer Aegisthus has fallen.
870   Come, let me bring whatever I have,
whatever is stored in the house
to adorn his hair, friends,
so I may crown the head of my victorious brother.

CHORUS:

[Antistrophe]

Bring garlands for his head
while our dance, the Muses' joy,
875   goes on and on,
now that the kings we loved in times gone by
have overthrown the usurpers
and will rule the land in justice.
Now raise the shout in gladness to the music of the pipe.

*(Enter Orestes, Pylades, and servants stage left from
the highway, carrying the body of Aegisthus.)*

Fourth Episode

ELECTRA: *(To Orestes, as she puts garlands on his head.)*
880   Glorious in victory, born of a father

---

63. *864:* The site of the ancient Olympics.

victorious in the war at Troy, Orestes,
take this garland for your curls.
You have come home, not after running
a useless footrace, but from killing our enemy
Aegisthus, who killed your father and mine.   885
And you, too, his companion in arms, son of a most loyal man,
Pylades, take this crown from my hand.
You shared equally with him in the contest.
I wish you happiness and prosperity.

ORESTES:
First, Electra, believe the gods are authors   890
of this good fortune and then praise me
as a servant of the gods and of luck.
Yes, I have come back from killing Aegisthus
not in word, but in deed; to add
to your certain knowledge of this, I bring you his dead
   body,   895
and if you so desire, make him prey for wild beasts
or fix him on a stake for birds to scavenge,
children of the sky. Now he is your slave,
who before was called your master.

ELECTRA:
I am ashamed, though I do want to speak.   900

ORESTES:
What is it? Go ahead and speak. You have nothing to fear.

ELECTRA:
I'm reluctant to insult the dead for fear of animosity.

ORESTES:
There is nobody who would find fault with you.

ELECTRA:
Our city is hard to please and quick to blame.

ORESTES:
Have your say, sister, if you desire. We were engaged   905
with him in a hatred that could make no truce.

ELECTRA:

Very well. Where start the tale of woes
and where end it? What words go in the middle?
Every day before dawn I never left off
910   rehearsing what I wished I could say to your face
if ever I could be free of the old fears.
Now at last I am free. I can even the score,
abusing you as I wanted to when you were alive.
You ruined my life. You made me and my brother
915   fatherless orphans when we had done you no wrong.
You entered an illicit union with Mother after you killed her
husband,
commander of the Greeks, when you never even went to Troy.
And you reached such a depth of lunacy that you expected
you would not get an evil wife when you married my mother,
920   even after the two of you had fouled my father's bed.
You can be sure of this: if a man carries on an affair
with another man's wife and then has to marry her,
he is a fool if he thinks that when she was
unfaithful to the first she will be faithful to him.
925   You didn't see it, but your life was miserable.
You knew you had made a sinful marriage, and in you
my mother knew she had acquired a godless husband.
United in evil you shared each other's fate,
you her depravity and she yours.
930   This is what everybody in Argos was saying about you:
"He belongs to his wife, not she to her husband."
It's a disgrace, for the woman, not the man,
to be head of the household. And the children—
not called after their father's name
935   but their mother's—I have no respect for them.
When a man marries his better,
he loses his reputation; it's all about the woman.
And this is what deceived you most—though you were
oblivious—
you prided yourself in *being* somebody because of your wealth,
940   which is nothing but a passing acquaintance.
It is nature, not property, that is steady.
Nature stays with you forever and relieves your troubles.
But wealth is unjust and keeps fools for company,
and after blossoming a day or two it is gone in the wind.

Your relations with women—not a proper topic for a virgin—   945
I will not speak of it, but will put it as a riddle.
You had your way because you ruled the royal roost
and were endowed with good looks. I hope I never have a
    husband
with a face like a girl, but one with a manly character:
their children grow up to be like Ares;   950
but the handsome ones only adorn the dance floor.
To hell with you. Time has found you out; you have paid up
but never learned—here is a lesson for a criminal:
even if he runs the first lap without a misstep
he should not think he has overtaken justice until he reaches   955
the finish line and rounds the final goal of life.

CHORUS:
He has done awful things and paid an awful price
to you and your brother. Justice has proved stronger.

ELECTRA:
So far so good. Now we must carry his body inside
and consign it to darkness, so when Mother   960
arrives she will not see him dead before her throat is cut.

ORESTES:
Wait. Let's turn to a different story.

ELECTRA: (Looking off down the road.)
What's this? Do I see a rescue party from Mycenae?

ORESTES:
No, but my mother who gave me life.

ELECTRA:
Perfect timing then. She is coming straight into the snare.   965
She really is magnificent in her carriage with all the trappings.

ORESTES:
What do we do about Mother? Are we going to kill her?

ELECTRA:
Has pity come over you because you see your mother in
    person?

ORESTES:
Woe![64]
How can I kill her? She gave me life and brought me up.

ELECTRA:
970   The same way she killed your father and mine.

ORESTES:
Phoebus! Your prophecy shows a total lack of wisdom.

ELECTRA:
If Apollo is a fool, who are the wise?

ORESTES:
Who decreed that I kill my mother, which I must not do.

ELECTRA:
How can you be tainted if you avenge your father?

ORESTES:
I will have to stand trial for matricide. Before this, I was free of
975   guilt.

ELECTRA:
And yet if you do not vindicate your father you are guilty of
impiety.[65]

ORESTES:
But my mother—how will I atone?

ELECTRA:
And what if you fail to appease your father?

ORESTES:
Did an avenging demon speak in the guise of the god?

---

64. *968:* "Woe!"—another use of *pheu.* See note on 244.
65. *976:* See Aeschylus' *Libation Bearers* 269–96 for what happens to a
man who does not avenge his father's murder.

ELECTRA:
Sitting on Apollo's sacred tripod?[66] I don't think so.   980

ORESTES:
I cannot believe that was a true prophecy.

ELECTRA:
You must not lose heart and turn into a coward.

ORESTES:
Will I treat her with the same treachery?

ELECTRA:
Yes, the same as when you killed Aegisthus.

ORESTES:
I will go in. I am about to begin a terrible business,   985
and I will do terrible things. If it is the gods' will
so be it, but the ordeal is at once bitter and sweet.

(Exit Orestes into the house.)

CHORUS: *(Addressing Clytemnestra as she arrives stage left*
from the highway in a carriage attended by two or more
Trojan women and driven or led by male attendants.)
Hail!
Royal lady of the Argive country,
Tyndareos' daughter,
sister of the two noble sons of Zeus,   990
who live among the stars
in the bright fire of the sky and hold the privilege
of rescuing mortals on heavy seas.
Greetings. I bow to you as to the blessed ones
for your vast wealth and happiness.   995
Now is the time to look
to your fortunes. Hail, my queen.

---

66. *980:* "Apollo's sacred tripod"—The priestess of Apollo (the Pythia)
delivered her prophecies seated on a tripod, a three-legged stand or altar.

CLYTEMNESTRA:
Climb down from the carriage, Trojan women.
Take my hand to help me step down.

1000   The houses of the gods are decked out with Phrygian spoils,
and these women chosen from the Trojan land are my share
in place of my daughter who was taken from me,
a small trophy, but they add to the grace of my house.

ELECTRA:
Am I not a slave, too, cast out of my father's house

1005   to dwell here in poverty—Mother,
may I not take your blessed hand?

CLYTEMNESTRA:
My slaves are here. Do not trouble yourself.

ELECTRA:
You sent me like a captive slave from my home,
and with my home captured I am captured

1010   like these women, left without a father.

CLYTEMNESTRA:
That was your father's doing when he made
the decision to harm those dearest to him.
I will have my say, and yet when a bad reputation
possesses a woman, there is bitterness in her mouth,

1015   not a good thing. I speak from experience. If you understand
the facts, you have the right to hate her, if she is
deserving of hatred.[67] Otherwise, why the hostility?
Tyndareos gave me in marriage to your father
not so that I or the children I bore him would be killed.

1020   Then Agamemnon, after enticing my daughter
with a promise of marriage to Achilles, took her away
to Aulis where the ships were drawn up. And there
he hoisted her over the altar
and cut through Iphigone's white cheek.[68]

---

67. *1015–17:* Compare to Euripides, *Medea* 219–21, 292–305.
68. *1024:* Iphigone—alternate form of Iphigenia.

If it had been to avert the capture of the city or to benefit his
    house   1025
or to save our other children that he had to kill one
for the good of many, there might have been an excuse.
But, in fact, because Helen was a wild thing and her husband
didn't know how to control his straying wife—
for that he killed my daughter.
I was aggrieved over losing her, but still   1030
I wouldn't have gone wild and killed my husband.
But he came home with that god-possessed madwoman[69]
and introduced her into our bed and we were installed
together, two brides in the same house.
We women are giddy creatures, I can't deny it,   1035
but—that being the case—when the husband strays
and pushes away his wife, the woman is likely
to imitate her husband and take on another "friend."
Then blame puts the spotlight on us,
but the responsible party keeps his sterling reputation.   1040
If Menelaus had been carried off from his house in secret,
would I have had to kill Orestes to rescue
my sister's husband? How would your father
have put up with that? Was it right that I suffer
at his hands but he not die for killing my child?   1045
Yes, I killed him. I turned, where I found a way,
to his enemies. Do you think any of your father's friends
would have abetted me in his murder?
It's your turn to speak if you wish and respond freely.
Tell me, if you can, how your father's death was undeserved.   1050

CHORUS LEADER:
    What you say is just, but it's a disgraceful kind of justice.
    A woman must go along with her husband in everything
    if she is sensible. Whoever does not agree with this
    does not count in my book.

ELECTRA:
    Remember, Mother, that your last words   1055
    gave me the right to speak freely.

---

69. *1032:* "That god-possessed madwoman"—Cassandra, the captive
priestess and prophetess.

CLYTEMNESTRA:
Yes, and I say it again and I won't take it back.

ELECTRA:
When you hear what I have to say, will you hurt me?

CLYTEMNESTRA:
No. I promise not to. Set your mind at rest.

ELECTRA:
1060   I can speak, then. This is what I have to say first.
Mother, if only you had better sense.
Your good looks do you credit,
Helen's and yours both, but you were born alike,
both vain and unworthy of Castor.
1065   She was "raped" of her own free will and ruined herself,
and you destroyed the best man in all Greece,
holding out the pretext that it was because of your daughter
that you killed your husband. They don't know you as well as
     I do.
Before your daughter's sacrifice was authorized,
1070   as soon as your husband was out the door
you started arranging your hair in the mirror.
When the man is away from home, if a woman starts
making herself pretty, write her off as a whore.
She has no reason to show her beautiful face
1075   outside the house unless she is looking for trouble.
I'm the only one in all Greece who knows what you are:
if the Trojan side was doing well, you were all smiles
and if it went badly, then your face clouded over
because you did not want Agamemnon to come home from
     Troy.
1080   And yet you had every opportunity to be virtuous:
you had a husband no worse than Aegisthus,
chosen by all of Greece to be commander in chief;
and when your sister Helen did what she did,
it was possible for you to attain an excellent reputation.
Badness provides an example to do the right thing for all
1085   to see.
But if, as you claim, my father killed your daughter,

what harm did my brother or I do you?
How is it that after you killed your husband you did not
    attach us
more closely to our father's house, but instead brought to your
    marriage
what didn't belong to you, buying a husband at our cost?   1090
And why is your husband not in exile for your son
or why is he not dead for me, since he killed me twice as much
as my sister even if I am still alive? And if in repayment
for murder there will be more murder, am I to kill you
with the help of your son Orestes, to avenge our father?   1095
If what you did is right, that is right, too.
[Anyone who marries a bad woman for money
instead of nobility is a fool. Poor but virtuous
marriages are better for the home than great ones.][70]

CHORUS LEADER:
    [Women's marriages are a matter of luck;   1100
    I have seen some turn out well, others badly.][71]

CLYTEMNESTRA:
    My dear girl, naturally you love your father.
    This happens. Some children favor the male parent
    and others love their mothers more than their fathers.
    I understand. And I'm not really   1105
    very happy with what I did, dear child.
    But why are you so unwashed and ill-clothed
    when you have just given birth?[72]

---

70. *1097–99:* These lines seem to be added to make sense of the chorus'
two lines that follow, and are probably an editor's interpolation.

71. *1100–1101:* The chorus usually speaks between the speeches in an
agōn (debate scene) to mark off the different speakers. Choruses like to
make general remarks that are not necessarily very significant—or even
relevant—to what the actors are saying.

72. *1107–8:* Some editors move 1107–8 to open the speech that begins
at 1132 because these lines interrupt the flow of Clytemnestra's remarks.
In defense of keeping them here, she has just called Electra *teknon* ("my
child"), and now takes a real look at her. The sight of Electra's sorry state
makes Clytemnestra feel regret more poignantly.

I regret some of my decisions, especially that
1110   I drove my husband to anger more than I needed to.[73]

ELECTRA:
It's too late for regret when there is no remedy.
Father is dead, but why don't you bring home
your son from his life of exile far from his homeland?

CLYTEMNESTRA:
I'm afraid. I have to look out for my own welfare, not his.
1115   They say he is angry over the murder of his father.

ELECTRA:
Why do you keep your husband so savage against us?

CLYTEMNESTRA:
That's his nature, but you are stubborn, too.

ELECTRA:
I am grieving, but I'll put an end to my rage.

CLYTEMNESTRA:
Then he will not be so hard on you.

---

73. *1110:* This is a difficult line: the manuscripts have *posin* (accusative
of the Greek word for "husband"), which in this context would refer to
Aegisthus. With this reading, Clytemnestra regrets egging him on and
encouraging his mistreatment of her children from her first marriage (see
1107–8 and 1116). An objection to this is that earlier, the Farmer said
she protected them (27–28). Clytemnestra might also refer to her urging
Aegisthus' participation in the murder of Agamemnon. The dative *posei,*
referring to Agamemnon, has been suggested, and is accepted in many
editions and translations. It would mean something like: "that I whipped
up my anger excessively against my husband" or "I drove [myself] into
anger at my husband." A degree of ambiguity could be maintained by
translating "I whipped up anger against my husband more than I should."
Clytemnestra regrets nursing and goading anger (her own and Aegisthus')
against Agamemnon. This would suggest that she almost cannot remember
why she killed him. What is interesting is that the two arguments begin to
blend together, as do the two husbands.

ELECTRA:
He has proud thoughts. He is in my house.   1120

CLYTEMNESTRA:
There you go. You are igniting new rancor.

ELECTRA:
I'll be silent. I fear him as I fear him.

CLYTEMNESTRA:
Let's stop this talk. Why did you summon me, daughter?

ELECTRA:
You have heard of my miserable childbearing:
help me sacrifice for it—I don't know how—   1125
at the tenth moon, as is customary for a birth.
I have no experience, since this is my first child.

CLYTEMNESTRA:
That's not my job, but the woman who delivered you.

ELECTRA:
I delivered myself and gave birth all alone.

CLYTEMNESTRA:
Is your house so remote and far from friends?   1130

ELECTRA:
No one wants to be friends with the poor.

CLYTEMNESTRA:
Very well. I will go in and sacrifice to the gods
for the completion of the infant's term, and after I do this for you
I must go to the farm where my husband is sacrificing
to the Nymphs. You, servants, take the beasts   1135
and put them to their mangers. Be ready when you think
I have finished this sacrifice to the gods.

(Servants lead away the animals and carriage stage right.)

I have to be there for my husband, too.

(Exit Clytemnestra through the central doors.)

ELECTRA:

Go now inside my impoverished home. But, please, watch out
1140   not to soil your dress on my sooty walls.[74]
You will sacrifice as you must to the gods.
The basket is ready for beginning the ritual and the knife is
  sharpened
which took down the bull. You will fall, struck down
beside him, and be his bride in Hades' halls,
1145   the man you slept with in life. That favor
I will give you. And you will pay for Father's death.

(Exit Electra through the central doors.)

Third Stasimon

CHORUS:

[Strophe]

Requital for evils—winds of change
are blowing through the house. Then, in the bath
our leader fell dead:
1150   a loud scream from the house and from the stone copings
when he cried out, "Hard woman, why do you kill me
when I come back to my homeland in the tenth seed time?"
. . . . . .
. . . . . .[75]

[Antistrophe]

1155   Time turning back brings her to justice
for her illicit bed; with her own hand
she killed her husband coming home at last
to the high Cyclopean walls[76]

---

74. *1140:* "My sooty walls"—an allusion to Aeschylus' *Agamemnon* 773–74, "Justice shines her light on humble, smoke-filled homes." Not even there, as the displacement of the setting tells us: any hut or hovel can serve as the scene building and become the scene of brutal, unseen murder.

75. *1154:* Two lines are missing here, the metrical match for 1163–64.

76. *1158:* "High Cyclopean walls"—The massive stone architecture in and around Mycenae was attributed to the Cyclopes, one-eyed giants, sons of Uranus and Gaia.

with the sharp blade, taking the axe in her hands. O suffering   1160
husband, what evil took hold of the wretched woman?
A mountain lioness dwelling in the woods
by the meadowlands brought this about.

CLYTEMNESTRA: *(From within.)*
Children, in the name of the gods, do not kill your mother.   1165

CHORUS:
Do you hear her cry from inside?

CLYTEMNESTRA:
Oh my god!

CHORUS:
I cry out for her, too, as she is overpowered by her children.
A god, you know, metes out justice, whenever it happens.
You suffered harshly. You committed atrocities,   1170
wretched woman, against your husband.

> *(Enter Electra and Orestes with the dead bodies
> through the central doors on the* eccyclema.*)*[77]

Exodos

Kommos[78]

CHORUS:
Look, here they are, coming out, soaked
in the fresh blood of their mother,
evidence of her defeat, the meaning of her miserable cries.
There is no house more unhappy than that
of Tantalus' descendants, and there never has been.   1175

ORESTES:
Earth and Zeus, who see all
of mortals' affairs, look on these deeds, murderous

---

77. *Eccyclema:* The *eccyclema* (device rolled out) was a revolve or platform on wheels, used to display the result of interior action.

78. *Kommos:* A lament sung by chorus and actors.

and foul, the two bodies lying
1180   together on the ground, struck
by my own hand in vengeance for my loss.

ELECTRA:
So sad, so sad, and I am the cause.
Through fire I plunged against my mother, in my misery,
my mother who gave me life, her daughter.

CHORUS:
Bad luck, it was your bad luck,
1185   mother who bore unforgettable
miseries, unforgettable and worse,
suffering at the hands of your children,
justly you paid for their father's death.

ORESTES:
1190   Phoebus, you intoned your justice
obscurely, but clear are the sorrows
you caused and you bestowed on me,
the murderer's sentence of exile from the land of Hellas.
What other city can I go to?
1195   What stranger, what decent man
will look me in the face,
the man who killed his mother?

ELECTRA:
Woe, woe. Where will I go,
to what choral rites, what marriage?
1200   What husband will take me into his bridal bed?

CHORUS:
Again, your thinking
has shifted again with the wind.
Now your mind is right, but then
it was not, and you did terrible things,
1205   dear girl, to your brother against his will.

ORESTES:
You saw how the poor woman opened
her gown, bared her breast as she was being murdered.

Woe. She let the limbs that gave me birth
fall to the ground, and her hair—I—[79]

CHORUS:
   I see clearly how you passed through torment   1210
   when you heard the heart-rending moan
   of the mother who gave you life.

ORESTES:
   These words she screamed as she stretched out her hand
   to my face: "My child, I beg you."   1215
   She hung from my cheek
   so the weapon fell from my hand.

CHORUS:
   The unhappy one, how did you dare to look
   with your own eyes on the murder of your mother
   as she breathed her last?   1220

ORESTES:
   I held my cloak over my eyes[80]
   and began the sacrifice, letting the knife
   go into my mother's neck.

ELECTRA:
   And I urged you on.
   I put my hand on the weapon with yours.[81]   1225

---

79. *1208–9:* "She let the limbs . . . and her hair"—Orestes cannot finish
the line (an example of *aposiopesis,* an abrupt breaking off in the midst
of a phrase). During the murder, when Clytemnestra dropped to the floor,
he would have taken hold of her hair—the only part of her he would have
had to touch—as he pulled her head back to slit her throat. He would have
leaned over her and she reached up to touch his cheek (1216). According
to another reading of 1209, Orestes says, "I felt faint."

80. *1221:* "I held my cloak over my eyes"—Like Perseus beheading the
Gorgon, Orestes covers his eyes.

81. *1225:* Besides having the most vivid description (in the form of a
reenactment) of the murder of Clytemnestra, this is the only version in
which Electra is physically present and takes part.

CHORUS:
You have caused the most terrible of sufferings.

ORESTES:
Take hold, cover Mother's limbs with her robe
and fit back her slit throat.
You gave birth to us, your own murderers.

ELECTRA:
Look, we are putting your robes around you,
1230   Mother, loved and unloved.

Dei ex Machina

*(The Dioscuri appear above the
rooftop on the* mēchanē.*)*[82]

CHORUS:
This is the end of great evils for the house.
But, look! Here on top of the building
there are appearing some divinities or some of
1235   the heavenly gods. This is not the way
mortals approach. Why in the world are they coming
into the clear sight of men?

DIOSCURI (CASTOR speaking):
Son of Agamemnon, listen. Your mother's
two brothers address you, the sons of Zeus:
1240   I am Castor, and this is my brother Polydeuces.
Just now we put down the violent disturbance
of a ship at sea and arrived in Argos when we saw
the murder of our sister here, your mother.
She has met with justice but you did not do justice,
1245   and Phoebus—Phoebus is my king;
I will hold my tongue—he is wise, but his oracle was not.
Still we must go along with it. It is necessary now
to do what Fate and Zeus have decreed about you.
To Pylades give Electra to take home as his wife.

---

82. *Mēchanē:* The *mēchanē* (machine) was a crane that lifted actors above
the scene building.

And you—leave Argos. You are not permitted   1250
to walk in the city after killing your mother.
The terrible fates, the dog-faced goddesses,[83]
will drive you wandering in madness.
When you reach Athens, embrace the holy statue
of Pallas Athena. As they swarm you with their hissing snakes,   1255
she will keep them off, so they cannot touch you,
raising over your head the circle of the Gorgon's face.
There is the Rock of Ares[84] where the gods first sat
to pass judgment in a case of murder
when brutal Ares killed Halirrhothius   1260
son of the lord of the sea in anger
over his daughter's ungodly coupling, where a vote
most sacred in the eyes of the gods is secure from that time.
There you must risk trial for murder.
Equal votes cast will save you from   1265
the penalty of death.[85] Loxias will take the blame
upon himself for commanding the murder of your mother.
And this law will be established for all time
that the defendant always wins when the votes are equal.
And the dreaded goddesses overcome by this distress   1270
will go down into a cleft of the earth right beside the hill,[86]
which will be a solemn holy oracle for humankind.
You must go to live in a city of the Arcadians
by the streams of Alpheus near the sacred Lycian precinct;[87]

---

83. *1252:* "The dog-faced goddesses"—the Erinyes or Furies.

84. *1259:* "The Rock of Ares"—the Areopagus (Ares' hill or outcrop), the Athenians' homicide court, northwest of the Acropolis in Athens. Euripides attributes the founding of the court of the Areopagus to the gods' trial of Ares for killing Poseidon's son Halirrhothius, who had raped Ares' daughter. Aeschylus, *The Furies* (*Eumenides*) 481–84 represents Athena establishing the court for Orestes' trial.

85. *1265–66:* "Equal votes cast will save you"—See Aeschylus, *The Furies* (*Eumenides*) 735, 741, 752–53, on the vote of Athena, which favors the defendant in the event of a tie.

86. *1271:* "Cleft of the earth"—See Aeschylus, *The Furies* (*Eumenides*) 805; the cleft or chasm is at the northeast angle of the Areopagus.

87. *1273–75:* "You must go . . . the city will be named after you"—In other versions, Orestes is only temporarily exiled and returns to rule in Mycenae. The city dubiously named for him is Orestheion (mentioned in

1275 the city will be named after you.
This much I have to say to you. Aegisthus' body
will be given a proper burial by the citizens of Argos.
But as for your mother—Menelaus—he's just arrived
in Nauplia from the time he captured Troy—
1280 he and Helen will bury her.[88] Helen has come
from the house of Proteus in Egypt and did not go to Troy.[89]
To cause strife and death among mortals, Zeus
sent a phantom of Helen to Troy.[90]
Let Pylades take his bride and go home
1285 to Achaean country, and let him take along
that man called your brother-in-law
into the land of the Phocians and give him a mass of wealth.
You now, set out over the neck of the isthmus
and go to the prosperous hill of Cecrops.[91]
1290 For after completing your appointed sentence for murder
you will prosper, free of troubles.

ORESTES:[92]
Sons of Zeus, may we approach
and speak with you?

CASTOR:
Yes, you are not polluted by these slaughters.

ELECTRA:
1295 May I be part of the dialogue, too, sons of Tyndareos?

Thucydides, *The Peloponnesian War* 5.64.3 and Herodotus, *The Histories*
9.11), near the source of the Alpheus River. The Lycian sanctuary of
Zeus is on Mount Lykaion, a mountain in Arcadia in the west central
Peloponnesus, about twenty-two miles from Olympia.
88. *1276–80:* In Homer's *Odyssey* (3.309–10), Orestes himself gives the
funeral feast—of both Aegisthus and his mother—for the Argives.
89. *1280–81:* The story of Helen in Egypt appears in Herodotus'
Histories; Stesichorus' Palinode (quoted in Plato, *Phaedrus* 243a–b), and
the *Cypria,* as well as in Homer's *Odyssey.*
90. *1283:* "Phantom of Helen"—The reunion of the real Helen and
Menelaus in Egypt after the Trojan War is the subject of Euripides' *Helen.*
91. *1289:* Cecrops—a mythical king of Athens.
92. *1292 ff.:* The distribution of lines is uncertain.

CASTOR:
  Yes, you, too. I attribute this act
  of murder to Phoebus.

ORESTES:
  How is it that though you are gods
  and the brothers of the murdered woman
  you did not hold off the Furies from the house?   1300

CASTOR:
  Fate's grim necessity led to what had to be
  and the commands of Phoebus, less than wise.

ELECTRA:
  What Apollo, what oracles decreed
  that I become Mother's murderer?

CASTOR:
  Shared actions, shared fates;   1305
  one madness of your fathers
  tears through you both.

ORESTES:
  My sister, seeing you after so long,
  I am to lose the joy of your love so soon,
  and when I leave I will leave you behind.   1310

CASTOR:
  She has a husband and home. She has not
  suffered brutally, except that she is leaving
  the city of Argos.

ELECTRA:
  And what other grief is greater
  than to leave the borders of your homeland?   1315

ORESTES:
  And I will go away from my father's home
  and submit Mother's murder
  to the votes of aliens.

CASTOR:
Be brave. You will go
1320   to the holy city of Pallas. Have courage.

ELECTRA:
Press your breast to mine,
dearest brother.
The curses of Mother's murder
sever us from our father's home.

ORESTES:
1325   Throw yourself into my arms. Embrace me. Raise the dirge
as you would at my tomb if I were dead.

CASTOR:
Alas, alas. Your cries of grief are terrible
even for gods to hear.
There is in me and the heavenly gods
1330   pity for mortals full of suffering.

ORESTES:
I will not see you again.

ELECTRA:
And I will not come again into your sight.

ORESTES:
This is the last time you will speak to me.

ELECTRA:
Farewell, city.
1335   A long farewell to you, fellow women of the city.

ORESTES:
Most loyal—are you going now?

ELECTRA:
I am going. My face is wet with tears.

(Exeunt Electra and Pylades stage left.)

ORESTES:
Pylades, good-bye.   1340
Make my sister your bride.

(Exit Orestes, running, stage right.)

CASTOR:
Marriage will be their care. The dogs are here!
Run from them now, racing to Athens.
They will set upon you a frightening pace,
snake-handed, black-coated,   1345
bearing fruit of terrible pains.
We two must leave in haste, soaring
through stretches of the sky to the Sikel sea[93]
to rescue the seafaring ships.
We do not come to the aid of the polluted   1350
but those who hold what's right, holy, and dear
in life; releasing them
from hard toils, we keep them safe.
Let no one choose to be unjust;
let no one sail with oath breakers on board.   1355
As a god, I have this to say to mortals.

(Exeunt the Dioscuri on the mēchanē.)

CHORUS:
Farewell! If anyone can fare well
and not be broken by bad luck,
he alone will prosper.

(The chorus files out in both directions.)

–END–

---

93. *1348:* Sikel—the sea between Sicily and Greece. Some scholars have
taken this to be a reference to the failed Athenian invasion of Sicily in
415–413 B.C.E.

EURIPIDES

Iphigenia among the Tauri

Cast of Characters

IPHIGENIA   daughter of Clytemnestra and Agamemnon, priestess of Artemis

ORESTES   her brother

PYLADES   his cousin, loyal friend, and constant companion

CHORUS   of Greek captive women, temple servants, and attendants to Iphigenia

The CHORUS LEADER   speaks for the group in the dialogue sections

HERDSMAN

THOAS   king of the Tauri

MESSENGER   one of the king's men

ATHENA

Extras include (possible) attendants of Iphigenia, two or more male temple slaves to escort the prisoners, and an entourage of Thoas' guards, some of whom accompany the procession of Iphigenia with the statue and prisoners.

Iphigenia among the Tauri was first produced between 414 and 412 B.C.E.

Iphigenia among the Tauri[1]

SCENE: *The action takes place in front of the temple compound of Artemis in the faraway land of the Tauri on the Crimean peninsula (called the Tauric Chersonese by the Greeks) on the Black Sea (or Euxine), where Iphigenia is priestess of the maiden goddess. Iphigenia was spirited away by Artemis from the sacrifice intended for her at Aulis by her father. She knows nothing of what has happened to her family since her departure from her home in Argos years ago when her brother Orestes was an infant. The side entrances represent the route to the sea (stage right) and the way to the king's palace (stage left).*

Prologue

(Enter Iphigenia from the temple.)

IPHIGENIA:
    Pelops, son of Tantalus, on his swift steeds came
    to Pisa in Elis[2] and married Oenomaus' daughter;

---

1. *Title:* The play is often called by its Latin title, *Iphigenia in Tauris,* which means *Iphigenia among the Tauri* (or *Taurians, Tauroi* in Greek). This does not imply that there is a place called "Tauris" (parallel to Aulis of *Iphigenia at Aulis*). The place is called *Taurica (Taurikē)* by Herodotus.

2. *1–2:* Pisa was a town in the western Peloponnese, ruled by Oenomaus, who made his daughter's suitors compete with him in a chariot race. The losers, thirteen in all, were killed. Pelops (or Hippodamia, Oenomaus' daughter) suborned Myrtilus, the king's charioteer, to sabotage his master's chariot. Pelops won and, forgetting his debt to Myrtilus, threw him off a cliff to his death. This is one of the beginnings of the curse on the house of Pelops, already cursed for Tantalus' misdeeds. The swift steeds serve a double purpose: Pelops traveled to the Peloponnese ("island of Pelops," as it subsequently came to be called) on them and used them to "win" his bride. The play opens with Pelops' name and he is mentioned several times

71

from her Atreus was born and from Atreus, two sons,
Menelaus and Agamemnon. From *him* I was born:
5 I'm Iphigenia, daughter of Tyndareos' daughter.[3]
I'm the one he sacrificed to Artemis for Helen's sake
by Euripus' whirling currents, where steady winds[4]
churn the sea dark in the infamous inlets of Aulis' bay,
my own father—at least he thought he had done it.
10 That was when Agamemnon the king had amassed
the Greek fleet with all its thousand sailing ships,
planning to win the crown of victory over Troy
for the Greeks and thus avenge the insult done
to Helen's marriage: it was a favor to Menelaus.
15 Faced with an inability to sail and lack of wind
he resorted to omens, and the seer Calchas told him:
"You who command the army of Greece gathered here,
Agamemnon, you will not unmoor your ships from land
until Artemis receives your own daughter Iphigenia
20 in sacrifice: for once you vowed to offer to the moon
goddess the fairest thing the year brought forth.
Now in your home your wife Clytemnestra gave birth
to a daughter—he awarded me the title "fairest"—[5]
and you must sacrifice her."[6]

(193, 807, 823, 985, 1415). Euripides begins many of his later plays with a genealogy: see *Orestes* 1–24, *Phoenician Women* 3–12.

3. *5:* Tyndareos had two famous daughters, Helen (who married Menelaus) and Clytemnestra, Agamemnon's wife. In *Iphigenia at Aulis,* Euripides adds a third daughter, Phoebe (50).

4. *6–8:* Euripus was notorious for its tidal currents, which changed direction several times a day (see Plato, *Phaedo,* 90c). Aulis is famous as the site of the gathering of the ships headed for Troy and the sacrifice of Iphigenia. Iphigenia is obsessed with the sacrifice of which she speaks as if it had actually been completed (see 361).

5. *23: Kallisteion,* "the award for beauty" or "offering of what is most beautiful"; Paris gave Aphrodite the golden apple inscribed with the word (*kallistēi*) meaning "for the fairest."

6. *20–24:* A better known reason for Artemis' demand for sacrifice is that Agamemnon killed her sacred deer or boasted of his skill as a hunter (see Sophocles' *Electra* 566–69). In Euripides' *Iphigenia at Aulis,* however, no cause is given. The vow, wish, or curse, made without fully realizing its implications, is a common folktale motif.

Using Odysseus' trick he took me
from my mother on the pretext of marriage to Achilles.[7]   25
To my sorrow I came to Aulis and was lifted up
above the altar fire to be butchered with a sword,
but Artemis gave the Achaeans a deer in my place
and whisking me away through the shining ether
brought me here to live in the land of the Tauri:[8]   30
a land of savages where savage Thoas is king,[9]
who moves his nimble feet as fast as birds' flight
and earned this name because of his fleetness of foot.[10]

---

7. *25:* The story of Iphigenia is not told in Homer, who does not even
list her among the daughters of Agamemnon. It was covered in the
Cypria, a lost epic that treats the origins and early events of the Trojan
War. Knowledge of the *Cypria*'s contents survives primarily in the late
summary of Proclus. The sacrifice of Iphigenia provides motivation for
Clytemnestra's murder of her husband in Aeschylus' *Agamemnon,* and in
the *Electra* plays of Euripides and Sophocles. In these plays it is assumed
that she died at Aulis. Calchas and Odysseus are represented as ambitious
and potentially disloyal in Euripides' *Iphigenia at Aulis.* An epilogue was
later added to *Iphigenia at Aulis* in which Iphigenia was rescued.

8. *28–30:* The reasons for Artemis' demand for the sacrifice and her
subsequent rescue of the victim remain obscure. Artemis was worshiped
in Attica at Halae, where the sacred wooden image (mentioned at 87–88)
was enshrined (Strabo 9.1.22) and Brauron, where young girls dressed
in saffron dresses performing as "bears" (*arktoi* in the ceremony of the
Arkteia) worshiped Artemis (Aristophanes, *Lysistrata* 645) as Artemis-
Tauropolos or Artemis-Iphigenia (see 1446–67).

9. *31:* "Savages"—The Greek word is *barbaroi,* which gives us the English
word *barbarian* and originally meant "non-Greeks" or "not Greek-
speaking people." It implied that their speech was incomprehensible, like
the sound of birds. After the Persian Wars it came to have a more and
more derogatory sense: not just *foreign,* but *brutal, uncivilized, savage.*
Of particular interest is the fact that in Greek literature, non-Greeks use
the term *barbaroi* to speak of themselves (see 1170, 1174, 1422). The Tauri
(or Taurians) are mentioned in Herodotus (*The Histories* 4.99–103). See
Cropp 2000, pp. 47–50 for the historical Tauri and the archaeological
evidence for their pastoral life. There were Greek settlements in the Crimea
from the sixth century B.C.E. This rugged region, Cropp points out (p.
48), "loosely imagined in its pre-Greek condition . . . is the setting for
Euripides' play."

10. *31–33:* Iphigenia relates the name Thoas to the Greek word *thoos,*
"quick, nimble," from the root of *theō,* "run."

In this temple she ordained me to be her priestess.
35 From then on the goddess Artemis has taken pleasure
in certain "celebrations"—only the name sounds fine—
the rest I will keep silent out of fear of the goddess.
[The state had the same custom before: I sacrifice
any Greek man who comes to shore in this country.][11]
40 I only begin the ritual, but the unspeakable slaughter
is others' concern inside the god's sacred dwelling.

Last night, strange visions visited my dreams.[12]
In hope of some relief I will tell them to the air above.
In my sleep I seemed to be delivered from this place
45 and living in Argos, sleeping among the other girls,[13]
when the earth's surface was shaken wave upon wave,
that sent me rushing outside, where I saw the capstone
of the house falling and the whole roof on the ground
in ruins collapsed from its high supporting pillars.
50 In my dream one column of my father's house was left
standing all by itself; from its capital, locks of hair
flaxen-colored hung down. From it came a human sound.
In keeping with the art I practice, of killing strangers,
in tears I performed the ritual of washing the man
55 who was to die. This is how I interpret the dream:
Orestes is dead and I was beginning his funeral rites.
The columns of the house are its male offspring;

---

11. *38–39:* These lines are suspected by editors because Iphigenia has just said she will be silent about the rites (37) and the next lines (40–41) contradict them.

12. *42–58:* Iphigenia's dream, even though she misinterprets its meaning, sets the tone for the first part of the play. It shows that Orestes and her home are very much on her mind and that despite her father's brutal betrayal, she loves her brother. The arrival of the two travelers immediately after her exit into the temple disproves at once her interpretation that Orestes is dead, but it does not rule out the possibility that the dream is predictive and that she will in fact perform the ritual washing, not of his dead body, but of him as sacrificial victim (58). At 569 she dismisses the dream as false, but does not attempt a new interpretation.

13. *45:* Girls and women were confined to separate apartments in the classical Athenian house. See also 452–55 and 1138–52 for the chorus' longing for home.

men I sprinkle with these holy waters are put to death.[14]
Now I desire to offer libations for my brother,   61
though I am here and he is not—this much I can do—
with my attendants, Greek women given to me
by the king. But for some reason they are not here
yet; I will go back to wait for them inside these walls   65
where I draw out my days, the temple of the goddess.

(Exit Iphigenia into the temple. Enter Orestes and
Pylades stage right, in urgent conversation.)

ORESTES:
Look around. Be sure there is no one on the path.

PYLADES:
I'm looking, scouring the landscape in every direction.

ORESTES:
Pylades, does this look like the temple of the goddess
we were sailing to when we crossed the sea from Argos?   70

PYLADES:
It does, Orestes. And I assume you think the same.

ORESTES:
And the altar where the blood of Greeks runs down?[15]

PYLADES:
Its stone courses are yellowed with dead men's gore.

---

14. *59–60:* Lines in the text are omitted in the translation that read:
[I cannot apply this dream to any other kin
because Strophius had no son when I was killed.]
This sounds like a note made by a student or teacher to explain why
Pylades, the son of Agamemnon's sister, might not be a second pillar of
the house. But he was not born when Iphigenia departed the scene and so
she has never heard of him, which explains why she does not recognize his
name in the first episode (249, 285, 321).

15. *72–75:* Herodotus (*The Histories* 4.103) writes that the Tauri impaled
the heads of sacrificed foreigners.

ORESTES:
Do you see the spoils fixed up there under the pinnacles?

PYLADES:
75   Yes, spoils of foreigners they have put to death.
We must keep a good lookout all around us.

ORESTES:
Ah, Phoebus, what is this new trap that your oracles
have led me to? First I avenged my father's blood
and killed my mother, and now am hounded by Furies
80   in constant attacks, a refugee, outcast from my home.
I covered the twists and turns of countless roads
until I went to your oracle to ask how I could reach
the end of this dizzying madness and the toils
that I live through, as I roam all across Greece . . .[16]
85   then you told me to travel to the borders of the land
of the Tauri where your sister Artemis has an altar,
and to seize the goddess' image, which fell, they say,
from the high heavens into the temple precinct;[17]
to seize it by subterfuge or a stroke of good luck,
90   to face every danger and deliver it to the land
of the Athenians. If I did this, you said I'd have respite
from my troubles—after that your instructions ended.
Obedient to all your commands I have come here
to an unknown and inhospitable land. But I ask you,
95   Pylades, since you are the accomplice of my toils,
what do we do? You see the high encirclements
of towers. Should we resort to scaling the buildings'
walls? How would we do that and escape detection?
Or break the bronze-worked locks with crowbars—
100   a thing outside our experience? And, if we are caught

---

16. *79–84:* Orestes was hounded by his mother's Furies after killing her to
avenge his father's death at her hands. In Aeschylus' *Furies* (*Eumenides*) he
submits to trial on the Areopagus in Athens and is acquitted, after which
the Furies cease haunting him. In *Iphigenia among the Tauri* only some of
the Furies accept the verdict; others continue their pursuit.

17. *87–88:* Ancient wooden cult images, like the Trojan Palladium and
the statue of Athena Polias in Athens, were believed to have fallen from
the sky.

opening the gates and contriving a way inside,
we are dead men. Well, before we die, let us escape
on the ship which carried us here to these shores.

PYLADES:
To run is out of the question. It is not our way.
And besides we must not disregard the god's oracle.[18]   105
Let's leave the temple for now and hide ourselves
in the caves where the dark sea waves splash,
far from our ship[19] in case anyone catch sight of it,
report it to the rulers, and we be taken by force.
When the darkening eye of night comes on   110
we must dare to take the hewn image from the temple
using whatever stratagems we can muster.
Look up in between the triglyphs where there is a space
to let yourself down inside. Brave men would dare
to face trials. Cowards count for nothing in this world.   115

ORESTES:
Yes. We have not come this long way by sea
only to return home again without reaching our goal.
You're right. Thank you: I will take your advice.
We must find somewhere in this place to hide.
It will not turn out to be the god's responsibility   120
if the oracle fails. We must find the courage to act.
No toil is so hard that it serves as an excuse to the young.

(Exeunt Orestes and Pylades stage right.)

---

18. *105:* Pylades' role in Aeschylus' *Libation Bearers,* in his only lines in
that play (900–902), is to remind Orestes of Apollo's oracle.
19. *108:* For *far from our ship,* "far from town" is suggested by some
editors. Pylades might mean that they should hide far from the ship so that
if it is taken they could still escape. How they would get away without the
ship, however, is unclear.

Parodos[20]

(Enter the chorus along the side entrances, stage left and right. Enter Iphigenia through the temple doors, perhaps with an attendant, carrying libations.)

IPHIGENIA:
Silence all
who dwell by the twin Clashing Rocks[21]
125   on the coast of the Euxine.

CHORUS:
—Daughter of Leto,
Diktynna of the mountains,[22]
to the court, to the gold-decked stone courses,
of your fine-columned temple,
130   I guide my devout virginal foot,
slave of the temple's devoted key holder.
Left behind are the towers and walls
of Greece, land of fine horses,
and Europe's fields wooded with trees,
135   settlements of our fathers' homes.[23]

---

20. *123:* The chorus at this time consisted of fifteen citizen men who were not professional actors, here representing captive Greek women. The parodos is the entrance song of the chorus. This one blends into a *kommos,* or song of mourning, in which Iphigenia participates with the chorus. The chorus may enter severally or in groups: dashes indicate different speakers or groups of speakers. The assignment of parts is in doubt: many editors attribute 123–25 to the chorus, but the manuscripts assign them to Iphigenia, who as priestess would be more likely to call for ritual silence.

21. *124:* The Clashing Rocks are the Symplegades. They clashed together, smashing any objects or creatures that went through. In the more common Greek legend the *Argo,* commanded by Jason, was the first ship; once the *Argo* passed through, the Symplegades remained open. Their immobile status seems in question in this play (see 421–22).

22. *127–29:* Diktynna is a cult name for Artemis the huntress (from *diktuon,* "net"). The chorus' description of the spectacular temple is a nice contrast to the revulsion felt by Orestes and Pylades to the visible gore on the altar and pinnacles.

23. *134–35:* Europe is the MS reading, but since the Greeks recognized the Tauric Chersonese as part of Europe, some editors have been troubled

—We have come. What news? What troubles you?
Why do you summon us to the temple, summon us here,
daughter of that man who assailed Troy's towers
with the famous fleet
of a thousand ships,   140
ten thousand spears, the son of Atreus?

IPHIGENIA:
My attendants,
in the sorrow of sad laments
I lie, the cry of a song without melody,   145
a joyless dirge not set to the lyre, alas,
alas with funereal grief,
a great loss has befallen me,
grieving for my brother's life—
such a vision
I saw in my dreams   150
during the night just past.
Lost, I am lost,
and my father's house is gone to ruin.
Alas, our family's light is put out.
Woe, woe for the troubles in Argos.   155
Ah destiny,
you rob me of my only brother,
sending him to Hades. For him I am preparing
to pour this bowl of libations
for the dead   160
over the earth's surface,
streams of milk from young mountain cows,
Bacchus' wine offerings,
honey, life's work of humming bees: 165
charms to appease the dead.

(To an attendant or member of the chorus.)

---

by the suggestion that the chorus claims to have left Europe and have
proposed emending the text to Eurotas, a major river in the Peloponnese
beside which Sparta was built (see Hall 1987, pp. 430–33). The chorus
might, on the other hand, be expressing nostalgia for their particular part
of Europe with its lush vegetation, as a person who has moved to the high
desert region might miss America's "fruited plain."

Hand me now the golden
vessel, Hades' libation.
170   Shoot of Agamemnon,
below the earth, to you now dead, I send these offerings.
Take them. Though far from your tomb,
I offer my tears and flaxen hair.
175   Far from your country, I have traveled
far from mine, where, by report,
I lie tragically slaughtered.

CHORUS:
I intone a responding tune
180   and the foreign strain of Asian
hymns to my mistress,
the music in dirges
pleasing to the dead, which Hades
sings in songs without joy.
185   Tragedy in the halls of Atreus' sons:
the scepter's light has gone
from your fathers' halls.
Once there was the regime of wealthy
190   kings in Argos—
from trouble springs more trouble
crashing on the whirling
winged horses of Pelops;[24]
and the sun changed
the eye of his holy light
195   from its course. After pain came more pain
in the halls, from the golden lamb,
murder after murder, grief after grief.
Vengeance for those slain before
200   comes into the halls of the Tantalids
and the god swoops down
upon you with unwanted zeal.

---

24. *193–96:* "Winged horses"—In one version of the legend Pelops prayed
to Poseidon for an advantage in the chariot race and Poseidon sent him
flying horses. In Euripides' *Electra* (726–36), the chorus reports that the
sun changed course after Thyestes' seduction of Atreus' wife and his theft
of the golden lamb, a gift from Pan that was a symbol of sovereignty.

IPHIGENIA:

From the first, for me my fate
was ill-fated, on that night[25]
of mother's ungirdling; from the first   205
the Fates of my birth
quickened the painful birthing
when the woman wooed through Greece,
unhappy daughter of Leda,   210
bore me in her chambers, the firstborn flower,
a victim to ancestral crime, and reared me to be
a votive sacrifice without joy.
In a carriage drawn by horses
they put me down on the sands of Aulis   215
a bride, alas no, not a bride,
for the son of Nereus' daughter.
Now I live here a stranger beside an unwelcoming sea
in a barren home,
unmarried, childless, without city, without family,   220
I sing no hymn to Hera, god of Argos,
nor at the rhythmic loom
with the shuttle weave an image
of Athenian Pallas and the Titans,[26]
but I cause strangers' blood to redden   225
the altars, with no sound of music,
but the piteous sound of men crying out,
of men shedding piteous tears.
But now I forget these sorrows
to weep for one slain in Argos,   230
my brother—I left him a baby at the breast,
still an infant, still a newborn, still a shoot
in his mother's arms at her breast
in Argos, Orestes born to bear the scepter.   235

---

25. *203–206:* It is uncertain whether this refers to Clytemnestra's wedding
night or the night of Iphigenia's birth. The loosing of the girdle usually
refers to the losing of virginity. The Fates chose the time of birth and were
present to determine the child's destiny.

26. *221–24:* The festival of Argive Hera was the main yearly celebration
at Argos; the weaving for Athena refers to the new *peplos* made for
presentation to the goddess at the Panathenaea, an annual festival in
Athens. Iphigenia misses the women's celebrations in her homeland.

First Episode

(Herdsman is seen approaching stage right.)

CHORUS LEADER:
Look over there—I see a herdsman coming
from the oceanside to bring us some news.

(Enter Herdsman stage right.)[27]

HERDSMAN:
Daughter of Agamemnon and Clytemnestra,
hear the strange news I have come here to tell.

IPHIGENIA:
240   What is there in your story that is so alarming?

HERDSMAN:
There have come to our country, aboard a ship,
escaping the dark Clashing Rocks, two young men,
a sacrificial offering that will be pleasing to Artemis
our goddess. Hurry and get ready the purifying
245   waters and other preparations for the sacrifice.

IPHIGENIA:
From where? Does their appearance tell you?

HERDSMAN:
They are Greeks. That is all I know for sure.

IPHIGENIA:
Did you hear the strangers' names to tell me?

HERDSMAN:
Pylades. That is what one called the other.

---

27. *238:* It is possible that all the entrances and exits are from the same
direction. I prefer to have the Herdsman enter from the seashore (stage
right) but exit to Thoas' palace (stage left) where the prisoners have been
sent. It seems reasonable that the Herdsman would report directly to
Iphigenia and that others would deliver the prisoners to the king.

IPHIGENIA:
And his companion, what was his name?   250

HERDSMAN:
None of us knows that. We did not hear them say it.

IPHIGENIA:
Where did you catch sight of them and take your quarry?

HERDSMAN:
On the rough surf of the inhospitable passage.

IPHIGENIA:
And why were you, herdsman, down by the sea?

HERDSMAN:
We had gone to wash our cattle in the seawater.   255

IPHIGENIA:
Come back to the point, how you captured them
and by what means. That is what I want to learn.
They've come after a long interval in which the goddess'
altar has not been reddened with the blood of Greeks.

HERDSMAN:
We led the cattle down from their hillside pastures   260
to the sea that runs between the Clashing Rocks;
there is a hollow crevice broken by the constant
surge of waves, a shelter for purple-dye collectors.[28]
That was where one of us herdsmen saw them,
the two young men, and he turned back to us,   265
stepping carefully on tiptoe and he asked us,
"You see them, don't you? They surely must
be gods sitting out there." One of us, a religious sort,
lifted up his hands to address them in prayer,
"Son of Leucothea of the sea, guardian of ships,[29]   270

---

28. *263:* The costly Tyrian purple dye was harvested from two species of
myrex, a type of sea snail.
29. *270–74:* After Athamas killed his son Learchus, his wife Ino and her
son Melicertes leapt into the sea and became the sea deities Leucothea

master Palaemon, be propitious unto us,
if you are the Twins of Zeus sitting on our shore
or the dear delights of Nereus, who fathered
the noble chorus of the fifty Nereid nymphs."
275   Someone else, a cynic, mocking his superstition,
laughed at his prayers and reckoned they were
shipwrecked sailors sitting in the cleft out of fear
of our customs, because they had heard we sacrifice
foreigners. To most of us *he* made sense and so we chose
280   to hunt them down as natural offerings to our god.
While this was going on, one of the foreigners got up[30]
and left the rock. He started shaking his head up and down,
roaring aloud, his hands and arms gesticulating wildly.
He seemed stark raving mad, yelling like a hunted man,
285   "Pylades, don't you see it? Don't you see this serpent
from Hell, how keen it is on killing me, its gaping
maw coiled against me with hideous snake-women?
Look there, from her robes breathing fire and death
she hurtles on wings, holding in her arms—my mother,
290   as if to cast her, like a crushing stone, on top of me!
Oh god! She will kill me. Is there anywhere to escape?"
His demeanor was constantly changing: his face
contorted at the lowings of our cattle and barking
of dogs which he took for the Furies' mocking cries.
295   And we, in our utter astonishment, sat quietly
cowering, while he drew out a sword in his hand,[31]

---

and Palaemon. The Twins are the Dioscuri, who protect sailors at sea (see Euripides' *Electra,* esp. 1347–53). Nereus was the sea god called "the old man of the sea," father of Thetis and her sister Nereids. The identity of the two called literally "delights of Nereus" is obscure; he is known for his daughters. Some scholars suggest that these are his grandsons.

30. *281–308:* Several mad scenes are described in Greek tragedy, in Euripides' *Heracles* and *Bacchae* and Sophocles' *Ajax;* in Euripides' *Orestes,* the madness is played out on stage. Here and in *Heracles,* the victim is left exhausted, as if after an epileptic seizure. In all cases, the victim suffers delusion and hallucination, mistaking the identity of those around him or her.

31. *296–301:* The slaughter of the cattle might remind the audience of the story of Ajax who, in a fit of madness over the award of Achilles' armor to Odysseus, butchered the Greek army's cattle in the belief that he was

and set upon the calves like a lion. He struck them
in the flanks, driving his weapon into their ribs,
supposing that way he could drive off the Furies.
Soon the sea was blossoming red with their blood.   300
Every man of us, when we saw the herds of cattle
being slaughtered and dying, took up arms.
We blew on conches, trying to alert our neighbors.
We were afraid as herdsmen we would be no match
for these foreigners who were strong and young.   305
In no time our numbers were swelled to a crowd.
Then he collapsed, freed from the throes of madness,
his beard dripping with foam. When we saw he was
down, we took advantage, everyone had work to do,
pelting and pounding. The other one, his companion,   310
wiped away the foam and cleaned his mouth
and covered him with his finely woven clothing,
trying to dodge the wounds that kept coming on,
while tenderly serving his friend with healing care.
The first, his senses revived, sprang up from his fall,   315
and cried out, seeing that a surge of hostile forces
was closing in and calamity would soon overwhelm
the two of them. We never let up pelting them
with stones, pressing on from every direction.
At that point we heard his desperate exhortation: 320
"Pylades, we will die, but let us die with glory.
Draw your sword and follow me into the fray."
And when we saw our enemies' two raised swords,
we filled the craggy ravines in our hasty flight.
Still if some few were routed, others stood ground   325
raining stones on them, and if these were pushed back,
those who had just given way pounded them again.
It was incredible: for all our numbers, not one of us
managed to hit either of the goddess' doomed victims.
In the end we overcame them, not so much by bravery   330
but we encircled them and robbed them of their swords
using rocks to knock them from their hands onto the ground.
They dropped to the ground exhausted. We escort them now
to our country's king. At sight of them, he will send them

---

killing Agamemnon and other Greeks (see the opening scene of Sophocles'
Ajax).

335   on to you with all speed for ritual washing and sacrifice.
       My young mistress, pray to receive such foreigners
       for immolation. And if you can get strangers like these
       to kill, Greece will atone for your murder, paying
       in full the penalty of your sacrificial slaughter at Aulis.

       CHORUS LEADER:
340   It is a strange tale you have told of this madman
       coming from Greece to our unwelcoming sea.

       IPHIGENIA:
       Very well. Go and bring the strangers to me.

            (Exit Herdsman stage left.)

       I will take charge of the needed ceremonies here.
       O suffering heart, you were always gentle
345   and full of pity toward strangers in the past,
       meting out a tear of fellow feeling in kinship
       whenever Greek men came into your hands.
       Now because of dreams, I have turned savage,
       believing Orestes is no longer among the living,
350   and you will find me unkind, whoever you are
       to have come here. I feel this is true, dear friends:
       unhappy people, because they are doing badly,
       do not feel well disposed to those who are worse off.
       No wind has ever come here brought by Zeus;
355   no ship has passed through the Clashing Rocks
       that carried Helen, the one who caused my ruin,
       or Menelaus, so I could wreak my revenge on them
       and make an Aulis here to pay for that other Aulis,
       where like a calf, Greeks took hold of me for slaughter
360   and the priest was my own father who gave me life.
       Ah me, I cannot get out of my mind what happened—
       how many times I darted out my hands to touch
       his beard and tried to hang onto my father's knees,
       with these words, "A wicked marriage you have planned
365   for me, Father. And now while you are killing me, Mother
       is singing the wedding song with her Argive women
       and the whole house is filled with the music
       of pipes. And at your hands I am meeting my death.

Achilles was not Peleus' son then: he was my Death,
though you called him my husband as a ruse to ferry me   370
here by swift chariot wheels to a bloody wedding day."
Peering out from behind the delicate bridal veil,
I was too bashful to take my brother in my arms—
my brother who now is dead—or to plant a kiss
on my sister's lips—since I was setting off to Peleus'   375
home. But so many embraces I put off until later
when I would come back home again to Argos.
My poor Orestes, if you are dead, from what fortune
you are fallen and from your father's lofty state!
I hold the goddess to blame for her cruel deceits—   380
she who keeps a mere human from her altars:
if he has taken part in a slaying or laid hands on
a woman in childbirth or touched a corpse—she deems him
unclean, while she herself delights in human sacrifice.[32]
It cannot be that Zeus' wife, Leto, gave birth   385
to such insensitivity in her child. I discredit
the feast of Tantalus, too, served at the gods' table:
how could they enjoy dining on the flesh of a child?
I believe that the people here, because they have
murder in their hearts, transfer their own villainy   390
to the gods—I do not believe any of the gods are evil.

First Stasimon

CHORUS:

[Strophe 1]

Dark, dark
confluences of seas where Io's[33]
flitting gadfly from Argos
crossed the hostile waves   395
and passed from Europe
to Asia.
Who are they then who left well-watered
Eurotas, green with reeds   400

---

32. *383–84:* Handling the dead and assisting at births made one unclean and were, therefore, women's work.

33. *392–93:* "The channel from the Propontis into the Black Sea . . . through the 'Thracian' Bosporus" (Hall 1987, p. 427).

or the holy springs of Dirkē
and came here, came to this savage land
where the altars and columned temple
405   of the radiant maiden are stained
by mortal blood?

[Antistrophe 1]

Their pine oars casting up waves,
on either side, did they sail
over the ocean surge in a seafaring ship
410   with the winds filling their sails,
vying in a contest to increase the wealth
in their homes?
For adding to their pain, fond hopes
415   are insatiable among men,
who carry off the weight of riches,
wandering over the waves and entering hostile cities
with empty expectation.
For some of them the thought of wealth fails to come
420   in time, for others it comes as an unforeseen prize.

[Strophe 2]

How did they pass between[34]
the rocks as they raced together?
How did they get past the sleepless sands of the Harpies,
speeding along the seashore
425   upon the surge of Amphitrite
where the choruses
of fifty daughters of Nereus
sing in a circle,
430   the rudders at the stern
creaking in their locks
under winds that fill the sails
with southern gusts
or western breezes
435   to the bird-filled land,
its shore bleached white,

---

34. *422–38:* See Hall (1987, pp. 427–29) on the geography of this passage.

the sparkling racecourse of Achilles
along the unwelcoming sea?[35]

[Antistrophe 2]

If only—in answer to my mistress' prayer—
Leda's own daughter Helen
one day would come   440
leaving the Trojan city,
so that —her hair sprinkled
with the sacred water of death—
she would die with her throat cut
by my mistress' hand   445
and repay all that she owes.
The sweetest news we could hear is this:
if someone comes, a sailor,
from the land of Greece,
to end my slavery's   450
grinding sadness.
And in my dreams I would be
at home in the land of my fathers,
a pleasure of sweet songs,
the shared joy of a happy state.   455

(Enter Orestes and Pylades, led
by attendants, stage left.)

Here come the two, their hands tied,
holding each other up,
a new offering to our goddess. Silence, dear friends:
trophies from Greece
approach the temple.   460
It was not false news
the herdsman brought.
O goddess, if these rites performed

---

35. *435–38:* Thetis whisked Achilles' body (along with Patroclus'
remains) from his funeral pyre away to the small island of Leukē (White
Island, named either for its white cliffs or pale flocks of seabirds) in the
Black Sea near the Danube delta (see Euripides' *Andromache* 1260–62).
There Achilles' spirit raced along the beach with the ghosts of his fallen
companions.

by the people here are pleasing to you
465   receive the sacrifice, which our law
declares unholy.

Second Episode

IPHIGENIA:
Well.
First I must take every care that the goddess'
ceremonies be done right. Untie their hands.
As dedications they must not be in bonds.
470   Go inside the temple and get ready what is needed
for the occasion and what local custom requires.

(Exeunt attendants into the temple.)

Ah.[36]
Who was the mother that gave you life, and who
was your father? And your sister, if you have one,
who will lose a pair of young men like you
475   and be without a brother—no one can tell who will suffer
such a fate. The workings of the gods proceed along
mysteriously and no one knows the disaster to come.
Fortune takes us at random into an uncertain future.
Where have you come from, unlucky guests?
480   You have sailed a long way to reach this land
and will spend forever buried here far from home.

ORESTES:
Why show this pity, lady, whoever you are,
and add to our pain on top of the evil to come?
I do not think it clever for a man about to die, to try[37]
485   to overcome the fear of annihilation with pity,
nor if anyone pities a man on the brink of death
without hope of his survival, since he adds to one evil
a second, the charge of foolishness in addition

---

36. *472:* "Ah," in Greek *pheu*, often indicates that the speaker will become
philosophical or reflective.
37. *484:* "To die" is the MSS reading. Several editors accept the
emendation "to kill," moving the supposed pity and imputation of fear on
the victim's part to the executioner's imagination.

to the inevitability of death. What will be will be.
Do not bemoan our lot. We are fully aware of   490
the customary sacrifices practiced in this place.

IPHIGENIA:
Which of you is called by the name Pylades?
That is the first thing I would like to know.

ORESTES:
He is, if knowing this gives you some pleasure.

IPHIGENIA:
What area of Greece does he call his homeland?   495

ORESTES:
What good would it do you to learn this, lady?

IPHIGENIA:
Are you brothers, born of the same mother?

ORESTES:
In affection, yes, but we are not brothers by blood.

IPHIGENIA:
What was the name that your father gave you?

ORESTES:
The right name to call me would be "Unhappy."   500

IPHIGENIA:
That wasn't my question. Ascribe that to your luck.

ORESTES:
If I die without a name, I will not be mocked.

IPHIGENIA:
Why do you begrudge me this? Are you so proud?

ORESTES:
You will sacrifice my body, not my name.

IPHIGENIA:
505   Won't you tell me the name of the city you are from?

ORESTES:
There is no benefit to what you ask since I am to die.

IPHIGENIA:
What makes you reluctant to do me this favor?

ORESTES:
I claim the renowned Argos as my native city.

IPHIGENIA:
Dear gods, were you really born there, my friend?

ORESTES:
510   Yes, in Mycenae: once upon a time it was prosperous.[38]

IPHIGENIA:
Are you an exile from home, or what happened?

ORESTES:
Yes I am in exile, in a way both voluntary and not.

IPHIGENIA:
Would you tell me something I want to know?

ORESTES:
Yes, it's just a minor point in the bad luck that is my life.

IPHIGENIA:
515   Yet if you come from Argos your presence is welcome.

ORESTES:
Not welcome to me, but if it is to you, enjoy it.

IPHIGENIA:
Perhaps you've heard of Troy—its story is well known.

---

38. *508–10:* Argos and Mycenae are often used interchangeably in
tragedy. If distinguished, Argos is the territory (the Argolid) and Mycenae
is the city.

ORESTES:
I wish I had never heard of it, not even in a dream.

IPHIGENIA:
They say that it lies in ruins now, fallen to the spear.

ORESTES:
That is so. What you heard was not an idle rumor.   520

IPHIGENIA:
And Helen, has she come back home with Menelaus?

ORESTES:
Yes, she has, bringing ruin to someone in my family.

IPHIGENIA:
Where is she? I, too, have an old charge against her.

ORESTES:
She lives in Sparta with her husband from before.

IPHIGENIA:
An abomination to all of Greece, not just to me!   525

ORESTES:
I have had experience of her irregular marriage, too.

IPHIGENIA:
The Achaeans' homecoming, did it happen as reported?

ORESTES:
You question me as if trying to grasp everything at once.

IPHIGENIA:
Before you die, I want to take in all the news I can.

ORESTES:
If you desire it, ask your questions. I will tell you.   530

IPHIGENIA:
There was a seer named Calchas. Did he return home?

ORESTES:
  He died. At least that was the going story in Mycenae.

IPHIGENIA:
  Thank god for that. And what about Odysseus?

ORESTES:
  He has not come back home, but is reported to be alive.

IPHIGENIA:
535   I hope he is lost and never reaches his homeland.

ORESTES:
  No need to curse him—his affairs are going badly.

IPHIGENIA:
  Thetis the Nereid had a son . . . is he still alive?

ORESTES:
  No. The marriage he celebrated at Aulis was a waste.

IPHIGENIA:
  A fraud, too, as those who suffered it are aware.

ORESTES:
540   Who are you then? You know a lot about Greece.

IPHIGENIA:
  I am from there. I was still a child when I was lost.

ORESTES:
  You have good reason to want to know what's going on.

IPHIGENIA:
  What about the commander, the one they call "Happy"?

ORESTES:
  Who is that? The one I know of is not so happy.

IPHIGENIA:
545   He was called King Agamemnon, son of Atreus.

ORESTES:
I do not know. Please give up this story line.

IPHIGENIA:
In gods' name, tell me, friend, to make me happy.

ORESTES:
He is dead, poor man, and has ruined someone else.

IPHIGENIA:
He is dead? How did it happen? I am so sorry.

ORESTES:
Why are you upset? Were you related to him?   550

IPHIGENIA:
I am upset because of his prosperity in days gone by.

ORESTES:
Yes, he died horribly, murdered by his own wife.

IPHIGENIA:
How very sad, she who killed . . . he who died.

ORESTES:
Stop now. No more questions on this subject.

IPHIGENIA:
Just one more thing: Is the poor man's wife alive?   555

ORESTES:

No. The son, to whom she gave life, took her life.

IPHIGENIA:
The house is in shambles. But why did he do it?

ORESTES:
He wanted to take vengeance for his dead father.

IPHIGENIA:
Ah! An ugly kind of justice, even if he executed it well.[39]

ORESTES:
560   Though he did the right thing, he does not prosper.

IPHIGENIA:
Did Agamemnon leave another child in his house?

ORESTES:
He left one unmarried daughter, the girl Electra.

IPHIGENIA:
Is there any word of the daughter he sacrificed?

ORESTES:
None, except that she is dead and gone from the world.

IPHIGENIA:
565   I feel sorry for her and for her father who killed her.

ORESTES:
She is gone for a bad woman's thankless sake.

IPHIGENIA:
The son of the father killed in Argos, is he alive?

ORESTES:
Yes, poor man, he is nowhere and everywhere.

IPHIGENIA:
Good-bye, false dreams—so you amounted to nothing.

ORESTES:
570   You are right, but those gods we call wise
       are even more false than flitting dreams.

---

39. *559*: Orestes, advised by Apollo, believed he had to avenge his father, but to kill one's mother can never be justified. See Euripides' *Electra* 1244: Castor says to Orestes, "She has met with justice but you did not do justice."

Among gods there is confusion in abundance,
among mortals too. This one thing pains me:
that an intelligent man, because he trusted mouthings
of seers, went to his ruin, as you can be sure he did.   575

CHORUS LEADER:
    Ah, ah! What about us, what of our parents?
    Are they alive or dead? Who could tell us this?[40]

IPHIGENIA:
    Listen to me. I have come upon a train of thought
    that is of benefit to you, strangers, and also helps me
    achieve my desire. This turns out to best advantage   580
    if the same matter is pleasing to all concerned.
    Would you be willing, if I let you survive, to bring
    a message for me to my loved ones in Argos,
    and carry a letter which out of compassion for me
    a captive wrote, in the belief that it was not my hand   585
    that was his murderer, but that he was to die by law,
    a victim of the goddess who believes this to be right?
    I had no one who could go back to Argos to carry
    my message and could, if he survived the trip,
    deliver my letter to someone in my family there.   590
    But you—you do not seem unfriendly to me, [41]
    and are familiar with Mycenae and my people there—
    save yourself and take this reward, not a trivial one,
    your survival for carrying my letter, no weight at all.
    Since the state requires these rituals, let him   595

        (Gestures toward Pylades.)

    be the offering to the goddess, separated from you.

ORESTES:
    Thank you for all you have said, but for one thing:
    it is a heavy burden to me if he is to be slaughtered.
    I am the one who steered our cargo of disasters;

---

40. *576–77:* As is usual, the characters ignore the comments of the chorus.
41. *591:* One manuscript has a word meaning "low-born"; the other has "hostile."

600   he sailed along with me out of kindness for my toils.
      It is not right for me to earn your favor at the cost
      of his death and for me to be free of troubles.
      This is how it should be: give your letter to him.
      He will deliver it to Argos—set your mind at rest.
605   Let them kill me—whoever wishes it. Anyone who
      would bail out of his friendship in disaster to save
      himself is an absolute coward. This man is truly
      my friend: his life means as much to me as my own.

IPHIGENIA:
      What a heroic spirit! You are sprung from a noble
610   root and are a genuine friend to your friends.
      I wish my brother who survives would be just like you.
      You see, strangers, I am not without a brother;
      it's just that I do not ever get to see him in the flesh.
      Since this is what you prefer, I will send him
615   to deliver my letter and you will die. Great concern
      for his life must be uppermost in your mind.

ORESTES:
      Who will sacrifice me and carry out the awful rites?

IPHIGENIA:
      I will. It is the duty I must administer to the goddess.

ORESTES:
      I'm sorry for you, young woman; it is not a pleasant job.

IPHIGENIA:
620   I am under the constraint of laws that must be preserved.

ORESTES:
      Do you, a woman, sacrifice men with the sword?

IPHIGENIA:
      No, but I sprinkle their hair with the lustral waters.

ORESTES:
      Who is the actual killer? If I may ask you this.

IPHIGENIA:
Inside the temple there are men who perform that duty.

ORESTES:
What sort of funeral will dispose of me when I'm gone?   625

IPHIGENIA:
The sacred fire within and a deep cleft in the rock.

ORESTES:
Ah!
How I wish I could be laid out by my sister's hand.

IPHIGENIA:
A futile wish you have uttered, poor man, whoever
you may be, for she lives far from this alien land.
Still, since you come from Argos, my homeland,   630
I will not omit any service that I can offer your corpse.
Your grave I will dress with an array of adornment
and I will anoint your body with golden olive oil,
and onto your pyre I will cast the flower-scented
honey, liquid sweetness of the dark mountain bee.   635
But now I'll go and bring the letter from the temple
of the goddess. Please do not feel ill will toward me.

(To the chorus.)

Attendants, keep watch over them, unfettered . . .
It may turn out that I will send unexpected news
to one of my family in Argos, the one I love most.   640
And the letter will bring him the happy message
that one he believes to be dead is in fact still alive.

(Exit Iphigenia into the palace.)

Sung Interlude

CHORUS:
You who are destined for the sprinkling
of lustral waters mixed with blood, I sing your dirge.   645

ORESTES:
It is not a cause for pity, but farewell, friends.

CHORUS: *(To Pylades.)*
   And you, young man, we honor
   for your happy fortune
   that you will return to the land of your fathers.

PYLADES:
650   It is no cause for envy to friends when friends die.

CHORUS:
   Oh, hard journeys.
   Ah, ah, you are lost.
   Oh, oh. Which is worse?
655   My mind pushes me two ways
   whether to lament you first or you. *(To Orestes and Pylades in
      turn.)*

ORESTES:
   Dear gods, Pylades, are you feeling the same as I?

PYLADES:
   I don't know. You leave me at a loss for words.

ORESTES:
660   Who can this young woman be? How like a Greek
   she asked us about the struggles in Troy
   and the homecoming of Achaeans and the seer
   Calchas and used Achilles' name, and poor
   Agamemnon, how she pitied him and asked
665   about his wife and children. The stranger must be
   an Argive by birth; otherwise she would not
   try to send a message or find out these things,
   as though she shares in the well-being of Argos.

PYLADES:
   You are ahead of me. And you say the same as I,
670   except for one thing: the sad tales of kings are
   known to all, if they have any claim to fame.
   But there is another matter I was thinking over.

ORESTES:
   What is it? By sharing it you will make it clearer.

PYLADES:
It is a disgrace for me to go on living if you die.
With you I set sail and I must die with you.   675
I will acquire a reputation for utter cowardice
in Argos and in the rolling hills of the Phocians:
It will seem to most people—malicious as they are—
that I saved myself by betraying you and returned alone,
or even murdered you, seeing the troubles of your house,   680
and caused your death for the sake of your kingdom,
being husband of your sister, the last in line to inherit.
These things I fear and I consider them to be shameful.
There is no other way: I must breathe my last with you,
be sacrificed with you, and be burnt on the same pyre,   685
since I am your friend and shrink from such reproach.

ORESTES:
Don't say such things. My troubles are mine to bear.
When I can have a single grief I will not choose two.
What you call bitter and bringing reproach, this
is the same for me if I will be the death of you,   690
who share my labors. To me it is not an evil if,
suffering as I suffer from the gods, I lose my life.
You are well off and have a house that is free of stain,
not polluted, while mine is unholy and unhappy.
If you survive, you and my sister whom I gave to you   695
in marriage will have children together.
My name would live on and my father's house
will not ever be obliterated and die out without an heir.
But go, keep on living, take over my ancestral home.
When you reach Greece and Argos, land of horses,   700
by my right hand I lay upon you a solemn charge:
raise a mound for me and set up a monument,
and let my sister offer tears and cut hair at the tomb.
Bring news of how I died, consecrated in death
on the altar at the hands of a woman of Argos.   705
Promise that you will never abandon my sister,
when you see the family bereft of its patriarch.
Farewell. I have found you the dearest of friends,
my childhood companion, fellow huntsman,
you have shared the many burdens of my troubles.   710
Phoebus the prophet has played me false:

with his devious schemes, he has driven me far
far from Greece, out of shame at his earlier oracles.
To him I gave all that I had: I obeyed his commands
715   and killed my mother and now I will die in return.

PYLADES:
You will have a tomb, my poor friend, and I could
never abandon your sister's bed, since I will hold
you dear in death even more than while you lived.
Still, the god's oracle has not yet been your ruin
720   even though you are standing on the brink of death.
Times of extreme crisis lend themselves, yes, they do,
to extreme changes, if your luck should shift course.

ORESTES:
Enough. Phoebus' words are no help to me now:
the woman is coming here out of the temple.

      (Enter Iphigenia from the temple with
      attendants, whom she dismisses.)

IPHIGENIA:
725   You, withdraw and go inside to make preparations
for those whose office it is to carry out the sacrifice.
Here, strangers, is my tablet with its many folds,
but there is one more request I want to make. Please
listen. No one remains the same as he was in troubles
730   when he moves from fear once more into confidence.
I am afraid that the one who is to take my letter
to Argos once he has reached the comfort of home
may set my message aside as worthless to him.

ORESTES:
What do you want then? What is it that troubles you?

IPHIGENIA:
735   Have him swear an oath to me that he will deliver
my message to Argos to my loved ones there as I wish.

ORESTES:
And will you in turn swear the same oath to him?

IPHIGENIA:
What would you have me do or not do? Tell me.

ORESTES:
Let him depart with his life from this savage land.

IPHIGENIA:
Fair enough. How else could he deliver my message?   740

ORESTES:
Will the country's ruler allow this to happen?

IPHIGENIA:
Yes.
I will convince him and I will escort *him* to the ship.

ORESTES:
Swear then. Begin the oath as is ritually proper.

IPHIGENIA:
You must say, "I will deliver this to your loved ones."

PYLADES:
"To your loved ones I will deliver this letter."   745

IPHIGENIA:
And I will see you pass safely through the dark rocks.

PYLADES:
What gods do you call to witness to these oaths?

IPHIGENIA:
Artemis in whose temples I hold this sacred office.

PYLADES:
And I swear by solemn Zeus, lord of heaven.

IPHIGENIA:
If you break the oath and do me wrong, what then?   750

PYLADES:
I'll never reach home. And if you do not save my life?

IPHIGENIA:
That, while I live, I never set foot in my native Argos.

PYLADES:
Listen, we have left out an important consideration.

IPHIGENIA:
If your point is good we will consider it anew.

PYLADES:
755   Grant me this exception: if something happens
to the ship and the letter with the other goods
is lost at sea and I escape with only my life,
in that case the oath will be no longer binding.

IPHIGENIA:
Here is what I shall do: success takes many turns.
760   All that is written in the folds of the tablet,
I will tell you out loud so you can tell my friends.
This is safer. If you are able to preserve the letter,
though without speech, it will tell what is written,
but if the words that are written here are lost at sea,
765   by saving yourself, you will save my words for me.

PYLADES:
Well said, both for my sake and the gods'.
Indicate to whom I must deliver the letter
in Argos and tell me what I should say.

IPHIGENIA:
Bring this news to Orestes, Agamemnon's son:
770   "She who was sacrificed at Aulis, Iphigenia, is alive
and sends this, though no longer alive in your eyes."

ORESTES:
Where is she? Has she come back from the dead?

IPHIGENIA: *(Indicating herself.)*
I whom you see here. But do not interrupt me.
"Bring me back to Argos, dear brother, before I die,

remove me from this savage land and the goddess'   775
sacrifices at which I hold the duty to kill strangers."

ORESTES:
Pylades, what can I say? Where do we find ourselves?

IPHIGENIA:
"Or I shall become a curse upon your house,
Orestes. I repeat the name so you will learn it."

PYLADES:
O gods!

IPHIGENIA:
Why do you invoke the gods in my affairs?   780

PYLADES:
It's nothing. My thoughts strayed somewhere else.
Perhaps if I ask you, I will learn something incredible.

IPHIGENIA:
Tell him that the goddess Artemis rescued me
by substituting a deer, which my father slaughtered,
believing he was thrusting the sharp sword into me;   785
she brought me here to live in this country. Here is
the letter: that is what is written in the folded tablet.

PYLADES:
Ah, it is with an easy oath that you have bound me,
and sworn most kindly. I shall not long hold off
before paying back in full the oath that I took.   790
Look here, Orestes, I deliver to you this letter
that I have received from your sister, standing here.

ORESTES:
I accept it. But putting off the opening of the letter
I will first take a sweet pleasure but not in words . . .

(Orestes reaches to embrace Iphigenia.)

795 My dear, dear sister, I am overcome with surprise,
but still I will embrace you in my doubting arms,
and take delight on hearing this amazing news.

CHORUS LEADER:
Sir, it is not right for you to sully the god's attendant
and put your hands on her sacred garments.

ORESTES:
800 My own sister born of the very same father,
Agamemnon's daughter, do not turn away from me,
when you have your brother, unexpected as I am.

IPHIGENIA:
I have you as my brother? Please, stop saying that.
He is in Argos or Nauplia, where he is well known.

ORESTES:
805 Unhappy one, your brother is not there anymore.

IPHIGENIA:
Did the Spartan, daughter of Tyndareos, give you life?

ORESTES:
Yes, to the son of Pelops' son, whose son I am.

IPHIGENIA:
Is it so? Do you have any proof of this for me?

ORESTES:
Yes. Ask me anything about my father's house.

IPHIGENIA:
810 It is for you to tell me and for me to learn from you.

ORESTES:
I'll begin with this, a story I heard from Electra:
Do you know of the quarrel between Atreus and Thyestes?

IPHIGENIA:
I have heard of it. There was a quarrel about a golden lamb.[42]

ORESTES:
Do you remember you wove this story into a fine weaving?

IPHIGENIA:
Oh dearest one, you are stirring up memories in my mind.   815

ORESTES:
The image on the loom was the sun reversing course.

IPHIGENIA:
Yes, I wove that image with the twisting of fine threads.

ORESTES:
And did you receive ritual bathwater from Mother at Aulis?[43]

IPHIGENIA:
The corrupted marriage did not obliterate that memory.

ORESTES:
Did you cut off your hair for Mother to take home?   820

IPHIGENIA:
Yes, as a memorial for the tomb instead of my remains.

ORESTES:
Of things I saw myself, I will offer this evidence:
the ancient spear of Pelops in father's house,
which he wielded in his hands when he won the girl
from Pisa, Hippodamia, by killing her father   825
Oenomaus. It was stored in the girls' chambers.

---

42. *813–17:* "Golden lamb"—See note on 193–96. The weaving is reminiscent of the garment Orestes holds up in Aeschylus' *Libation Bearers* (230–31) as the final proof of his identity in the recognition scene. In the earlier play, the weaving had been made by Electra and represented an animal scene rather than an astrological myth.

43. *818:* The mothers of the bride and groom prepared the purifying baths: spring water was brought in special vessels called *loutrophoroi*.

Sung Interlude

IPHIGENIA:
My dear, dear one, nothing else, you are dearest to me;[44]
I hold you, Orestes, all grown up, far from home,
830   far from Argos, my dear.

ORESTES:
And I you, long dead, so it was believed.
Tears wet your eyes, just like mine,
and keening mixed with joy.

IPHIGENIA:
I left you still a newborn baby
835   in your nurse's arms,
an infant in the house.
Oh my soul, happy more than words can tell,
what can I say? Things are passing beyond wonder,
840   beyond speech.

ORESTES:
I pray we have a happy future with each other.

IPHIGENIA: *(To the chorus.)*
Dear friends, I have caught a strange joy.
And I am afraid he will flit away
from my arms into thin air.
845   O Cyclopean hearth, o fatherland,[45]
my own Mycenae,
I have you to thank for his life, for his nurture,
because you brought up my brother,
a light to the house.

---

44. *827–99:* The duet of Iphigenia (singing) and Orestes (speaking) separates the two parts of the episode: the elaborate, drawn-out recognition scene and the escape plot.
45. *845:* Cyclopean—The massive stone boulders of Mycenaean Age walls (in Mycenae, Tiryns, Argos, and other places) were said to have been put in place by the Cyclopes.

ORESTES:

    We are fortunate in our birth, but falling into tragedy;   850
    our lives, dear sister, are less than happy.

IPHIGENIA:

    I know, from my own misery,
    when my grim-hearted father
    held the knife to my throat.

ORESTES:

    Ah me. I can almost see you there though I was not present.[46]   855

IPHIGENIA:

    No wedding song, dear brother, led me
    into Achilles' quarters
    but a false marriage.
    By the altar there were tears and keening.   860
    Alas, for the ritual bathing, alas.

ORESTES:

    Alas, that Father dared such a deed.

IPHIGENIA:

    No father; my fate is to be without a father.
    One thing comes on top of another   865
    through chance from some god.

ORESTES:

    If to your sorrow you had killed your brother.

IPHIGENIA:

    I am sorry for my terrible daring. Terrible
    deeds I dared, terrible deeds, dear brother.   870
    Barely did you escape a sacrilegious death,
    slashed by my hands.
    What will be the consequence of this?
    What chance will present itself?
    What way forward will I find   875

---

46. *855:* In Euripides' *Iphigenia at Aulis,* Orestes, still an infant in his
mother's arms, is present as Iphigenia pleads for her life.

to conduct you from this city, from death,
into your homeland in Argos,
880   before the sword closes in to take your blood?
Oh sorrowing heart,
this is yours to find.
By land will it be, not by sea,
885   but with the rippling of feet
will you draw near death crossing through
savage tribes and impassable roads?
Yet by the narrow passage between the dark rocks
890   is a long journey
for racing ships.
Sorrow, oh sorrow.
895   What god or mortal,
or what unimagined means,
making a passage where there is none,
might show an escape from evils
to the last two of Atreus' children?

CHORUS LEADER:
900   Wonders even beyond words I have seen here,
with my own eyes and report no empty rumor.

PYLADES:
It's natural for loved ones to embrace
when they catch first sight of one another,
but it is time to break off these emotional scenes
905   and consider how we will attain renown that comes
with survival and escape from this savage territory.
This is the way of the wise, not driven by luck,
but seizing the opportunity to reach new joys.

ORESTES:
Well said. I think fortune along with ourselves
910   will take care of that: if a person is eager,
in all likelihood, divine power will prove stronger.

IPHIGENIA:
Do not stop me nor put an end to our talk,
before I find out what manner of life Electra
enjoys now. She is very much in my heart.

ORESTES:
She is married to my friend here and has a happy life.   915

IPHIGENIA:
Where does he come from and whose son is he?

ORESTES:
Strophius the Phocian is known as his father.

IPHIGENIA:
He is the son of Atreus' daughter and related to me?

ORESTES:
Yes, your cousin and my only friend, tried and true.

IPHIGENIA:
He was not yet born when my father killed me.   920

ORESTES:
No. Strophius remained childless for a long time.

IPHIGENIA:
Hello, then, husband of my own dear sister.

ORESTES:
Not just my relative, but the preserver of my life.

IPHIGENIA:
How did you have the heart to do what you did to Mother?

ORESTES:
Let's not talk about that. I had to avenge my father.   925

IPHIGENIA:
What was her reason for killing her husband?[47]

---

47. 926: Chief among Clytemnestra's motives for killing Agamemnon in other versions is his sacrifice of their daughter Iphigenia. What is Orestes' reason for not telling his sister? Perhaps it is simply to avoid distracting her and the audience from the escape plot, or to avoid the complications in the siblings' relationship if Iphigenia were forced to turn her mind to the fact that Orestes and Electra took her father's side.

ORESTES:
No more about Mother. It is not good for you to hear.

IPHIGENIA:
I'll stop. Does Argos look to you now as ruler?

ORESTES:
Menelaus is king. I am an exile from my homeland.

IPHIGENIA:
930   Did our uncle usurp when our family was in trouble?

ORESTES:
No, but fear of the Furies drives me from my country.

IPHIGENIA:
Is that why you were having a fit on the shore, as I was told?

ORESTES:
I was seen in my affliction and not for the first time.

IPHIGENIA:
I see. The goddesses hunt you because of Mother.

ORESTES:
935   To force me to bear a bloody bit in my mouth.

IPHIGENIA:
What brought you to set foot in this country?

ORESTES:
I came here directed by the oracles of Phoebus.

IPHIGENIA:
To do what? Can you tell or are you bound by silence?

ORESTES:
I'm free to tell. This is how my tale of woes began.
940   After what happened to Mother, which we are not
to speak about, because the Furies began to hound me,

I had been wandering in exile, until Loxias directed[48]
me to make my way to Athens to stand trial
before the goddesses that may not be named.[49]
There is a solemn tribunal which Zeus established   945
for Ares because he had blood on his hands.
When I got there, at first not one of the citizens
was willing to welcome me, a god-detested man.[50]
Those who showed respect for me provided a table
set apart from the others, but under the same roof;   950
without speaking to me, or I to them, they contrived
a way I might be isolated from their festivities:
each guest had his own jug filled with an equal
measure of wine so they could enjoy themselves.
And I did not feel that I could reproach my hosts,   955
but I grieved in silence and pretended not to notice,
greatly troubled, because I was my mother's murderer.
I have heard that my distress has been turned
into a ritual by the Athenians and it is still the custom
for the people of Pallas to celebrate the Day of Wine Jugs.[51]   960
Then, when I came to the Hill of Ares, I stood trial,
taking my seat on one side of the court, and the eldest
of the Furies on the other. The arguments were made

---

48. *942:* Loxias is a name for Apollo in his oracular role.

49. *944:* Various euphemisms are used to avoid naming the Furies
(Erinyes): the nameless ones, the awesome ones (*semnai*), the Eumenides
("Kindly Ones"). See *Orestes* 408–10.

50. *947–48:* Orestes is polluted by murder. In Aeschylus' *Furies
(Eumenides)* he has gone through ritual purification and reacceptance
into society before he reaches Athens. Euripides postpones the purification
until after the trial. Iphigenia is able to use the fear of contamination from
contact with a murderer in her escape plan (1031–41).

51. *949–60:* The festival of the Anthesteria was celebrated over three days:
Pithoigia (Opening of the Jars), *Choes* (Day of Wine Jugs), and *Chutroi*
(Day of Pots). On the Day of Wine Jugs, each person was seated at a
separate table and received his measure of wine in a jug. When the drinking
started no words were to be spoken (Burkert 1985, pp. 237–42): "The
participants drink at the Choes like persons defiled by murder" (p. 238).
In Orestes' case, they are motivated by *aidōs*, "respect," particularly for
the rights and needs of suppliants and guests who are protected by the gods
(Zeus in particular), as well as by fear of pollution.

concerning the shedding of my mother's blood.
965   Phoebus testified on my behalf and saved my life,
as Pallas, presiding, counted out the equal votes
and I walked away, acquitted of the charge of murder.
Those of the Furies who were persuaded by the trial
marked off a holy sanctuary to keep beside the court;[52]
970   but those who were not persuaded by the verdict
pursued me ceaselessly with homeless wandering,
until I went again to Phoebus' sacred precinct,
and abstaining from food, I prostrated myself before
his shrine. I swore to end my life there and then, unless
975   Phoebus, who had caused my ruin, would save me.
Then, emitting a voice from the golden tripod,[53]
Phoebus directed me here, to carry off the statue
dropped from the sky and to place it in Athenian land.
But join me in this: what he sketched out as my means
980   of survival. If we can take hold of the goddess' image,
I will be free of my madness and in a vessel plied
by many oars I will bring you back to live in Mycenae.
Oh my dear, much-loved, my own true sister,
keep alive our ancestral home, and preserve my life.
985   All that I have, the whole line of Pelops' sons, is lost
unless we take in our hands the image of the goddess.

CHORUS LEADER:
Some dreadful ire of the gods has boiled to the surface
and drags the seed of Tantalus through trial and tribulation.

IPHIGENIA:
Before you came here, I was full of eagerness
990   to be in Argos and to see you, my dear brother.
I desire the same as you, to free you of your toils
and to set right the troubled house of our fathers—

---

52. *961–69:* Up to this point, Orestes' trial follows the outline of Aeschylus'
Furies (Eumenides), 470–753. Thereafter, all the Furies accepted Athena's
persuasion (916–25). Euripides departs from the Aeschylean version
because the continued pursuit of Orestes is needed for the plot of *Iphigenia
among the Tauri.*

53. *976:* Tripod—At Delphi, Apollo proclaimed his oracles from a golden
tripod. See also 1242–58.

I am no longer enraged at the man who killed me.
That way I could keep my hand free of killing you
and preserve my house. But I'm afraid I could not   995
escape the goddess or the ruler when he finds
the stone pedestal empty and the image missing.
I will surely be killed. What reason would I give?
But if this can be done as one single action:
you take both the statue and me together aboard   1000
the fine-built ship. The risk would be well worth it.
Without this my life is lost, but for yourself,
perhaps you could arrange a safe homecoming.
I do not shrink from this, not even if to save you
I must die. If a man loses his life he is sorely missed   1005
in his family, but a woman's life counts for little.

ORESTES:
I could not be your murderer as well as my mother's;
her blood is enough. I feel the same as you. With you
I wish to live or in death to share the same destiny.
I will take you home, if I can get away from here,   1010
otherwise I will perish here and remain by your side.
But listen to what I think: if this were objectionable
to Artemis, how would her brother have advised me
to transport the goddess' image to Athena's city?
Or let me look upon your face? Putting all these things   1015
together I find hope that we will achieve a homecoming.

IPHIGENIA:
How will it be possible to avoid being put to death
and to achieve the thing we want? It is on this point
that our return home is in trouble. The will is there.

ORESTES:
Do you suppose there is any way we could kill the ruler?   1020

IPHIGENIA:
That's a terrible thing to say, strangers murder their host.

ORESTES:
But if it will save your life and mine, it must be dared.

IPHIGENIA:
  I could not do it. Still, I'm touched by your enthusiasm.

ORESTES:
  Well, what if you hide me secretly here in the temple?

IPHIGENIA:
1025   So we would save ourselves by making use of darkness?

ORESTES:
  Thieves own the nighttime, daylight belongs to truth.

IPHIGENIA:
  Inside there are temple guards who will surely see us.

ORESTES:
  Oh well. We are lost. How can we save ourselves?

IPHIGENIA:
  I have an idea—something just occurred to me.

ORESTES:
1030   What is it? Share your idea with me so I know it, too.

IPHIGENIA:
  I will make use of your troubles as a trick.

ORESTES:
  Women are clever at figuring out intrigues.

IPHIGENIA:
  I will say that you came from Argos a mother-killer.

ORESTES:
  Use my tragic story, if you can benefit from it.

IPHIGENIA:
1035   I will say it is not right to sacrifice you to the goddess.

ORESTES:
  What cause will you give? Well, I have a suspicion . . .

IPHIGENIA:
Because you are polluted. It will make the pious uneasy.[54]

ORESTES:
How does this lead to the taking of the goddess' image?

IPHIGENIA:
I'll say I want to cleanse you in running seawater.

ORESTES:
But the statue for which we sailed is still in the temple.   1040

IPHIGENIA:
I will say that I must wash that, too, since you touched it.

ORESTES:
Where will you take it? To the sea's wave-swept inlet?

IPHIGENIA:
Yes, where your ship is moored by its rope fastenings.

ORESTES:
Will you or someone else take the statue in hand?

IPHIGENIA:
I will. I'm the only one allowed to handle it.   1045

ORESTES:
And Pylades here, what part will he play in our effort?

IPHIGENIA:
I will say he has the same pollution on his hands as you.

ORESTES:
Will the king know, or will you do it in secret from him?

IPHIGENIA:
I will have to persuade him—there is no way to avoid it.

---

54. *1035–37:* A victim for sacrifice had to be unblemished.

ORESTES:

1050   My ship stands ready, equipped with swift strong oars.

IPHIGENIA:

It is up to you to take care that all the rest goes well.

ORESTES:

There is only one thing left: that these women keep
our secret. Beg them; find words to persuade them.
A woman has the power to bring out others' pity.

1055   For the rest, just maybe, all will turn out for the best.

IPHIGENIA: *(To the chorus.)*

My dear, dear friends, I turn my eyes to you,
and on you all my hopes depend, whether I succeed
or fail and be forever bereft of my homeland
and my dear brother and the sister I love the most.

1060   These first thoughts are the beginning of my speech:
we are women with a natural affinity to each other
and most reliable at preserving the common good.
Keep our secret and add your help to our efforts
to escape. A loyal tongue is a fine asset if you have it.

1065   You see how one fortune holds us, three loving friends:
to achieve a return to our native land or else to die.
If I succeed, you, too, will share in my fortune:
I will see you safe in Greece.

(To each of the women.)

But by your right hand
and yours, I beg you, and by your dear cheek

1070   and by your knees and by those you love most at home,
your mother and father, and children if you have any.
What do you say? Who is willing and who is not?
Tell me, please. If you do not assent to my words
I am doomed to die, both I and my unhappy brother.

CHORUS LEADER:

1075   Take heart, dear mistress, and save yourself.
I will keep your secret in everything you ask.
Let mighty Zeus be witness to my oath.

IPHIGENIA:
Bless you: I pray your words bring you benefit.

(To Orestes and Pylades.)

Your role, and yours, now is to go inside the temple,
since the king of the country will soon arrive to find out   1080
if the sacrifice of the strangers has been executed.

(Exeunt Orestes and Pylades into the temple)

Revered goddess, who saved me in the inlets of Aulis
from the terrible hand of my murderous father,
rescue me yet again along with these men. Or because
of you Loxias' words will no longer be regarded as true.   1085
But be merciful and go forth from this savage land
all the way to Athens. It does not become you
to dwell here, when you can inhabit a blessed city.

(Exit Iphigenia into temple.)

Second Stasimon

CHORUS:

[Strophe 1]

O bird, that along the rocky
ridges by the sea, halcyon,   1090
you sing an elegy of your doom,
a call easily known to the knowing:
that with birdsong you are mourning your mate—
I, a bird without wings, compare
my lamentation to yours: 1095
I miss the gatherings of the Greeks,
I miss Artemis, helper of birth,
who dwells at the foot of Mount Cynthos,
and the palm with its slender fronds,
the laurel fresh with sprouting leaves,   1100
and the holy shoots of the silvery olive,
comfort to Leto in her birth pangs,
and the lake whirling its circling water,
where the melodious swan
serves the Muses.   1105

[Antistrophe 1]

Oh, the constant stream of tears,
that fell onto my cheeks
when, our towers
overthrown, aboard ship I journeyed,
1110   by oars of the enemy under arms.
Bartered away for gold,
I made a journey to a savage land,
where I serve the handmaid
of the goddess slayer of deer,
1115   Agamemnon's daughter, and the altars
for sacrifice—and not for the blood of sheep;
how I envy the life that is tragic
throughout; for though familiar
with hardship you are not broken by it.
1120   Ill fortune can change,
but after good times to suffer ill
is a heavy life for mortals.

[Strophe 2]

And you, mistress, an Argive ship
with its fifty oars will carry you home.[55]
1125   The reed of pipes bound in wax
of mountain-dwelling Pan
will urge on the oars,
and prophet Phoebus, singing
to the music
1130   of the seven-toned lyre, will convey you
happily home to the glorious land of Athens.
Leaving me behind,
you will journey to the plashing of oars.
In the wind, the forestays spread
1135   the sails over the bow, along the prow,
of the swift-moving ship.

_____

55. *1124:* The pentekonter (fifty-oared ship) was replaced in the fifth
century by the trireme (with three banks of oars).

[Antistrophe 2]

I wish I could traverse the bright course
which the sun's fire crosses,
and over the chambers of my house   1140
bring to rest the wings on my back
from their swift beating.
I would take my place in the dance
for a noble wedding as I did when I was a girl,
whirling my feet away from my mother's side,   1145
dancing with the choruses of my friends,
entering into the rivalries of grace,
the delicate matching of tresses,
veiling myself
with my rich-colored cloak and curls,   1150
I shaded my cheeks from the sun.

Third Episode

(Enter Thoas with attendants stage left.)

THOAS:
Where is the guardian of this precinct, the woman
from Greece? Have the strangers been consecrated?
Are their bodies ablaze with fire in the holy shrines? 1155

*(Enter Iphigenia from the temple, carrying
the cult image of Artemis.)*

CHORUS LEADER:
Here she is. She will tell you everything clearly, my king.

THOAS:
My god!
Daughter of Agamemnon, why have you taken the image
of the goddess in your arms? It must not be moved from its
    base.

IPHIGENIA:
Stop, my king, stay there in the forecourt, away from the door.

THOAS:
What is it? What strange business is in the halls, Iphigenia?   1160

IPHIGENIA:
Avert the sacrilege.[56] To Holiness herself I utter these words.

THOAS:
What do you mean by this strange preface? Explain clearly.

IPHIGENIA:
My king, the victims you have stalked for me are not clean.

THOAS:
What is your proof or are you expressing your opinion?

IPHIGENIA:
1165   The image of the goddess turned around on its pedestal.

THOAS:
All on its own or did an earthquake cause it to shift?

IPHIGENIA:
All on its own. And besides that it closed its eyes.

THOAS:
And what was the cause? Was it the strangers' pollution?

IPHIGENIA:
That was it, no other cause. They have done awful things.

THOAS:
1170   What was it? Did they kill someone on our foreign shore?

IPHIGENIA:
They came here after committing murder in their family.

THOAS:
Who was the victim? I really desire to know this.

IPHIGENIA:
With swords they joined to strike down their mother.

---

56. *1161:* "Sacrilege"—Literally, she says, "I spit it off," a phrase used
instead of actually spitting, to ward off the pollution she pretends Thoas'
thoughtless words may have caused.

THOAS:
Apollo! Not even a savage would dare such a thing.[57]

IPHIGENIA:
They are persecuted and driven out everywhere in Greece.   1175

THOAS:
Is it because of this that you are carrying the statue outside?

IPHIGENIA:
Yes, to remove the stain of murder, under the pure sky.

THOAS:
In what way did you learn of the strangers' pollution?

IPHIGENIA:
I questioned them when the goddess turned her back.

THOAS:
Greece has made you clever to notice this so capably.   1180

IPHIGENIA:
And truly they tried to set a sweet bait for my mind.

THOAS:
Do they have enticing news to tell of those in Argos?

IPHIGENIA:
That my only brother Orestes is getting on well.

THOAS:
In hope you will preserve them for their pleasant news.

IPHIGENIA:
And that my father is alive and prospering nicely.[58]   1185

---

57. *1174:* "Savage"— The Greek word is *barbaros* (barbarian, the Greek word for non-Greeks). As often, Euripides subverts the Greek polarity of superior Greek against crude, stupid, violent Other. See note on 31.

58. *1185:* Iphigenia is assumed by Thoas and the other Tauri to hate Agamemnon and all Greek men because of the sacrifice at Aulis (see the

THOAS:
But you inclined to the side of the goddess naturally.

IPHIGENIA:
Yes, I hate everything Greek because they took my life.

THOAS:
What are we to do about the strangers, tell me this?

IPHIGENIA:
We must honor the law that has been established.

THOAS:
1190   Are your sword and lustral water ready for the business?

IPHIGENIA:
First I would like to wash them in sacred cleansings.

THOAS:
In freshwater streams or in the waters of the sea?

IPHIGENIA:
The sea washes away all the troubles of humanity.

THOAS:
Then they would make a holier sacrifice to the goddess.

IPHIGENIA:
1195   And things would work out better for me that way.

THOAS:
Don't the waves wash up right against the temple?

IPHIGENIA:
We need solitude. There are other things we have to do.

THOAS:
As you wish. I do not care to see what is forbidden.

Herdsman's closing comment, 336–39). This reference to her father's
supposed well-being adds credibility to her scheme to seem to be going on
with the sacrifice of the two young Greeks.

IPHIGENIA:
I must also purify the image of the goddess.

THOAS:
In case it has been tainted by the stain of matricide.   1200

IPHIGENIA:
Otherwise I would not have lifted it from its base.

THOAS:
Your scrupulousness and foresight are praiseworthy.

IPHIGENIA:
Let me tell you what I need.

THOAS:
                              Yours only to ask.

IPHIGENIA:
Put the strangers in chains.

THOAS:
                      Where could they escape from you?

IPHIGENIA:
Greece and its people are faithless.

THOAS: *(To his attendants.)*
                              Go and bring the chains.   1205

IPHIGENIA:
And have them bring the strangers here.

THOAS:
                                  It will be done.

IPHIGENIA:
Cover their heads in cloaks.

THOAS:
                          Out of sight of the sun.[59]

---

59. *1207:* They are covered to protect the sun's purity from the pollution
of the murderers.

IPHIGENIA:
Send along some of your attendants.

THOAS:

These will go with you.

IPHIGENIA:
Send someone to proclaim to the citizens . . .

THOAS:

What should he tell them?

IPHIGENIA:
That they all must stay inside their homes.

THOAS:

1210   To avoid the pollution of murder?

IPHIGENIA:
Yes, such things are unclean.

THOAS: *(To an attendant.)*
You, go and issue the command.

IPHIGENIA:
And that no one come near the sight.

THOAS:

You show concern for the city.

IPHIGENIA:
And especially those who are my friends.

THOAS:

You say this about me.

IPHIGENIA: [Yes, that is true.]⁶⁰

---

60. *1214:* Iphigenia's words are lost. "Yes, of course" or "Naturally" have been suggested.

THOAS:

                  The whole city respects you, as is right.

IPHIGENIA:

You, stay here in front of the temple and . . .

THOAS:

                          What should I do?   1215

IPHIGENIA:

Purify the building with a torch.[61]

THOAS:

                So you will find it pure when you return.

IPHIGENIA:

When the strangers come outside . . .

THOAS:

                        What should I do then?

IPHIGENIA:

Cover your face with your clothing.

THOAS:

                        Lest I catch the pollution.

IPHIGENIA:

If I seem to be gone too long . . .

THOAS:

                        What time limit should I set?

IPHIGENIA:

Do not be surprised.

THOAS:

            Take care of the goddess' affairs. There is no hurry.   1220

---

61. *1216:* This may refer to purification with sulfur, as in Homer, *Odyssey* 22.480.

IPHIGENIA:
I pray this cleansing goes as I wish.

THOAS:

I share your prayer.

*(Enter Orestes and Pylades under guard from
the temple with attendants leading lambs
and carrying the temple accessories.)*

IPHIGENIA:
I see the strangers are coming here out of the temple, and what
    befits
the goddess' worship, young lambs, so that I may wash out
    with blood
the stain of blood, and gleaming torches and whatever else I
    requested
for the purification of the strangers and the image of the
1225   goddess.

(Iphigenia begins the procession stage right.)

To the citizens I say, stay clear of this pollution.
Whoever is a temple guard with hands pure for the gods
or is about to be married or is carrying a child,
move away, withdraw, let the pollution not fall on you.
1230   O virgin queen, daughter of Zeus and Leto, if I wash the blood
from these men and make the perfect sacrifice, your house will
    be clean
and we will be blessed. The rest I will keep in silence, but still,
goddess, to you and the gods who know more, my meaning is
    clear.

(Exeunt Iphigenia, prisoners, and attendants stage right.)

Third Stasimon

CHORUS:

[Strophe]

Leto's son is a blessed child,
1235   whom she bore in the flourishing valleys
of Delos, golden-haired god,

skilled at the lyre, along with her daughter who enjoys[62]
good aim with the bow.
From the coastal ridges,   1240
leaving the storied birthplace, his mother carried him
to the peaks of Parnassus, [63]
place of rushing waters
that celebrates Dionysus in revels,
where the serpent, its face dark as wine, with dappled back,   1245
hidden in the leafy shade of the laurel,
a primeval freak of Earth,
girdled the oracle below the ground.
You were still an infant,
still in your dear mother's arms, when leaping up   1250
you killed it, Phoebus,
took over the holy oracle
and sitting now on the golden tripod,
on the throne that never lies,
you give prophecies to mortals,   1255
from the oracular sanctum,
near Castalian waters,
dwelling in a house that stands at earth's center.

[Antistrophe]

When he evicted Themis,
daughter of Earth,   1260
from the holy oracle, Earth gave birth
to nightly visions of dreams
which to many mortals told
what happened first, what next,
and what is yet to come   1265

---

62. *1237:* The manuscript gives the feminine form of "who," making a
reference to Artemis that seems startling. Some editors emend to "who"
in the masculine, making it refer to Apollo.

63. *1242–48:* On the transfer of the Delphic oracle, see also Aeschylus'
Furies (Eumenides) 1–19 and the *Homeric Hymn to Apollo.* In Aeschylus
the transmission of the oracle from Earth to Apollo is represented as
peaceful: the killing of the serpent that guards the oracle is omitted. Here,
Apollo kills the serpent (1245) and ousts Themis to take over the lucrative
oracle (1275; see Homer, *Iliad* 9.404–5; Sophocles, *Oedipus Tyrannus*
152).

as they slept in their beds
on the ground at night. Thus Earth
took from Phoebus
his prophetic privilege, in anger for her daughter.
1270   Swift of foot Lord Apollo rushed to Olympus,
reached out his childish hand to the throne of Zeus
to ask him to remove from his Pythian home
the goddess' otherworldly wrath.
Zeus laughed because his son had come so fast
1275   in his desire to retain the wealthy oracle.
He shook his head
and silenced the dream voices.
He took from mortals
nighttime soothsaying
1280   and gave the privilege back to Loxias,
and gave mortals confidence
in the oracular chants
at his throne visited by pilgrim throngs.

Exodos

(Enter Messenger, running, stage right.)

MESSENGER:
Yo! Temple guards, attendants of the altars,
1285   where has Thoas gone, the king of our country?
Open the well-latched gates and call outside
from within these halls the ruler of the land.

CHORUS LEADER:
What is it, if I may speak, though unbidden?

MESSENGER:
They are gone. The two young men have escaped
1290   by the machinations of Agamemnon's daughter,
in flight from this country and the sacred image—
they seized it and put it into the hold of a Greek ship.

CHORUS LEADER:
What you say is incredible. The man you are looking for,
the king, has gone away from the shrine in great haste.

MESSENGER:
Where? He must be informed of what is going on. 1295

CHORUS LEADER:
We do not know. But you should go and hunt for him.
Wherever you find him you can tell him the news.

MESSENGER:
Look at this: all womankind is untrustworthy.
You have played a part in what has been done.

CHORUS LEADER:
You are mad. What part have we in the strangers' flight? 1300
Will you not hurry as fast as you can to the rulers' gates?

MESSENGER:
No. Not until the gatekeeper here gives me the word,
whether in fact the ruler of the country is inside or not.

(Messenger calls and beats at the doors of the temple.)

Hey in there! Open up. Unbolt the doors. I am speaking
to you inside. And tell the master why I am here 1305
at the gates, bearing the burden of bad news to tell.

(Enter Thoas from the temple.)

THOAS:
Who is raising a cry here at the goddess' home,
rattling the gates and making noise heard inside?

MESSENGER:
Aha!
These women tried to make me leave the temple,
saying you were out. But you were here all along. 1310

THOAS:
What did they hope to gain by saying such a thing?

MESSENGER:
I'll explain that later. Listen to what is happening
right now. The young woman you keep here

1315   who attends to the sacrifices, Iphigenia, has gone
        out of the country with the strangers and is taking
        the holy image with her. The purification was a sham.

THOAS:
        What are you saying? What can have gotten into her?

MESSENGER:
        This will come as a surprise: she did it to save Orestes.

THOAS:
        What do you mean? The son of Tyndareos' daughter?

MESSENGER:
1320   Yes. He was the one the goddess dedicated at her altar.

THOAS:
        This is astonishing. What other word can I use for it?

MESSENGER:
        Do not turn your mind to that, but listen to me:
        after you understand everything clearly, decide
        what manner of pursuit will catch the strangers.

THOAS:
1325   Right. Go on with what you have to say. Their flight
        is no short passage: they will not escape my armed pursuit.

MESSENGER:
        When we came to the shoreline of the sea
        where Orestes' ship was secretly moored,
        Agamemnon's daughter signaled to those of us
1330   you had sent to hold the strangers' fetters to stand
        far off since she was going to light the sacred
        cleansing flame as she had come there to do.
        She walked behind by herself, holding the bonds
        of the two strangers in her hands. This was suspicious
1335   in itself, but your attendants were satisfied, my king.
        After a time, so she would seem to be doing something,
        she cried out loud and intoned unintelligible chants
        as though by magic to wash away the stain of murder.

But when we had been sitting there for a long time,
it occurred to us that the strangers might break free   1340
and kill her and escape as fugitives from the country.
Still in fear that we might see something we should not,
we remained there in silence. Finally we were all
repeating to each other: "Let's go, even if it's forbidden."
Once there we caught sight of the ship from Greece   1345
fitted out with oars like the wings of a great bird,
and fifty sailors, their hands ready on the oars
in the oarlocks, and the two young men now freed
from their bonds standing beside the ship's stern.
Some were holding the prow with poles, others   1350
drawing the anchor on the beams. Others pulled
the cables through their hands and were hurriedly
letting down ladders into the sea for the strangers.
When we saw their deceitful trickery we cast aside
our hesitation and seized the Greek woman along with   1355
the cables, and through the openings we were trying
to drag the rudder oars from the well-built ship.
We cried out: "What right have you to steal our statue
and our priestess and take them out of the country?
Who are you and whose son, to carry this woman off?"   1360
And he said, "Orestes, her brother—just so you know—
I'm Agamemnon's son; this woman is my sister
who was lost from our home and I am taking her back."
No less tightly did we hold onto the foreign woman
and we tried to force her to follow us into your presence.   1365
That's how I got these ugly bruises on my cheeks.
They did not have weapons in their hands and neither
did we. So fists were pounding in every direction.
The arms and legs of both young men at once
were flung against our sides at our abdomens,   1370
so that we had barely started fighting before we were
exhausted. Bruised and battered with hideous wounds,
we escaped to an overhang, some sporting bloody
gashes on the head, others bleeding about their eyes.
Stationed on the heights, from a safer vantage point,   1375
we rejoined the fight and kept pelting them with rocks.
Their archers, standing on the stern, were keeping us
back with arrows, so we were forced to retreat.
While this was happening a huge wave drove the ship

1380   to the shore and they were afraid it would go under.
        Orestes, lifting her up onto his left shoulder,
        walked into the sea and climbing up the ladder
        put his sister down inside the well-marked ship,[64]
        along with the image of Zeus' daughter that fell
1385   from the sky. A cry went up from the middle
        of the ship: "Sailors from the land of Greece,
        take hold of the ships' oars and make the water
        white: for we have obtained what we sailed for
        on this hostile crossing between the Clashing Rocks."
1390   From the sailors there issued a rhythmic murmur
        as their oars slapped the surge. And the ship, still inside
        the harbor, made progress, until it passed the mouth,
        where, fighting the powerful surf, it was driven back again.
        A fierce wind arose suddenly and was forcing
1395   the ships' sails toward the stern. Still the sailors kept
        fighting against the surge; but the wave ebbing
        back kept driving the ship again toward the land.
        Agamemnon's daughter stood up and prayed:
        "Daughter of Leto, carry me, your priestess, safely
1400   to Greece from this savage land and forgive my theft.
        Goddess, you have affection for your own brother:
        understand that I too love my nearest of kin."
        The sailors approved the woman's prayers with a paean
        of joy, and applied their arms, bare at the shoulders,
1405   to the oars to the rhythm of the boatswain's call.
        Still, more and more the ship was headed for the rocks.
        On our side one man rushed on foot into the sea,
        another was securing woven ropes [to trees],[65]
        and I was sent at once here to you, my king,
1410   to bring you news of what was happening there.
        Come, take chains and ropes in your hands.
        Unless a sudden calm falls upon the sea,
        the strangers have no hope of escape.

---

64. *1383:* "Well-marked" is the manuscript reading. "Well-benched" or "well-decked" has been suggested by editors, but the Messenger might be referring to a conspicuous figurehead.

65. *1408:* "To trees" is not in the text. Platnauer (1938, commenting on line 1407) explains the action of Thoas' men as bringing down ropes they had already secured to rocks or trees.

Mighty Poseidon, lord of the ocean, looks on Troy
with favor and is hostile to Pelops' progeny.   1415
He will deliver Agamemnon's son to you
and, I think, into the hands of the citizens, to arrest,
along with his sister, who is caught betraying
the goddess and forgetting the murder at Aulis.

CHORUS LEADER:
Poor Iphigenia, with your brother you will die,   1420
falling once more into the hands of our masters.

THOAS:
All you citizens of this barbarian nation,
hurry, rein your horses. Race to the shore
to take in the wreckage of the Greek ship,
with the help of our goddess. With all haste   1425
hunt down and capture these godless men.
Some of you drag swift-oared ships into the sea,
so that by sea and by land on horseback
we may catch them and throw them down
from the rough crag or impale them on pikes.   1430
And you, women, accomplices in this plot:
later, when I have the leisure, I will see
that you are punished. Now with this urgent
business at hand I will not stand idly by.

(Athena appears above the temple roof on the mēchanē.*)*

ATHENA:
I ask you, king Thoas, where are you taking   1435
this pursuit? Attend to the words of Athena, standing
above you. Call off the manhunt. Do not deploy
your troops. Orestes came here, destined
by Apollo's oracles and fleeing from the anger
of the Furies to bring his sister back to Argos   1440
and convey the sacred image into my land,
to earn a respite from his present sufferings.
This is what I have to say to you. But Orestes,
whom you expect to kill, catching him in the storm,
Poseidon has already, for my sake, made the sea's
surface untroubled for him and set the ship on its way.   1445

Orestes, be instructed by my commands—
though far away you can hear my divine voice—
make your way, taking the image and your sister.
When you reach Athens, built by the gods,
1450   there is a place at the farthest borders of Attica,
a holy site, neighbor to the Carystian mountain:
the people of Athens have named it Halae.[66]
Build a temple there to house the goddess' statue,
to be called after the land of the Tauri and the toils,
1455   which you endured, wandering all through Greece,
goaded by the Furies. Mortals forever after will
sing of her as the goddess Artemis-Tauropolos.
Lay down this custom: when the people celebrate,
in atonement for your sacrifice, let the sword
1460   be held to a man's neck and let human blood flow,
for the ritual lost, that the goddess may have honor.[67]
And you, Iphigenia, around the sacred terraces
of Brauron, you must be the keeper of the temple.
And there you will be buried when you die
1465   and they will honor you with fine-woven gowns
that women who die in childbirth leave in their homes.
I command you further to escort these Greek women
from this country in thanks for their good intentions.[68]
. . . . .

1470   I saved you once before, Orestes, on the Areopagus
when I judged the equal votes: this will be the law,
that whoever wins equal votes will be the victor.
Now, son of Agamemnon, take your sister and leave
this country. And, you, Thoas, do not be angry.

THOAS:
1475   Queen Athena, anyone who hears gods speak
and remains unbelieving is out of his mind.
I bear no grudge toward Orestes, if he has gone,

---

66. *1452:* Halae—see note on 30.

67. *1460–61:* The bloodletting is symbolic rather than lethal, but still shows that Artemis is not opposed to blood sacrifice.

68. *1468–70:* Editors have noticed a lacuna in the middle of the line. The missing line is indicated by a row of dots.

carrying the goddess' image, nor toward his sister.
What good comes of opposing the mighty gods?
Let them depart into your land with the goddess' statue   1480
and with good luck build a sanctuary to enshrine it.
These women I will send into the prosperous land
of Greece, just as your commandment bids me.
I shall call a halt to the armed force I raised against
the Greeks and stay my ships, since it is your will, goddess.   1485

ATHENA:
   Very good.
   Necessity rules both you and the gods.
   Go, winds, conduct Agamemnon's son
   into Athens. I shall sail with them myself
   to protect the sacred image of my sister.

CHORUS:
   Go, blessed in the happiness   1490
   of your rescued fortune.
   Pallas Athena, revered among the immortal gods
   as well as mortal folk,
   we will do as you bid.
   Most pleasant and unexpected   1495
   is the voice my ears have heard.

   O great Victory, awesome goddess,
   sustain my life and never
   withhold your crown.[69]

                              −END−

---

69. *1497–99:* The same three-line tag in Greek is used at the end of
Euripides' *Orestes* and *Phoenician Women*. Some critics take it as a
request for the judges' favor in the dramatic competition.

EURIPIDES

Orestes

Cast of Characters

ELECTRA   daughter of Clytemnestra and Agamemnon, sister of Orestes

HELEN   daughter of Zeus/Tyndareos and Leda, wife of Menelaus, sister of Clytemnestra, aunt of Electra and Orestes, mother of Hermione

CHORUS   of Argive Women

The CHORUS LEADER   speaks for the group in the dialogue sections

ORESTES   son of Clytemnestra and Agamemnon, brother of Electra

MENELAUS   husband of Helen, son of Atreus, brother of Agamemnon

TYNDAREOS   father of Helen, Clytemnestra, and the Dioscuri

PYLADES   friend of Orestes

MESSENGER   an Argive countryman

HERMIONE   daughter of Helen and Menelaus, cousin of Electra and Orestes

PHRYGIAN SLAVE   member of Helen's staff

APOLLO   god of prophecy and plague

Non-speaking Characters

HERMIONE in prologue and exodos, PYLADES in exodos, ELECTRA in exodos, HELEN in exodos

Various extras are required as entourages for Menelaus and Tyndareos.

A possible division of roles among the three speaking actors is:

Protagonist (first actor): Orestes, [possibly Messenger]

Deuteragonist (second actor): Electra, Menelaus, Phrygian Slave

Tritagonist (third actor): Helen, Tyndareos, Pylades, [possibly Messenger], Hermione, Apollo

It is unclear whether the protagonist or tritagonist plays the messenger.

Orestes was first performed in 408 B.C.E.

Orestes

SCENE: *The action takes place outside the palace of Agamemnon at Argos six days after the murder of Clytemnestra by her children. Entrances and exits are through the palace doors, on the rooftop, and along the side passages (in Greek* parodoi *or* eisodoi*): stage right is used for the way to the city center and stage left leads to the highway or outskirts, where the tombs would be. The play opens with a tableau of Electra and Orestes. Orestes is asleep on bedding strewn on the ground in front of the scene building and Electra sits watching over him.*

Prologue[1]

ELECTRA:

There is nothing so dire—no god-sent terror,
no torment, no tragedy we can put into words
that human nature will not one day have to bear.
He was lucky once—my ancestor Tantalus,[2]

---

1. The prologue is everything that takes place before the entrance of the chorus. It is part of the play. As is typical of Euripides, *Orestes* begins with a monologue that is followed by a dialogue. The monologue establishes the scene and the history, letting the audience know where we are in the myth and hinting at the emotions and themes to come. Here, as in many of the late plays of Euripides, no attempt is made to disguise the unnaturalness of a character delivering a long address to no one (or to no one but the audience). Usually at the beginning of a play a character enters from the scene building or from the outside. This prologue is unusual in starting with a "revealed scene" or tableau. Perhaps the *eccyclema* (scenic device that revealed the result of interior action) was used to reveal this intimate scene.

2. *4–10:* Tantalus is better known to students of Greek mythology for testing the gods' omniscience by serving his son Pelops to them in a stew. Euripides tantalizes his audience by using the word "table" to hint at this story but not explicitly referring to the cannibalism. In this version,

5   they say he was Zeus' son—I mean no slur on his fate.
He twists now in the wind in dread of the rock
that looms over his head.³ This is the price he pays.
He was just a man but he had the honor of sitting
at the gods' table—that's the story—but he refused
10   to curb his tongue,⁴ a plague that brought him down
in disgrace. He fathered Pelops, whose son was Atreus.
For him the goddess Fate carded the wool and spun out
strife—setting him at war with Thyestes, who was
his brother. Is there a reason to retell the unspeakable?
15   [Atreus killed his children and feasted him on them.]
What happened in between I leave out.⁵ Atreus' sons
were the celebrated Agamemnon—if that's what he was—⁶
and Menelaus, both born of Aerope, a woman from Crete.
Menelaus married the god-detested Helen while
20   King Agamemnon took Clytemnestra as his wife,
a match that became infamous in the world of Greeks.
From his one wife we three daughters were born to him,

Tantalus' hubris is verbal. This may be a reference to the sophists, often accused of blasphemy for their cosmological speculations. One of the sophists, Prodicus of Ceos, was nicknamed Tantalus (Plato, *Protagoras* 315c).

3. *6–7:* The more famous story of Tantalus in the Underworld, reaching for water and fruit that forever flee from his grasp, is described by Homer (*Odyssey* 11.582–92). In the version referred to here he is in constant motion beneath a suspended rock.

4. *10:* The story was that he revealed divine secrets to mortals.

5. *15–16:* Many editors delete line 15 as an interpolation, in this instance a teacher's or editor's note, explaining what Electra means by "the unspeakable." The banquet of Thyestes, at which he was tricked by his brother Atreus into dining on the flesh of his sons, would then be one of the events that occurred "in between" along with the treacherous murder of Myrtilus (see 990) and the seduction of Atreus' wife by Thyestes and the phenomenon of the golden lamb (see Euripides, *Electra* 698–746). Lines in the Greek text that are of doubtful authenticity are bracketed in the translation.

6. *16–17:* Agamemnon as victorious commander at Troy was illustrious, but his subsequent ignominious murder by his wife tarnished his glamour.

Chrysothemis,[7] Iphigenia, and myself, Electra,
and he fathered a son, Orestes, by our godless mother.
She ensnared her husband in an endless web[8]   25
and killed him. Why she did it, my maiden lips
cannot repeat: I will leave it to the imagination.[9]
What use would it be to accuse Apollo of wrong?[10]
He convinced Orestes to kill the mother who gave him
life, an act that brought him the people's hatred.   30
Still he did not say *no* to the god, but killed her,
and I helped in the murder as much as a woman could.[11]
Pylades, as well, abetted us in everything we did.
Since then, poor Orestes[12] has been wasting away
with a savage sickness. He lies here, wallowing   35
in his bed while his mother's blood dizzies him
to madness. I shudder to name the Eumenides,[13]

---

7. *23:* Chrysothemis is mentioned in Homer, along with Iphianassa
and Laodice, as a daughter of Agamemnon (*Iliad* 9.145, 287; Electra is
not named as one of the daughters in Homer) and, though not named
in Euripides' *Electra,* Chrysothemis has a small but important role in
Sophocles' *Electra.* With the words "and myself" Electra finally identifies
herself.

8. *25:* On the web, see Aeschylus, *Libation Bearers* 980, where it is held
up by Orestes after the killing of Aegisthus and Clytemnestra.

9. *26–27:* Electra is too fastidious to do more than imply her mother's
adultery with Aegisthus, but she also omits the other motives her mother
might have: Agamemnon's slaughter of their daughter and his bringing
home the captive Trojan princess Cassandra to be a third partner in their
marriage.

10. *28:* Apollo, through the Delphic oracle, plays a role in inciting Orestes
to revenge in all the extant Electra and Orestes plays.

11. *32:* In Euripides' *Electra,* Electra holds the sword (1224–25); in
Sophocles she stands outside screaming, "Hit her again!" as her mother
is killed (1415); in Aeschylus' *Libation Bearers* she has already been
dismissed to wait inside before the matricide is perpetrated.

12. *34:* "Poor Orestes"—The epithet *tlēmōn* (suffering, enduring, daring)
has become almost a formal title, or heroic epithet, for Orestes in this play
(74, 293, 845, 947, 1334).

13. *37:* These are the Furies (Erinyes) that haunt a person who has shed the
blood of a kinsman. Eumenides ("Kindly Ones") is a euphemism used to
avoid uttering their name. They are also called *semnai* ("awesome ones").

goddesses who terrorize him with their pursuit.
This is now the sixth day since his dead mother's
40   murdered body was purified by the funeral fire.
All this time he has taken nothing to eat; he hasn't
even washed himself, but lies huddled in his cloak.
Whenever the fever gives him a moment's relief,
he comes to his senses and sobs; then he leaps
45   from his covers, breaking like a colt from its harness.

The city of Argos has decreed that as mother-killers
no one is to welcome us to their home or hearth,
no one is to speak to us. Today is the designated day
on which the Argive citizens will decide by vote
50   whether or not we are to be put to death by stoning[14]
[or have a sharp sword thrust through our necks].[15]
And yet we still have some hope of escaping death.
Menelaus has come back home from Troy to Argos,
and is filling the harbor of Nauplia with his fleet,
55   which he is mooring along the shore, home
at last from Troy after being long lost at sea.[16] Helen,

Despite the taboo, Orestes and Electra use the name Erinyes several times
in the play (238, 264, 582).

14. *46–50:* In *The Furies (Eumenides),* Aeschylus ends the cycle of revenge
by staging the establishment of the first homicide court (the court of the
Areopagus in Athens) with divine sanction. A striking feature of this
version of the Orestes tragedy is that a murder court has already been
established in Argos, meaning that the children of Agamemnon did not
have to avenge their father by killing their mother. They could have sued
her in court (see 500–502).

15. *51:* These lines are of doubtful authenticity because what is at issue is
not the method by which the matricides are to be executed, but whether or
not they are to be sentenced to death. Exile is a common punishment for
homicide, since it takes care of the problem of pollution through contact
with the killers by removing them.

16. *53–56:* Menelaus was away not only for the ten years of the Trojan War.
He and Helen were driven off course by a storm and spent an additional
seven years in Egypt gathering booty (Homer, *Odyssey* 3.286–303), which
caused him to miss major family events: his brother's murder; the reign
of Aegisthus and Clytemnestra, which lasted seven years; the return of
Orestes (exiled since boyhood); and the latter's revenge on Aegisthus and
his mother.

the cause of all our sorrows, he has sent to our house,
waiting for nightfall in case any of those who lost
sons at Troy should see her coming during the day
and stone her to death. She is here, safe inside,   60
crying over her sister and the tragedy of our house.
Yet in her grief she has found some consolation:
her daughter Hermione, whom she left behind
when she sailed off to Troy—Menelaus brought her
from Sparta and gave her to my mother to bring up.   65
In her, Helen takes pleasure and can forget her miseries.
Now I'm looking in every direction, hoping to see
Menelaus coming. Otherwise we remain afloat
but with failing strength: unless we are rescued by him
our luckless house has nothing to fall back upon.   70

HELEN: *(Enters from the palace.)*[17]
Ah, daughter of Clytemnestra and Agamemnon,
Electra,[18] poor dear, still without a man for such a long,
long time. How are you? And your brother Orestes
lying here, the poor boy, his mother's murderer?[19]
Well, I do not feel polluted from speaking to you   75
since I place the wrongdoing at Phoebus' door.[20]
Still I mourn the death of my sister Clytemnestra.
I had not laid eyes on her since I set sail for Troy,
as sail I did, driven to recklessness by the gods—[21]
now I'm left to lament my sorry fate without her.   80

---

17. *71:* The entrance of Helen may be seen as an example of audience
misdirection. The audience is made to expect the arrival of Menelaus, but
his wife enters instead (Wright 2008, p. 34; Halleran 1984, pp. 41–42).

18. *72:* The name Electra is derived from *alektros* (unbedded, i.e.,
unwedded).

19. *72–74:* Helen's remarks are variously interpreted as arrogant, tactless,
or self-absorbed, but usually not malicious.

20. *75–76:* Murderers, especially kin-killers, are polluted (see 46–48;
also Euripides' *Electra* 1292–97). Blaming Phoebus (Apollo) would be in
Helen's self-interest.

21. *79:* This may seem like a lame excuse, but Helen is vindicated by
Apollo at the end (1639–42): she was just a tool.

ELECTRA:
Helen, why repeat what you can see for yourself?
[The house of Agamemnon is sunk deep in tragedy.]22
I sit, a sleepless companion to this wretched corpse:
yes, a corpse is what he is, but for his shallow breath.
85   I mean no offense to him for all his sufferings:
but you, blessed one,23 and your exalted husband,
together you have come to us in wretched straits.

HELEN:
How long is it since he has taken to his bed?

ELECTRA:
Ever since the day he shed his mother's blood.

HELEN:
90   I pity him. His mother, too, dying like that.

ELECTRA:
You see how it is: he is exhausted by his illness.

HELEN:
Dear gods, would you do something for me, my girl?

ELECTRA:
I would, but I am busy taking care of my brother.

HELEN:
Would you mind going to my sister's grave?

ELECTRA:
95   You want me to go to my mother's grave? What for?

---

22. *82:* The line is suspect because it is unnecessary and says what Electra claims does not bear repeating. It was probably added by a later editor to explain the obvious.

23. *86: Makaria* (blessed, happy) is almost a title for Helen. As daughter of Zeus she will go to the Isles of the Blessed as will Menelaus (see Homer, *Odyssey* 4.562–69) or she will be enthroned in the heavens (*Orestes* 1635–37).

HELEN:
  To bring these offerings of my hair and libations.

ELECTRA:
  Isn't it better for you to go to your sister's tomb?

HELEN:
  I am ashamed to be seen by the people of Argos.

ELECTRA:
  It's a bit late for remorse after forsaking your home.

HELEN:
  You are right, but you are not very kind to me.   100

ELECTRA:
  What holds you back from facing the people of Mycenae?

HELEN:
  I'm in dread of the parents of the men who died at Troy.

ELECTRA:
  So you should be. Your name is a curse all over Argos.

HELEN:
  Do this for me, then, and free me from my fear.

ELECTRA:
  I could not bear to lay eyes on my mother's grave.   105

HELEN:
  It would not do to have slaves bring my offerings.

ELECTRA:
  Why not send your daughter Hermione to do it?

HELEN:
  It's not proper for young girls to be out in public.

ELECTRA:
  She could do this to repay her dead aunt for her care.

HELEN:
110   You are right, I accept your advice, dear girl
       [and will send my daughter. Yes, you do talk sense].[24]
       Hermione, my dear child, come out of the house

       (Enter Hermione from the palace.)

       and take these libations and this offering of my hair
       and go to Clytemnestra's grave. Pour down
115   this honey mixed with milk and the froth of wine.
       Stand at the top of her mound and say these words:
       "Your sister Helen offers you these libations
       in dread of approaching your monument, fearing
       the mob of Argives." Ask her to think kindly
120   of me and of you and my husband and of these
       two unfortunates whom the god brought low.
       Promise to discharge all the offerings to the dead
       that I am obliged to perform for my sister.
       Run along, dear. Make the offerings at the grave
125   and mind you come back as quick as you can.

       (Exit Hermione stage left. Exit Helen into the palace.)

ELECTRA:
       Character! How much harm you cause humanity
       and yet a saving grace to those blessed with virtue.
       See how she has cut only the tips of her curls,
       keeping their beauty intact. She is the same woman
130   she always was.[25] May the gods hate you for ruining me
       and him[26] and all of Greece. Oh god, I am so unhappy.

       *(The chorus is seen making its entrance
       along the side entrances.)*

---

24. *111:* The line is suspect because it merely repeats the sentiment of the previous line.

25. *129–30:* "The same woman" contrasts with Euripides' "new Helen" (presented in his play *Helen* of a few years earlier) who did not cause the Trojan War, who did not even go to Troy, but was spirited off to Egypt by divine agency and remained there, forever faithful to Menelaus for the duration of the war.

26. *131:* "Him"—Orestes. Electra gestures or looks in his direction.

Look, here come my friends to add their voices
to my laments. Now they will disturb the sleep
in which he finds peace and make my eyes stream
with tears when I see my brother turn raving mad.   135
My dearest women, walk softly on silent feet,
do not make any noise, let there be no sound.
Your friendship is welcome, but for me
it will add to our tragedy if you wake him up.

Parodos

CHORUS:[27]

[Strophe 1]

Hush, hush, put down your foot   140
quietly, make no sound.

ELECTRA:
Move away from there, away from his bed.

CHORUS:
Look here, I'm doing as you say.

ELECTRA:
Ah, ah, like the breath of a thin reed's   145
piping, my dear, speak to me softly.

CHORUS:
See how hushed my voice is,
like the softest note.[28]

---

27. *140–207:* Although other late plays of Euripides (*Electra* and
Iphigenia among the Tauri, for example) divide the opening song of the
chorus between the fifteen members and a monody sung by a character (in
a lyric duet or *amoibaion*), this is a most unusual parodos (entrance song):
here the chorus is told to tiptoe and speak in a whisper.

28. *147–48:* The text is unclear. Another reading is "as if inside the
house." Either one could be a metatheatrical reference to staging. The
chorus enters accompanied by a pipe to which Electra alludes at 145–46.
The chorus is being asked to speak quietly in the huge outdoor theater and
they suggest that they will use their "indoor" voice.

ELECTRA:
  Yes, like that.
  Come down, come down. Soften your footfalls, step lightly.
150   Tell me the reason for your coming.
  He has fallen asleep at long last.

CHORUS:
                    [Antistrophe 1]

  How is he? Share your news, dear friend.
  What has happened? How bad is he?

ELECTRA:
155   He is still breathing, but his strength is failing.

CHORUS:
  Do you say so? The poor thing!

ELECTRA:
  You will ruin me if you make him open his eyes
  now that he is enjoying the sweet solace of sleep.

CHORUS:
  Poor man, suffering for his deeds,
160   odious still, though god-inspired.

ELECTRA:
  Woe for our sorrows.
  He was wrong then; what the god told us was wrong,
  when he prescribed the unnatural murder of my mother,
165   prophetic Apollo,[29] at the tripod of Right.

CHORUS:
                    [Strophe 2]

  Do you see? He is stirring in his covers.

---

29. *165:* Apollo is called Loxias in his prophetic capacity. Another name
for him is Phoebus (76, 416, etc.). *Right* is the Greek goddess *Themis,* also
a common noun ("right, law" as established by custom), who presided over
the Delphic oracle before Apollo.

ELECTRA:
With your yapping,[30] you wretch,
you have upset his sleep.

CHORUS:
No, he is still asleep, I think.

ELECTRA:
Will you please wheel back your steps   170
away from us, away from our house,
and restrain your stomping feet?

CHORUS:
He is still drowsing.

ELECTRA:
I am glad to hear it.
Revered mistress, Night,
bringer of sleep to suffering mortals,   175
leave the pit of Erebus,[31] come, oh come, wrapped in wings
to the house of Agamemnon.
Through our pains and our tragedy,   180
we are lost, worse than lost. You made a sound. Shh, shh!
Keep down the noise,
move away from the bed   185
and please let him sleep in peace.

CHORUS:
                    [Antistrophe 2]
Speak up, tell us, what end of troubles is in store?

ELECTRA:
Death, only death. What else?
He has no more desire for food.

---

30. *167:* "Yapping"—The verb *thōussein* is used of a dog barking or a
gnat buzzing.
31. *174–78:* Night (Nyx) and Erebus are children of Chaos and Gaia
(Hesiod, *Theogony* 123).

CHORUS:
190   His future seems clear.

ELECTRA:
    Apollo sacrificed us
    when he ordained the grim, unnatural shedding
    of Mother's patricidal[32] blood.

CHORUS:
    She deserved it.

ELECTRA:
    But it was not right.[33]
195   You killed, you died.
    O Mother, you gave me life, and you took the life
    of our father, and of us, your children here, your own blood.
200   Dead, we are dead, no more than wraiths.
    He, too, is among the dead, and most of my life
    is gone in groaning and grief
205   and nighttime tears; unmarried,
    childless, I drag out my lifetime,
    forever in lonely misery.

CHORUS:
    Virgin Electra, go near him and see
    if your brother here has died.
210   I don't like seeing him so still.

First Episode

ORESTES: (Waking up.)
    Sweet drug of sleep, opiate of my fevered brain,
    how gently you came over me in my need.
    Lady Lethe, oblivion of sorrows, skilled
    goddess, prayed for by those in torment.
215   Where am I? How have I come to be here?
    My memory is gone—have I lost my reason?

---

32. 193: From Electra's point of view Clytemnestra is patricidal because
she killed her and Orestes' father.
33. 194: For the thought that Clytemnestra received her just deserts, but
her children were wrong to kill her, see Euripides, Electra 1244.

ELECTRA:
   My dear, you lifted my spirits so when you fell
   asleep. May I hold you and raise up your body?

ORESTES:
   Yes, yes, lift me up and wipe the clotted foam
   from around my wretched mouth and from my eyes.   220

ELECTRA: *(Wiping his face.)*
   There. The service is a pleasure and I do not reject
   nursing my brother's limbs with a sister's hand.

ORESTES:
   Put your arm under my side and brush the matted hair
   from my face. The vision of my eyes is blurred.

ELECTRA:
   Your poor head of greasy curls—how filthy you   225
   have become after going so long without washing.

ORESTES:
   Put me back down on my bed. When the sickening
   madness lets up, I feel faint and my limbs are weak.

ELECTRA:
   Here you go. The couch is a friend to the sick,
   a possession that is full of pain, but needed still.   230

ORESTES:
   Lift me upright again, turn my body the other way.
   The sick are hard to please because they're helpless.[34]

ELECTRA:
   Would you like to set your feet on the ground[35]
   after all this time? A change of things might be nice.

---

34. *232:* See Euripides, *Hippolytus* 181–86, 198–207 for a similar scene displaying the dysphoria of the sick.

35. *233:* Literally, "It's a long while since you made a footprint," a possible reference to the use of footprints as recognition tokens in Aeschylus' *Libation Bearers* which was mocked by Euripides in his *Electra* (see Wright 2008, pp. 121–22).

ORESTES:

235 Yes, very much so. It has the look of health—
better to seem well even if it doesn't match reality.

ELECTRA:

Listen to me now, my dear brother, for as long as
the Furies permit you to be in your right mind.

ORESTES:

You have news to tell. If it's good, thank you.
240 But if it's more bad news, I've had enough bad luck.

ELECTRA:

Menelaus has arrived, our father's brother,
His ships are moored in the harbor of Nauplia.

ORESTES:

Do you mean it? Light has dawned on our troubles,
yours and mine. He is kin and in our father's debt.

ELECTRA:

245 Yes, he's here. This will back up my words:
he has brought Helen from the walls of Troy.

ORESTES:

If he had survived alone, he would be more enviable;
if he brings his wife, he's in the company of great evil.

ELECTRA:

Tyndareos fathered his brood of daughters as a signal
250 cause of blame and infamy throughout Greece.

ORESTES: *(Starting his descent into madness and
hallucination.)*
Don't you be like them in their badness—you have it
in your power—don't just say it, but keep your mind on it.

ELECTRA:

Oh, my dear brother, your eyes are rolling wildly!
A minute ago you were fine, now you look crazy.

ORESTES:

Oh, Mother, I beg you, do not drive against me   255
these bloody-eyed, serpent-headed girl-women.
Here they come. Here they come, hurtling at me.

ELECTRA:

Wait, poor man. Try to stay calm in your bed.
There's nothing there. You are imagining it.[36]

ORESTES:

O Phoebus, they will kill me, these dog-eyed   260
gorgon-faced priests of the dead, terrible goddesses.

ELECTRA:

I will not leave you, but will fold my arms
around you to stop your useless thrashing about.

ORESTES:

Let me go! You are one of them, one of my Furies.
You grip me by the waist only to hurl me into the Pit.[37]   265

ELECTRA:

My life is in ruins. What help can there be for me,
when all that I own is the hatred of the gods?

ORESTES:

Give me the bow, tipped with horn, Loxias' gift,
with which Apollo told me to ward off the goddesses
if they terrify me with their maddening rage.   270
Will a god be wounded by a mortal's hand?
Yes she will, if she will not get out of my sight.

---

36. *259:* In Aeschylus' *Furies* (*Eumenides*), the Furies are very much present as the play's chorus. The story grew up that at their entrance in the original production women had miscarriages and children fainted, so terrifying was their appearance. In Euripides' *Electra* they are seen in the distance by Castor (1342–43). Here only Orestes sees them and yet to him they are real enough (see 314–15).

37. *265:* "By the waist"—Orestes feels as if Electra has him in a wrestling hold when she puts her arms around him. "Pit"—in Greek *Tartarus,* the lowest part of Hades, where the truly wicked are tormented.

(Orestes mimes shooting with a bow.)

Don't you hear? Don't you see the feathered
arrows that I let fly from my far-shooting bow?
                                              Ah, ah!
275   What are you waiting for? Mount the high air
        on your wings. Blame the oracles of Apollo.
        Ea!
        What a frenzy I am in, the breath gasping from my lungs.
        Where in the world have I wandered from my bed?
        Out of the waves once more I see a calm.[38]
280   Sister, why do you cover your head and sob?
        I am ashamed of making you share my torments
        and troubling a virgin with my sickness.
        Do not waste away because of my troubles:
        you approved the deed, yes, but Mother's blood
285   is on my hands. I place the blame on Apollo
        who stirred me on to that most unholy act—
        in words he lifted my spirits, but not with deeds.
        I think that if I could consult my father
        face to face and ask him if I should kill my mother,
290   he would supplicate me with prayer after prayer
        never to wield my sword to slaughter the mother
        who gave me birth: it would not bring his life back
        and I would have to pay such a miserable penalty.
        And now, my sister, uncover your head
295   and—despite our misery—give up your tears.
        Whenever you see me fall into despair,
        you calm down the life-destroying terrors
        of my mind and console me and whenever you mourn,
        I must stand by you and give you loving comfort.
300   These are the mutual benefits of loving kinship.
        And now, my poor sister, go inside the house
        and lie down. Give your insomniac eyes a rest,
        have something to eat, and bathe your skin.
        For if you fail me and by your constant care

---

38. 279: According to the scholia (ancient commentaries), the actor
(Hegelochus) at the original performance misaccented the word for
"calm," and it came out "weasel" or "polecat," much to the delight of
later comic poets.

you suffer any setback, we are lost. You are the only   305
help I have, abandoned, as you see, by all the others.

ELECTRA:
It cannot be. With you I choose to end my life, with you
to go on living. It comes to the same: if you die,
as a woman what will I do? How will I survive alone
without a brother, without a father, without a friend?   310
Still, if you think it best, I must do this. Stay there
and do not take in what disturbs and frightens
you out of bed, but lie quietly on your sickbed.
Even if your disease is a figment of your mind,
the pain and disability it causes are just as great.   315

(Exit Electra into the house. Orestes returns to his bed.)

First Stasimon

CHORUS:
                        [Strophe]

Aiai!
Racing, swift of wing,
awesome goddesses,
cast as a troupe, not of Bacchus' revelers,
but in weeping and dirges,   320
black-masked Eumenides,
you shake the high spacious sky for blood,
exacting justice, avenging murder,
we implore you, and implore again,
suffer Agamemnon's son   325
to forget the fury of
his vagrant madness. Woe for your troubles,
unhappy man—you reached them and were damned,
when you heard the voice from the tripod
that Apollo spoke on the hallowed ground,   330
called earth's secret center.

                        [Antistrophe]

O Zeus,
What pity, what contest
of killing is this that comes,

335   hounding you to your grief, where
       an avenging demon adds more tears to your tears,
       carrying into the house
       your mother's blood to drive you mad?
       I keen, I keen in mourning.[39]
340   Wealth piled high does not last for mortals.
       A god has shaken him
       like the sail of a swift boat
       and drowned him in the turbulent killing waves
       of a sea of churning troubles.
345   What other house must I honor still
       before this one, sprung from marriage with the gods,
       sprung from Tantalus?

Second Episode

CHORUS LEADER:
       And, look, here comes the king,
       Lord Menelaus, clearly recognized
350   in his splendor[40]
       as born from the sons of Tantalus.
       You who launched the force of a thousand ships
       to the land of Asia,
       hail. You keep company with good luck
355   since you have gotten from god what you prayed for.

       (Enter Menelaus with an entourage stage
       right. He addresses the palace.)

MENELAUS:
       Home at last! Returning from Troy, I see you
       with pleasure, but also grieve at the sight.
       Never have I seen another family hearth
       so tragically wound up into a coil of misery.

---

39. 338–44: Some fragments of the musical notation for these lines
survive in a papyrus from around 200 B.C.E. (see West 1987, pp. 203–4).

40. 350: The luxury of Menelaus' costume and possible entourage contrast
with the squalor of Orestes and with his own notorious arrival in rags in
Euripides' Helen, where even his wife does not recognize him. Here he does
not recognize Orestes as one of the family because of his changed state.

Agamemnon's fate I learned, and his death,   360
how he lost his life at his wife's hands,
when I put to shore at Malea. From the waves
the sailor's seer declared it to me: the prophet
Glaucus, son of Nereus, unlying god, said
these things standing above me, clear to see.   365
"Menelaus," he said, "your brother lies dead,
fallen in the bath his wife drew for him, his last."
He filled me and my sailors full of tears that fell
in streams. When I touched land here in Nauplia—
my wife was already sent on ahead of me—   370
expecting to embrace Agamemnon's son
Orestes in my loving arms, and his mother
doing well, I heard from a random fisherman
of the unnatural murder of Tyndareos' daughter.
Now tell me, women, where is he, Agamemnon's   375
son, who has taken upon himself these terrible deeds?
He was just a baby then in Clytemnestra's arms
way back when I left the palace to sail for Troy,
so I would not know him now even if I saw him.

ORESTES: (Getting up from his bed.)
  Here I am, Menelaus. I am Orestes, for whom you ask.   380
  Of my own free will I inform you of my evils.[41]
  For my first act I touch your knees as a suppliant,
  adding prayers from my lips without the sacred branch.
  Help me. You have come at the crisis of my troubles.

MENELAUS:
  Oh god! What do I see? A ghost from beyond?   385

ORESTES:
  You're right. In my torment I am alive, but not living.

MENELAUS:
  You look like a wild man with your hair in tangles.

ORESTES:
  It's not my looks, but my deeds, that disfigure me.

---

41. *381:* "My evils"—Chief among his evils is that he is Orestes.

MENELAUS:
Your look is ferocious, your eyes red and parched.

ORESTES:
390   My body is lost, but my name has never left me.

MENELAUS:
It upsets me to look at your ravaged features.

ORESTES:
Here I am, the murderer of my pathetic mother.

MENELAUS:
I have heard about it, but spare me the sorry details.

ORESTES:
I was sparing, but my fate has been rich in sorrow.

MENELAUS:
395   What is wrong with you? What disease eats away at you?

ORESTES:
Awareness—I am aware of what awful things I have done.[42]

MENELAUS:
What do you mean? Clarity, not obscurity, is wisdom.

ORESTES:
More than anything, it is grief that is killing me.

MENELAUS:
Grief is an awesome goddess, but there is a cure.

ORESTES:
400   And with it fits of madness to atone for Mother's blood.

MENELAUS:
When did your lunacy begin? What day was it?

---

42. *396:* Such awareness of the wrong one has done is the very essence of tragedy.

ORESTES:
As soon as I raised up the tomb for my poor mother.

MENELAUS:
In the house or while you were sitting by the pyre?

ORESTES:
That night as I kept watch until the gathering of her bones.

MENELAUS:
Was anyone there with you to support your body?   405

ORESTES:
Yes, Pylades was there, my accomplice in matricide.

MENELAUS:
What were they like, the apparitions that made you sick?

ORESTES:
I thought I saw three girls, looking like the night.

MENELAUS:
I understand, but ask you not to speak their names.

ORESTES:
They are the awesome ones you shrank from naming.   410

MENELAUS:
So they make you mad because of the matricide?

ORESTES:
How terribly they persecute me and drive me insane.

MENELAUS:
Those who commit outrage also suffer outrage.

ORESTES:
Yes, but there is a way out of my misfortunes.

MENELAUS:
Don't suggest death—that is not good sense.   415

ORESTES:
Phoebus. He ordered me to commit matricide.

MENELAUS:
He was not very skilled in fairness or justice.

ORESTES:
We are slaves of the gods, whatever gods may be.

MENELAUS:
Doesn't Apollo offer you any protection from evils?

ORESTES:
420   He is always going to—that's what divine nature is.

MENELAUS:
How long is it since your mother breathed her last?

ORESTES:
Six days now. The funeral pyre is still warm.

MENELAUS:
They didn't wait to pursue you for your mother's blood.

ORESTES:
I'm not shrewd, but I am a true friend to my friends.[43]

MENELAUS:
425   Do you get any advantage from avenging your father?

ORESTES:
Not yet. What is always in prospect is never done.

MENELAUS:
In the city's eyes, where do you stand after doing this?

---

43. *424:* The text is in doubt here. Some editors believe that something is missing: Orestes' response to 423, a line by Menelaus to which this line is Orestes' reply. West (1987) substituting *theos* for *philos*, an earlier emendation, suggests "God may not be intelligent, but he is true to his own" (424, pp. 88–89).

ORESTES:
I am so loathed that no one will speak to me.

MENELAUS:
Have you performed the customary purification rites?

ORESTES:
How can I? Wherever I go, I am shut out of the house.   430

MENELAUS:
Among the Argive citizens, which ones are most against you?

ORESTES:
Oeax—he lays his hatred of Troy on my father's head.[44]

MENELAUS:
I see. He wants to take Palamedes' murder out on you.

ORESTES:
I took no part in it, but on all three counts I am fallen.[45]

MENELAUS:
Who else? Aegisthus' allies, I would imagine.[46]   435

ORESTES:
Yes, they insult me. They have the citizens' ears now.

MENELAUS:
Does the city let you wield Agamemnon's scepter?

---

44. *432:* Oeax was brother of Palamedes, traditionally the inventor of writing, counting, and jokes. By means of a forged letter, Odysseus framed him as a traitor and had him stoned to death at Troy. Orestes is blamed because his father was commander in chief of the Greek forces.

45. *434:* "Three counts"—a wrestling metaphor. Orestes' three causes of ruin are probably to be understood as Clytemnestra, whose Erinyes pursue him; Oeax; and Aegisthus' allies. Or it might mean "even at two removes I am ruined" (see West 1987, p. 213).

46. *435:* Menelaus seems to be suggesting the existence of political factions such as those that plagued Athens during this period of turmoil.

ORESTES:
How would they? They do not even let us live.

MENELAUS:
What do they plan to do? That you can tell me clearly.

ORESTES:
440   On this very day a vote will be taken against us.

MENELAUS:
To be exiled from Argos or concerning life and death?

ORESTES:
To be executed by stoning at the citizens' hands.

MENELAUS:
Why not cross the border and go into voluntary exile?

ORESTES:
We are hedged around by a circle of bronze shields.

MENELAUS:
445   By your personal enemies or by the Argive army?

ORESTES:
By all the citizens, I am to be killed. The story is short.

MENELAUS:
I'm sorry for you. Your case is extreme.

ORESTES:
On you my hope relies as refuge from evils.
In your prosperity you come to those in need—
450   share your good fortune with your loved ones
and do not keep to yourself the good you received,
but take on your fair share of our troubles
to pay back my father's favors done for you.
They are friends in name but not in deed
455   who fail to help their friends in time of need.

CHORUS LEADER:
  Look, here comes Tyndareos of Sparta, struggling
  along on his old man's feet, dressed in black,
  his hair cropped in mourning for his daughter.

ORESTES:
  Menelaus, I'm ruined. Tyndareos is coming
  this way, to us. More than anyone else, I am   460
  ashamed to be in his sight for what I have done.
  He brought me up when I was little; he covered
  me with affection, carrying me around in his arms,
  "Agamemnon's boy!" he'd say. Leda, was just the same,
  both of them, honoring me no less than the Dioscuri.[47]   465
  And to them—oh, my wretched heart and soul—
  the return I gave was far from good. What dark
  shadow can I hold in front of my face? What cloud
  can I hide behind to avoid the old man's eyes?

      (Enter Tyndareos stage left with
      an escort of his servants.)

TYNDAREOS:
  Where can I find my daughter's husband   470
  Menelaus? I went to pour libations at the tomb
  of Clytemnestra when I heard that he had landed
  at Nauplia with his wife, safely home after many years.
  Take me to him. I want to stand by his right hand
  and greet him, seeing a friend after all this time.   475

MENELAUS:
  Hello, Tyndareos, the man who shared his wife with Zeus.[48]

---

47. 465: Dioscuri—Zeus' twins, Castor and Polydeuces, sons of Leda, the
latter by Zeus, the former by Tyndareos (or in other versions, both are sons
of Zeus). At 1689 they are called "Tyndaridae (sons of Tyndareos), Zeus'
sons." Leda is also mother of Helen (Zeus' daughter) and Clytemnestra
(daughter of Tyndareos).
48. 476: This may not sound like a compliment, but Menelaus shared his
wife with Paris, by no means the honor that having Zeus as a co-husband
was considered.

TYNDAREOS:

Hello, to you, too, Menelaus, my son-in-law. *(Seeing Orestes.)*
Ugh! It's a tragedy not to see what's coming.
This snake, this mother-killer, in front of the house,
480   object of my odium, his eyes glare noxious flashes.
Menelaus, do you speak with this polluted filth?

MENELAUS:

Yes, why not? He is the son of a father who was dear to me.

TYNDAREOS:

What? Is he that man's son? This degenerate?

MENELAUS:

He is his son. Even in his misery he deserves respect.

TYNDAREOS:

485   Have you gone savage after all that time in savage lands?

MENELAUS:

Well, it is certainly a Greek custom to respect one's kin.

TYNDAREOS:

True, but not to try to put oneself above the common law.

MENELAUS:

To the wise, everything that happens is necessity's slave.

TYNDAREOS:

You can hold to that opinion, but I will not accept it.

MENELAUS:

490   Strong feelings and old age do not add up to wisdom.

TYNDAREOS:

Wisdom! What does wisdom have to do with him?
If what is right and what is wrong are clear to all,
what man has failed in wisdom more than he,
who did not even think about what was right
495   and did not turn to the law common to all Greeks?
When Agamemnon gasped his last dying breath,

his head cleaved by my own daughter's hand,
an ugly deed—I will not ever condone it—
he should have pressed an indictment for murder,   500
prosecuted a righteous cause, and put his mother
out of the house.[49] He would have achieved wisdom
instead of misery, adhered to law, and stayed unsullied.
As it is, he has come to share the same fate
as she; he was right to think her evil, but in killing   505
his mother he has turned out to be even more vile
than she. I ask you to think about this, Menelaus:
if the woman who shares a man's bed kills him
and his son turns around and kills his mother,
and then the one born from him should repay   510
murder with murder, when will the evil ever end?
In days gone by our fathers wisely laid down this law:
if anyone had blood on his hands, they did not let him
come into their sight or take any part in society;
he had to atone by exile, but not be killed in return.   515
Otherwise one person would always be entangled
in murder, taking in his hands the latest pollution.
For my part I hate women who commit godless deeds,
first my own daughter who murdered her husband.
Helen, too, your wife. Never will I condone what she did   520
or speak to her. And you, I am not one of your admirers,
for invading Troy to go after a loose woman like her.[50]
I shall—as far as I am able—defend law and order,
striving to put an end to this bloody, brutish practice[51]
that only serves to corrupt country and citizens alike.   525

---

49. *500–502:* In Aeschylus' *Furies (Eumenides)*, the trial of Orestes is represented as the first trial of a mortal for murder, setting a solemn precedent for homicide trials. Common practice prescribes exile as punishment for murderers.

50. *521–22:* Tyndareos' condemnation of Menelaus for going to war to recover Helen is particularly ironic in view of the oath of Tyndareos, which required Helen's suitors to swear to raise an army and protect whichever of them became her husband if she should be carried off. See Euripides, *Iphigenia at Aulis* 61–65.

51. *524:* See Hesiod, *Works and Days* 276–80, for the ways of beasts that have no justice.

(Turning to Orestes.)

What feelings did you have in your heart, you wretch,
when she held out her breast and begged for her life,
your own mother? I was not myself a witness to that horror,
but my old eyes are wasted with tears in my misery.
530   One fact proves my words true: the gods hate you
and you are paying for your crime against your mother,
drifting about lost in madness and terror. Why need I hear
from other witnesses what I can see for myself?
Just so you know, Menelaus, do not act in opposition
535   to the gods, in your eagerness to help this man,
but let him be stoned to death by the citizens;
otherwise, do not set foot again in Sparta's territory.
Justice was served by my daughter's death,
but it was not right for her to die at his hand.
540   In everything else I have been a happy man,
except in my daughters. There I am far from blessed.

Chorus Leader:
Blessed are they who are happy in their children
and have no experience of human catastrophes.[52]

Orestes:
Old man, in fear and trembling I speak to you,
545   knowing I will cause distress to your mind.
I am well aware that I am unholy for killing Mother,
but in a different sense, holy for avenging Father.[53]
Let us put your old age outside the discussion:
it hinders me from speaking and I'd like to continue
550   on course, though right now I am in awe of your gray hair.
What should I have done? Set the two side by side:
my father engendered me; your daughter gave me birth,

---

52. *542–43:* The chorus leader often utters a bland couplet between
long harangues to set them off from each other and, perhaps, to alert the
audience to a change in speakers.

53. *546–47:* Some editors put these lines after 548–50 for better sense.
Orestes would first clear away the impediment of his grandfather's old age
before launching his argument.

as a plowed field that receives seed from another.[54]
Without the father the child could not exist.
I reasoned that I should be on the side of my begetter,   555
rather than the one who undertook my nurture.
Your daughter—I shrink from using the word *Mother*—
in a self-arranged marriage that was hardly moral
entered the bed of another man. I sully myself
when I speak ill of her, but still I will say it: 560
Aegisthus was the secret husband in our house.
I killed him and sacrificed Mother over his body.
Yes, I did wrong, but I avenged my father's death.
In the matters for which you claim I must be stoned,
listen: here's how my actions will benefit all Greece.   565
If women will reach such extremes of boldness
that they murder their husbands and escape punishment
from their children's hands, baring their breasts to win pity,
it would cost them nothing to dispatch their husbands,
seizing on any excuse that offers itself. In perpetrating   570
a crime, as you claim, I have put a stop to this practice.
I hated my mother and I had every right to kill her,
since she betrayed her husband when he was deployed
overseas with the army as commander of the Greek forces,
and she did not keep their marriage bed unadulterated.   575
Then, when she sensed she had done wrong, she did not
atone for it, but to avoid punishment from her husband,
she punished *him* instead and killed him, my father.
In gods' name—I'm sorry to bring the gods into it
to justify a murder—if I had kept quiet and condoned   580
Mother's deeds, what would the murdered man do to me?
Wouldn't he have stirred the Furies against me in hatred?
The goddesses are present as Mother's allies; but aren't
they also allies to him who suffered a greater wrong?
The daughter you fathered, Tyndareos, was evil   585
and you have brought my ruin because of her daring.
Robbed of my father, I became my mother's killer.
Don't you see? Telemachus did not execute the wife
of Odysseus—she did not marry a second husband
but remains in the home, a wife faithful to his bed.   590

---

54. *552–53*: This view of generation was widespread. See Apollo's
argument in Aeschylus, *The Furies (Eumenides)*, 658–59.

Don't you see? Apollo, who dwells at earth's navel
and gives the surest oracles to mankind, made me do it.
I was obedient to him in everything he told me:
relying on him I killed the mother who gave me birth.
595   Tell the world *he* is the polluted one and kill *him!*
He is the sinner, not I. What was I supposed to do?
If I transfer the account to him, isn't the god solvent—
to redeem this pollution? What escape can there be
if the one who commanded me won't save me from death?
600   Do not say that these things were not well done
by us who did them, but say "not happily done."
Whenever a person's marriage is on firm ground
his life is happy. But if it does not fall out well,
life inside the house and out in the world is misery.

CHORUS LEADER:
605   Women have an unfortunate effect when they become
involved in whatever tragedies happen among men.

TYNDAREOS:
Since you are brazen and do not curb your speech,
but answer in such a way as to pain my heart,
all the more you inflame me to call for your death.
610   This will make a fine addition to the task for which
I came here, the decoration of my daughter's tomb.
I will go to the assembled masses of Argos and whip up
the city, willing or not, to inflict the ultimate punishment
of death by stoning on you and your sister:
615   she is worthy of death even more than you.
She turned you savage against your mother, always
filling your ears with stories to increase your hatred,
reporting her dreams of Agamemnon, adding this, too,
Aegisthus' scandalous adultery—an abomination
620   to the gods of the Underworld as it was galling here, too—
until she set the house ablaze with a fire from Hell.[55]
Menelaus, I have this to say to you and I will do it.
If you set any value on my enmity and my kinship,

---

55. *621:* Literally, "a fire not of Hephaestus" (the fire god). "A Fire from
Hell" is the title of an essay on *Orestes* in Verrall 1905.

do not defend this man from death, against gods' will,
but let the citizens of Argos execute him by stoning,   625
or else never again set foot on Spartan ground.
I mean what I say. Pay attention: do not choose
this miscreant, pushing away your god-fearing allies.
Come, servants, escort me away from this house.

(Exit Tyndareos with his entourage stage right.)

ORESTES:
Go on then, so the rest of my speech can reach   630
this man in peace. Deliver us from your dotage.
Menelaus, where are your thoughts taking you?
Are you in doubt which side to take, which way to go?[56]

MENELAUS:
Let me be, to pursue my inner thoughts with myself.
I am at a loss which way to turn in the circumstances.   635

ORESTES:
Do not come to a rash conclusion, but first hear
what I have to say and then make your final decision.

MENELAUS:
You are right. Have your say. Silence can prove
better than speech, but sometimes it's better to talk.

ORESTES:
I'll begin at once. Long speeches are preferable   640
to short ones and more convincing to their hearers.
From what is yours, Menelaus, give me nothing,
but repay what you received from my father.
I do not mean money. If you save my life you would
be saving the possession that is dearest to me.   645
I have done a wrong. In payment for this evil I deserve
to receive a wrong from you.[57] Agamemnon my father

---

56. *633:* Literally, "entering upon a double road of double cares?"
57. *646–50:* Orestes argues like the Unjust Argument (*Adikos Logos*)
in Aristophanes' *Clouds*. Agamemnon's wrong was going to war over a
woman (see 650, 521–22, and Aeschylus, *Agamemnon* 225–26).

wrongly gathered the Greek forces and went to Troy,
not because he had done wrong, but trying to mend
650   the wrong committed by your wife. What's fair is fair:
for this one favor you must repay us one favor.
The fact is he risked his life, as friends should
on behalf of friends, toiling for you under arms
in a war fought so that you could recover your wife.
655   Repay to me now exactly what you received there.
Stand up on our behalf to shield us. One day is all
I ask, not the ten years he gave up for you in Troy.
The sacrifice of my sister that was made in Aulis
I won't even count. You don't have to kill Hermione.
660   I accept your being better off than I, as things are,
in my present circumstances, and I must swallow it.
To my poor father pay back my life and my sister's,
long unmarried. If I die I will leave my father's house
orphaned, without an heir to carry on his line.
665   You will say "it cannot be done." That's just it:
friends must help friends in their hour of need.
While your luck holds out you don't need friends.
If god is on your side, you do well enough without them.
In the eyes of all the Greeks you love your wife,
670   and I'm not saying this to win you over with flattery.
In her name I beg you—oh, how I suffer in my misery,
to have fallen so low! What else can I do? I must bear it.
I make this supplication on behalf of our whole house.
Uncle, my father's brother, believe that the dead man
675   himself hears these things and that his spirit is hovering
over you and it is saying exactly what I am saying.
These things with tears and laments and misery
I have spoken; my claim is made for self-preservation,
what all men desire for themselves and not I alone.

CHORUS LEADER:
680   Though I am only a woman, still I implore you
to help those in need. You have it in your power.

MENELAUS:
Orestes, I have the greatest regard for you
and am willing to join with you in your troubles,
for one must share the miseries of one's kin

in blood as long as the gods grant the capacity, 685
as far as giving one's life and taking an enemy's life.
This ability I need to obtain from the gods.
As it is, I have come without a force of allies
in arms, wandering among ten thousand toils,
with little strength in the friends I have left. 690
In battle we could not overpower Pelasgian
Argos, but if, by means of persuasive speeches,
we could do so, we can offer this much hope.
With small means we cannot achieve great
success and it would be foolish to try to do it. 695
When the people fall into a rage, early in its vigor,
it is like trying to put out a furious fire.
If one yields quietly to it as it spreads, giving in
and watching out for the appropriate moment,
it might blow itself out; and if it abates its blasts, 700
one could easily get from it whatever one wishes.
There is pity in the mob and also furious passion,
a great advantage to one who watches for his chance.
I will go to Tyndareos for you and try to persuade
both him and the city to keep their excess in check. 705
A ship with the sail stretched too forcefully
pitches, but is upright again if you slacken sail.
God hates an excessive display of eagerness;
the citizens hate it, too. My words are not idle—I must
save you with shrewdness, not by using force 710
against the stronger. With arms, whatever you may think,
I cannot save you. It is not easy with a single spear
to triumph over the many evils that surround you.
I'd never go to the land of Argos in supplication,
but present circumstances make it necessary 715
for a wise man to become the slave of fortune.

    (Exit Menelaus stage right.)

ORESTES:
You were never good for anything except going to war
over a woman—too cowardly to protect your friends,
do you turn tail and run from me? Agamemnon's claims 720
are lost. You were without a friend, when your luck turned.
Ah me, I am betrayed. Gone are my hopes that I would

have somewhere to turn to escape death from the Argives.
This man was my refuge and my hope for preservation.

725   Look there. It's Pylades, my greatest friend in all the world,
heading this way, hurrying back from the Phocian land,
such a sweet sight, a man true to me in all my troubles,
better even than when sailors catch sight of a calm sea.

(Enter Pylades stage left.)

PYLADES: *(Out of breath.)*
Here I am. I've run more quickly than I should through town
730   after hearing the city assembly and seeing with my own eyes
that they plan to put you and your sister to death at once.
How are you doing? Dearest to me of my companions,
friends, and family—you are all this and more to me.

ORESTES:
We are lost: that's all it takes to reveal all my troubles to you.

PYLADES:
You will take me down with you then. Friends share in all
735   things.

ORESTES:
Menelaus has proved most treacherous to me and my sister.

PYLADES:
It adds up. That a bad wife would have a bad husband.

ORESTES:
He came here, but he might just as well have stayed away
for all the good he has done.

PYLADES:
                    Then he really has returned to this country?

ORESTES:
Long delayed, but he wasted no time showing himself a false
740   friend.

PYLADES:
And that treacherous woman, his wife, did he bring her aboard?

ORESTES:
He didn't bring her. It was she who brought him here.

PYLADES:
And where is she—the one woman who caused the deaths
of so many Greek men?

ORESTES:
In my house. If I can still call it mine.

PYLADES:
What exactly did you say to your father's brother? 745

ORESTES:
Not to let me and my sister be put to death by the people.

PYLADES:
For gods' sake, what did he say to that? I would like to know.

ORESTES:
He was cautious, exactly as faithless friends are to friends.

PYLADES:
What pretext did he advance? That's all I need to learn.

ORESTES:
He came, that man who fathered those excellent daughters. 750

PYLADES:
Tyndareos? I suppose he's angry at you over his daughter.

ORESTES:
That's right. My uncle cared more for his ties to him than to
my father.

PYLADES:
Didn't he have the courage to be your ally in the face of
trouble?

ORESTES:
He is not a natural-born warrior, but a hero to the ladies.

PYLADES:
755   You are in deep trouble. It looks like death is inevitable.

ORESTES:
The citizens have yet to cast a vote about us on the murder
   charge.

PYLADES:
What will the judgment be? Tell me. I shudder with dread.

ORESTES:
Death or life: a short summary of such a long tale of woe.

PYLADES:
Escape now, leave the palace with your sister in hand.

ORESTES:
760   Don't you see? We are kept under guard on every side.

PYLADES:
I saw the streets of the city palisaded by weapons.

ORESTES:
Our bodies are under siege like a city hemmed in by the enemy.

PYLADES:
You need to know how I have fared. I, too, am brought to ruin.

ORESTES:
Who did it? This adds a new trouble to the troubles I have.

PYLADES:
765   In a rage my father Strophius drove me from home into exile.

ORESTES:
Bringing charges against you in private or with the citizens?

PYLADES:
Because I abetted you in the matricide,[58] he says I'm polluted.

ORESTES:
My poor friend. It seems my tragedy brings you grief, too.

PYLADES:
I do not keep the ways of Menelaus: these things must be
borne.

ORESTES:
Aren't you afraid Argos will want to kill you just like me? 770

PYLADES:
Punishment of me is under Phocian jurisdiction, not Argive.

ORESTES:
The mob is frightening when their leaders are criminal.

PYLADES:
But when they have good ones, their decisions are good.

ORESTES:
Well, we must confer.

PYLADES:
                    What is it that's so important?

ORESTES:
If I should go before the citizens . . .

PYLADES:
                    To claim what you did was right? 775

ORESTES:
That I avenged my father?

PYLADES:
                    They may not like hearing you say it.

---

58. 767: Clytemnestra was Pylades' aunt by marriage. Strophius' wife was
sister to Agamemnon and Menelaus.

ORESTES:
But am I to die in silence like a coward?

PYLADES:
That would be craven.

ORESTES:
What action should I take then?

PYLADES:
Is there any hope if you stay here?

ORESTES:
No, not a bit.

PYLADES:
If you go, is there a chance of escaping?

ORESTES:
Maybe. It could happen.

780
PYLADES:
That's better than staying here.

ORESTES:
I should go then, I guess.

PYLADES:
Yes, it would be nobler to die that way.

ORESTES:
You are right. That way I avoid being called a coward.

PYLADES:
More so than staying here.

ORESTES:
And my cause is just.

PYLADES:
Only pray that it appears to be so.

ORESTES:
And someone might take pity on me.

PYLADES:
Your noble birth is a major factor.

ORESTES:
In distress because of father's death.

PYLADES:
That is part of the picture.   785

ORESTES:
I must go. To die ingloriously is unmanly.

PYLADES:
Well said.

ORESTES:
Should we tell this to my sister?

PYLADES:
Good god, no!

ORESTES:
You're right—there would be tears.

PYLADES:
It would be a bad omen.

ORESTES:
Better to keep quiet then.

PYLADES:
You will gain some time.

ORESTES:
One thing hinders me.

PYLADES:
What new scruple bothers you?   790

ORESTES:
I'm afraid the goddesses might grip me with torment.

PYLADES:
I will take care of you.

ORESTES:
It's hazardous to touch a diseased man.

PYLADES:
Not for me to touch you.

ORESTES:
Be careful not to share my madness.

PYLADES:
Never mind that.

ORESTES:
You will not shrink from me then?

PYLADES:
For a friend that would be a disgrace.

ORESTES:
Come on then, be a guide to my feet.

PYLADES:
795   Tending to my friend.

ORESTES:
Escort me to my father's tomb.

PYLADES:
Why is that?

ORESTES:
So I may beg him to preserve my life.

PYLADES:
That makes sense.

ORESTES:
But don't let me see Mother's mound.

PYLADES:

                              No, she was an enemy.
Hurry so the Argives will not condemn you before we get there.
Press your limbs that are feeble with sickness on my limbs.   800
I will conduct you through the town, feeling no shame
and giving little thought to the mob. Where will I show myself
a true friend if I do not help you in your time of direst need?

ORESTES:
This is what it means to have friends, not just family.
Even an outsider, who yokes his ways with your own,   805
is a friend more worth having than a thousand close kin.

(Exeunt Orestes and Pylades stage right.)

Second Stasimon

CHORUS:
                              [Strophe]

Wealth piled high and prowess
full of pride all through Greece
and beside the canals of Simois
has withdrawn a happy fortune from Atreus' sons,   810
as it did long ago at the ancient tragedy of the house
when strife came
to the Tantalids with the golden lamb,
the heart-piercing feast
and slaughters of royal children: 815
from then on murder for murder
in bloody bargain never ceases
for the two sons of Atreus.

                              [Antistrophe]

That glory brings no glory, to gash
with frenzied hand parents'   820
flesh and to expose the sword
blood-black with murder to the sun's rays.

Evil for evil is a cunning blasphemy,
the madness of ill-willed men.
825   Trapped in fear of death
the despairing daughter of Tyndareos cried out:
"My child you are daring impious deeds,
killing your mother. Do not pay homage
due your father, and so mire yourself
830   in ill fame that lasts forever."

[Epode]

What sickness, what tears,
what pity is greater on earth
than to pollute the hands with matricidal blood?
He has done that monstrous deed
835   and now he is driven insane with wild ravings,
prey to the Eumenides, dizzy
from murder with maniac eyes,
Agamemnon's son.
Oh, wretched when he saw
840   his mother's breast bared
from the folds of her gold-woven robes,
he made the sacrifice—his mother's life
to pay for his father's demise.

Episode Three

(Enter Electra from the palace.)

ELECTRA:
Women, has my poor Orestes rushed off somewhere
845   away from home, overcome by the god-sent madness?

CHORUS LEADER:
No, but he has gone to the Argive assembly
to plead his case in the trial for his life where
it is to be decided whether you are to live or die.

ELECTRA:
Oh no! What has he done? Who persuaded him to do it?

CHORUS LEADER:
Pylades. But it won't be long, I think, before this messenger   850
informs you what happened there concerning your brother.

(Enter Messenger stage right.)

MESSENGER:
Poor Electra, unhappy daughter of Agamemnon,
our commander, hear the message of bad luck,
mistress, which I have come to deliver to you.

ELECTRA:
Oh god! We are lost! Your words leave little doubt.   855
You have come, I can see, as a messenger of woe.

MESSENGER:
By the ballot of the Pelasgians it has been decided:
on this day you and your brother are to be executed.

ELECTRA:
God help us. The catastrophe has come, which in prospect
I have feared so long, wasting away my life in tears.   860
But what was the debate like, what arguments among
the Argives condemned us and sentenced us to death?
Tell me, old man, by stoning or the sword must I breathe
my dying breath, sharing the same fate as my brother?   865

MESSENGER:
As it happened I was passing through the city gates
on my way from the country and eager to learn
about you and Orestes. In the past I always had
good feelings for your father: your house fed me,
a poor man, but loyal to those who befriend me.   870
I saw the crowd coming and taking seats on a summit,
where they say Danaus first gathered the people
to a common session when he was being called
to account by Aegyptus,[59] and I asked a man from town:

---

59. 872–74: Danaus asks for asylum for his daughters who are fleeing from
marriage to their cousins, the sons of Aegyptus. The story is dramatized
in Aeschylus' *Suppliants*.

875   "Is there news in Argos? Has a proclamation sent
       by enemies raised hackles in the Danaans' city?"
       He said, "Don't you see Orestes over there headed
       this way, ready to plead his case for life or death?"
       I saw an unexpected sight, which I wish I had never
880   seen: Pylades and your brother walking together,
       the one with his head down, weakened by sickness,
       the other, supporting him as a brother would,
       tending his friend's illness with a nurse's care.
       When the assembly of the Argives was full,
885   a herald stood up and proclaimed: "Who wants to speak,
       on the question shall we or shall we not execute Orestes
       on the charge of matricide?"
                              At this, Talthybius got up:
       he had been with your father at the siege of Troy.
       His speech—he is always the toady of those
890   in power—was duplicitous, praising your father
       but not condoning your brother, spinning words
       fair and foul, how he laid down a precedent
       concerning his parents that was not good. He kept
       glancing a flattering look toward Aegisthus' allies.
895   He was true to type. Heralds will always fall in
       with the fortunate. They ally themselves to anyone
       who has influence in the city and holds high office.
       After him, royal Diomedes gave a speech.
       He was against killing either you or your brother,
900   but for maintaining piety by a sentence of exile.
       They roared in response, some saying he spoke well,
       while others disapproved.
                              After him there stood up
       some arrogant man who could not stop his mouth,
       an Argive, yet not Argive, the tool of Tyndareos,[60]
905   relying on confusion and mindless license of speech,
       but persuasive in getting them involved in foul play.
       [When someone with a facile tongue, but mean-spirited,
       persuades the crowd, it is a great bane to the state.
       Those who always give sound advice with forethought

---

60. *904:* The text is obscure. The word in the MSS meaning "compelled"
(here interpreted "tool of Tyndareos") might mean that he was suborned
to perjury by Tyndareos (see 915 and Willink 1986, p. 232).

in the long run are useful to the state—even if they don't   910
seem so at once. An insightful leader must also look out
for this. The matter turns out the same for the one
who speaks the words and the one holding office.]⁶¹
And he said that you and Orestes should be put
to death by stoning. Tyndareos had coached him   915
on what to say to ensure the death of the two of you.
Somebody else got up and said the opposite of this.
He was not much to look at, a genuine man, the type
that rarely comes near town or the environs of the agora,
a working farmer⁶²—the country's only safeguard—   920
who tempers his speech with native intelligence,
uncorrupted, living a frugal life beyond reproach.
He said: as Agamemnon's son, Orestes should
be given a crown, because he was eager to avenge
his father and killed that wicked, godless woman,   925
who was trying to prevent a man from taking up
arms and leaving home to lead an army to war,
if those left in charge are allowed to destroy the home
from the inside, and pollute their husbands' beds.
To men of honor his words were right on the mark.   930
Nobody else spoke, but your brother came forward.
This is what he said: "Inhabitants of Inachus' land
[in ancient times Pelasgians, later Danaans],⁶³
it was for your sake, no less than my father's, that I killed
my mother. If the murder of men by their wives   935
will be condoned, you had better hurry up and die
or else risk becoming the slaves of your wives.
You are preparing to do the opposite of what you ought
to do. As it is, the woman betrayed my father's bed
and has died for it. If you put me to death, the rule of law   940
will be eroded and you all might as well be dead,
since there will be no end of shameless daring."
He failed to convince the assembly, though I thought

---

61. *907–13:* These lines clearly do not belong here and are perhaps added
from another play as an example of similar political thought.

62. *920:* That is, an *autourgos,* a farmer who works his own land, like
Electra's husband in Euripides' *Electra.*

63. *933:* This line seems to be a pedantic editorial addition.

he spoke well. That vile man who harangued the mob,
945   pleading for the execution of you and your brother,
won the debate. Poor Orestes, he was barely able
to persuade them not to stone you to death. He vowed
that today he will use his sword to kill himself and die
with you. Pylades is escorting him from the assembly,
950   in tears. Their friends are coming along, weeping,
in pity for his plight. He is coming here to you,
a bitter sight to behold, a sorrowful spectacle.
But get ready a sword or a noose for your neck.
Since you must leave the world. Your high birth
955   is no help to you; neither is Pythian Apollo who sits
on his prophetic tripod. Both have brought you ruin.

(Exit Messenger stage right.)

CHORUS LEADER:
Oh, unhappy maiden, I see you are silent and turn
your shaded face to the ground, as though you
are about to let loose a stream of loud lamentations.

Lyric Interval[64]

ELECTRA:
[Strophe]

960   I begin the shrill keening, land of my fathers,
drawing my pallid nail across my cheek,
blood-red wreckage,
beating my head, destined now for the queen of the dead
below the earth, goddess Persephassa beautiful daughter.
965   Cry aloud, Cyclopean land,
putting steel to the hair cropped in mourning
for the havoc of our house.
Pity comes and more pity
for those sentenced to die,
970   once commanders of all Greece.

---

64. *960–1012:* For the view that this song was originally a choral ode,
later rescored as a monody or duet, see Damen 1990, p. 133.

CHORUS:

[Antistrophe]

It has passed, passed out of sight—the whole generation
of Pelops is gone, once envied for the luck
of their happy house.
Hate from the gods has seized it and the vote,
hostile and bloodthirsty, of the citizens.   975
Ah, ah races of creatures who live but a day,
full of tears, full of toils, see how fate comes
to thwart our hopes.
Every single man in turn has sufferings
all his own, in the fullness of time.   980
The whole life of mortals is uncertain.

ELECTRA:

I wish I could go to that mass
between heaven and earth
suspended in midair
held by golden chains that spin it in place,
lump of clay from Olympus
where I would let fly my voice in lament
to our ancient ancestor Tantalus   985
who fathered us, yes, he was the father of the forebears of our
    house
who saw ruin after ruin:
first the steeds' winged pursuit
when Pelops in his chariot drawn by four horses
crossed over the waves, Myrtilus' murder,[65]   990
as he cast him into the surge of the sea,
toward Geraestus,
white with waves,
racing his chariot on the beaches
of the tossing seas.

---

65. *990:* Pelops cheated in a chariot race in which he had to beat Oenomaus
to win the hand of his daughter Hippodamia. He bribed Myrtilus, his
potential father-in-law's charioteer, to remove the linchpin from one of
the wheels, causing Oenomaus' death. He then murdered Myrtilus (instead
of fulfilling his promise to let him lie with Hippodamia). With his dying
breath Myrtilus cursed Pelops and his descendants.

It started there, the tragic curse
995   on my house—
among the flocks brought to birth by Maia's son
the gold-fleeced portent
of a lamb was born—lethal,
1000   it was lethal for Atreus, breeder of horses.[66]
Then Discord changed
the flying chariot of the sun,
directing the western sky's route
on its single steed toward the dawn,
1005   and Zeus changed the course
of the seven Pleiades to go another way;
from these, deaths succeeded deaths
and the feast of Thyestes, named after him,
and the faithless bed of Aerope, woman of Crete,
1010   in faithless marriage, but last of all
it has come upon me and my brother[67]
through the inescapable tragedy of our house.

Episode Four

CHORUS LEADER:
Here he comes now, your brother,
condemned to the sentence of death,
1015   Pylades too, most loyal of all,
like a brother to him, guiding
Orestes' weakened limbs,
yoked together with anxious step.

(Enter Orestes and Pylades stage right.)

---

66. *994–1010:* Hermes (son of Maia, father of Myrtilus) placed a golden lamb among Atreus' flocks. The golden lamb was brought from the country to the city and became an object of treachery. It was to be the symbol of the sovereignty of Atreus. Thyestes seduced Atreus' wife in order to possess the lamb and the kingdom. At this, Zeus changed the sun's course. See Euripides, *Electra* 699–746. Later Atreus took his revenge by killing Thyestes' sons, cooking them, and serving them to their father.
67. *1011:* For sense the MS word "father" is emended to "brother." See Willink 1986, p. 258.

ELECTRA:
Ah me. Seeing you at the tomb I cry out,
brother, and at the pyre for the dead,
and again, ah me. Seeing you with my eyes,   1020
now for the last time, I am out of my mind.

ORESTES:
Hush your womanish wailing and be content
with what must be. It's a pity, but still
we must bear our present misfortunes.

ELECTRA:
How can I be quiet when we poor wretches   1025
will no longer look up at the god's sunlight?

ORESTES:
Don't you be my death. It is enough that I am dead
by the Argives' hand. Let our present woes suffice.

ELECTRA:
Oh, Orestes, my tears are for your youth, your fate,
your untimely death. You will die when you should live.   1030

ORESTES:
In gods' name, do not smother me in cowardice,
and make me weep, reminding me of my sorrows.

ELECTRA:
We are about to die. I cannot hold back my lament.
The loss of life makes all mortals feel sad.

ORESTES:
This is our destined day. Either we must tighten   1035
the noose around our necks or whet the sword in our hand.

ELECTRA:
You do it, then, dear brother. Do not let any Argive
add insult by killing the descendant of Agamemnon.

ORESTES:
Mother's blood on my hands is enough. I will not kill you.
But you must die by your own hand whatever way you wish.   1040

ELECTRA:
So it will be. I shall not lag far behind your sword.[68]
But I long to put my arms around your neck.

ORESTES:
Yours is an empty longing if this gives you pleasure,
to put your arms around a man so close to death.

ELECTRA:
1045   My dearest one, your name is the sweetest to me
and most loved. You share one soul with your sister.

ORESTES:
You have softened my heart. I too wish to answer
with a loving embrace of my arms. No more shame—
Oh sister's breast, loving object of my embrace!
1050   [These words are all we poor wretches have
instead of children and the marriage bed.][69]

ELECTRA:
Ah!
I wish we might both die by the same sword
and one coffin made of cedar contain us both.

ORESTES:
That would be most pleasant, but you see how we are
1055   destitute of friends to ensure that we share a tomb.

ELECTRA:
Didn't Menelaus speak up for you, taking up the cause
against our death, the coward, betrayer of my father?

---

68. *1041:* That is, "I shall die soon after by your sword" (see Egan 1999, p. 283).

69. *1050–51:* These lines, though a conventional lament of those dying young, are sometimes marked for deletion as inappropriate to a brother and sister. On the other hand, the marriages of Agamemnon's children and, by inference, their hopes for offspring are important in the divine dispensations at the end of the tragedy.

ORESTES:

He did not even show his face. He entertains hopes
for the scepter. He was too cautious to help his friends.
But come let us act nobly and die in a manner   1060
most worthy of our father, Agamemnon.
I will display my nobility for the city to see
and strike through my liver with the sword.
You, too, must act with bravery like mine.
Pylades, you be the witness of our death for us,   1065
and when we are dead, cover our bodies decently
and bury us together bearing us to Father's tomb.
Farewell. As you see, I am ready for the deed.

PYLADES:

But wait. First I have one charge to make against you
if you expect that I desire to live once you are dead.   1070

ORESTES:

But, what concern of yours is it to die with me?

PYLADES:

You ask me this? What is life without your friendship?

ORESTES:

You did not kill your mother as I did, to my sorrow.

PYLADES:

In common with you I acted. I must suffer the same as you.

ORESTES:

Return alive to your father. Do not die with me.   1075
You still have a city to live in and I do not;
you have your father's house, a great haven of wealth.
You have lost your marriage to my unhappy sister
whom I betrothed to you in respect for our friendship.
Take another bride and raise a family of your own,   1080
the connection between us exists no longer.
Oh much loved name of my companionship,
be happy. For us this cannot be, but it can be for you.
We dead have no further need of happiness.

PYLADES:

1085   You have completely missed my train of thought.
        Let the fertile earth never receive my blood
        nor the shining air, if ever by betraying you
        I engineer my own escape and abandon you.
        I committed the murder with you, no use denying it,
1090   and I was in on the planning of everything you stand
        convicted of: and so I must die with you and her.
        I consider her mine—I proposed marriage to her:
        she is my wife. What in the world will I have to say
        for myself if I go to Delphi, the Phocians' citadel,
1095   when I was your friend, before your fortune changed,
        but now have left our friendship when you are ruined?
        No way can I do it. But this is what is on my mind:
        since we are going to die, let us consider together
        how we can involve Menelaus in our common ruin.

ORESTES:

1100   Oh, my dear, dear friend. Then I could die happy.

PYLADES:

        Listen, then. And hold off falling on your sword.

ORESTES:

        I'll do that if I can get even with my enemies.

PYLADES:

        Be quiet now. I have little trust in women.

ORESTES:

        Don't worry about them. They are here as friends.

PYLADES:

1105   Let's kill Helen. It will cause bitter grief to Menelaus.

ORESTES:

        Good idea. But how? I'm ready if it will be successful.

PYLADES:

        By slitting her throat. She is there in your house.

ORESTES:
Yes, of course. She is putting her seal on our goods.

PYLADES:
She will stop when she takes Hades as her husband.

ORESTES:
How will we do it? She has her staff of foreigners. 1110

PYLADES:
Them? I wouldn't be afraid of any Phrygians.

ORESTES:
They are good for the care of mirrors and scents.

PYLADES:
Did she come here with all her Trojan luxuries?

ORESTES:
So that all of Greece is but a small cottage to her.

PYLADES:
A race of slaves is nothing in the face of those who are free. 1115

ORESTES:
If I can accomplish this I would gladly die twice.

PYLADES:
I, too, if only I can take vengeance for your sake.

ORESTES:
Explain the whole business—leave nothing out.

PYLADES:
We will go into the house as if we were preparing to die.

ORESTES:
I understand that much, but am at a loss for the rest. 1120

PYLADES:
We will make lamentations to her about what we suffer.

ORESTES:
>She will get all teary, but secretly she'll be glad.

PYLADES:
>It will be the same for us as for her.

ORESTES:
>How do we carry out the mission?

PYLADES:
1125   We will carry our swords hidden in our clothing.

ORESTES:
>What shall we do to get rid of the slaves beforehand?

PYLADES:
>We will lock them out in different parts of the house.

ORESTES:
>And if anyone doesn't keep quiet we'll have to kill him.

PYLADES:
>The action itself will be our guide what to do next.

ORESTES:
1130   To murder Helen. I see how the pieces fit together.

PYLADES:
>You've got it. Listen to how precise my planning is.
>If it were against a more modest woman that we were
>wielding our swords, the killing would be ignoble.
>As it is, she will pay on behalf of all the Greeks,
1135   for the orphaned children, for the childless parents,
>for the young brides who sleep alone because of her.
>There will be a cry of triumph; fires will be kindled
>to the gods, blessings conferred on you and me,
>because we have shed the blood of an evil woman.
1140   You will not be called "matricide" after you kill her
>but, free of that, you will fall into a better repute,
>and be named "the killer of man-slaying Helen."
>It was not ever, ever right that Menelaus succeed,
>while your father and you and your sister face death—

your mother, too, no, she is not fit to be named—   1145
that he usurp your home after recovering his wife
by Agamemnon's sword. Let me give up my life
if we do not unsheathe our swords against her.
But if we fail in our attempt to rid the world of Helen,
then we will set this house on fire and die in the blaze.   1150
Just so we succeed in one or the other we win glory,
either way we will die nobly or nobly save ourselves.

CHORUS LEADER:
To all women the daughter of Tyndareos
is worthy of hate—she has disgraced us all.

ORESTES:
Phew!
There is nothing better than a proven friend,   1155
not wealth, not power. Most worthless of all
is popularity compared to a noble friend.
You devised the punishment of Aegisthus
and stood beside me in my peril. And now again
you are there for me, helping to plot revenge   1160
against my enemies . . . I must stop praising you
since being praised too much can be distasteful.
But, in any case, with my last breath, I am glad
to die if I can do something to get back at my enemies
for ruining my life—if I can bring disaster on those   1165
who betrayed me and make them feel the pain I suffer.
I am, believe it or not, the son of Agamemnon,
elected commander of Greece; he was no tyrant,
but he had a god's power. I will never shame him
by dying a slave's death, but in freedom   1170
I will breathe my last breath and make Menelaus pay.
If we could achieve one thing, we would be happy:
if somehow safety should fall unexpectedly on the side
of the killers so we do not have to die. I pray for that.
What I wish is sweet and delightful to the spirit   1175
without cost, winged words passing through the lips.

ELECTRA:
Brother, I have an idea that will bring us safety,
for you, for Pylades, and in third place for me.

ORESTES:
Your words are a godsend. But what good is that?
1180   Still, I know there is understanding in your mind.

ELECTRA:
Listen then. And pay attention to what I have to say.

ORESTES:
Tell me. Good things in prospect bring pleasure.

ELECTRA:
Helen's daughter, you know her? Of course you do.

ORESTES:
I know her. Hermione. My mother brought her up.

ELECTRA:
1185   She has lately gone to visit Clytemnestra's grave.

ORESTES:
What is she doing there? What hope do you offer?

ELECTRA:
She went to pour offerings at the tomb for her mother.

ORESTES:
What does all this have to do with our safety?

ELECTRA:
Seize her as a hostage as soon as she comes back.

ORESTES:
1190   What remedy does this hold for the three of us?

ELECTRA:
When Helen is dead, if Menelaus does anything
to you or him or me—three friends, we stand as one—
tell him you will kill Hermione. You must draw
your sword and hold it right up to the girl's throat.
1195   And if Menelaus helps you, not wanting to see
the girl die, with Helen lying there in a pool of blood,

you let the girl go free for her father to take home.
But if he does not control his hot temper and
tries to kill you, go ahead and slit the girl's throat.
I think—though at first he was high and mighty—   1200
in time he will soften his anger. He is not bold
nor brave at heart. This is what I have to offer
as a bulwark of our survival. My story is told.

ORESTES:

Oh, my sister, you have a man's mind within
a body that is outstanding for womanly beauty.   1205
How worthy you are to live and not to die.
Pylades, my friend, what a woman you will lose
or else you will live to enjoy a happy marriage.

PYLADES:

I hope it will be so and she will go to the land of
the Phocians celebrated in joyful wedding songs.   1210

ORESTES:

What time will Hermione return to the house?
In other ways, what you said is excellent, if we
succeed in seizing the spawn of the godless father.

ELECTRA:

I estimate she must be getting very near the house:
the length of time since she left corresponds to this.   1215

ORESTES:

Excellent! Now you, my sister, Electra,[70] wait in front
of the house to welcome the girl when she returns.
And make sure nobody, whether some ally of theirs
or my father's brother, comes into the house until
after the murder is accomplished—make a noise: 1220
beat on the door or call aloud to those inside.
Let us go inside and for the final battle
arm ourselves with swords in our hands.
Pylades, stand by me and join in my labors.

---

70. *1216:* The scene is reminiscent of the Electra plays, in which Orestes
and Pylades enter the stage building to kill Clytemnestra.

1225   Oh, Father, dwelling in the halls of gloomy night,
         Orestes, your son, summons you to come as ally
         to those who need your strength. I suffer unjustly for you
         and am in misery. I am betrayed by your brother, though
         I did what was right. Now I intend to take his wife
1230   and kill her. Father, be our accomplice in this deed.

ELECTRA:
     Oh, Father, come then, if within the earth you hear
     your children calling, we who are about to die for you.

PYLADES:
     Oh, near kinsman of my father, Agamemnon,
     hear my prayers too. Save your children's lives.

ORESTES:
     I killed my mother.

ELECTRA:
1235   I held the sword.

PYLADES:
     I egged you on and broke down your resistance.

ORESTES:
     Avenging you, Father.

ELECTRA:
              I did not abandon you.

PYLADES:
     Hearing these reproaches, will you not save your children?

ORESTES:
     I pour out my tears to you.

ELECTRA:
                And I my lamentations.[71]

---

71. *1231–39:* This invocation to Agamemnon's spirit is a pale reminiscence
of the great *kommos* in Aeschylus' *Libation Bearers.*

PYLADES:
> Time to stop. Let us proceed to the task at hand.   1240
> If prayers[72] reach their target inside the earth,
> he hears ours. But you, Zeus, our ancestor,
> and solemn Justice, grant success to him and me
> and her, for three friends, one struggle, one cause,
> all to live or all to meet our death together as one.   1245

> *(Exeunt Orestes and Pylades into the palace.)*

Musical Scene

ELECTRA:
> Women of Mycenae, my friends,
> foremost in the Pelasgian settlement of Argos.

CHORUS:
> What are you saying, my lady?
> This title belongs to you in the city of Danaans.   1250

ELECTRA:
> Stand here, some of you along this wagon track,
> others on this path, to watch the house.

CHORUS:
> What are you asking us to do?
> Tell me, dear.

ELECTRA:
> I am consumed with fear that someone near the house   1255
> might see him at the bloody murder
> and devise more woes on top of the woes we have.

> *(Chorus divides into two groups, one on
> each side of the scene building.)*

HALF CHORUS:
> Come, let us hurry: I will watch this track
> that faces toward the morning sun.

---

72. *1241:* Pylades uses the word *arai*, prayers, but also curses, appropriately addressed to those below ground (cf. Aeschylus, *The Furies [Eumenides]* 417).

HALF CHORUS:
1260   And I this that bears to the sun's setting.

ELECTRA:
        Turn your eyes every way.

CHORUS:
        This way and that, and back again,
1265   as you say, we are keeping lookout.

ELECTRA:
        Roll your eyes around
        shaking your curls in every direction.

HALF CHORUS:
        Here is someone coming on the track. Who is this
1270   moving around your palace, some man from the farms?

ELECTRA:
        Oh my friends, we are lost! Now he will reveal
        to our enemies the armed beasts hidden inside.

HALF CHORUS:
        Don't be afraid. The path is clear, my dear,
        though you thought it wasn't.

ELECTRA:
1275   Which is it? Can I still rely on you?
        Give me a clear report,
        whether the area in front of the court is empty.

HALF CHORUS:
        It's good over here, but look to your side,
        to see if any Danaan is approaching.

HALF CHORUS:
1280   The same here—there is no trouble on this side.

ELECTRA:
        Come, then I will place an ear at the gates.

CHORUS:

Why are you delaying, you inside the house, while all's quiet,
to draw the sacrificial victims' blood?   1285

ELECTRA:

They are not listening. Oh, my misery.
Are their swords blunted before her beauty?
Any minute an armed Argive running
to bring help will reach the palace.   1290
Take a better look. Sitting still will not win the match.
But some turn this way, some that way.

CHORUS:

I run back and forth, looking this way and that.   1295

HELEN: *(From inside.)*[73]
Oh! Pelasgian Argos, I am being brutally killed.

ELECTRA:

Did you hear? Men are setting their hands to murder.
It is Helen's death cry, as you may suppose.

CHORUS:

O Zeus, ever-living power of Zeus,
come, be a helper to my friends in every way.   1300

HELEN: *(From inside.)*
Menelaus, I am dying. You are not here to help me.

CHORUS/ELECTRA:[74]

Murder, slay,
kill, thrusting the pair of two-edged swords
in your hands
into the woman who left her father, left her marriage,   1305

---

73. *1296, 1301:* Helen's cries from inside are so like the death cries of
victims in other plays that the audience will expect that she is dead, as
Electra surmises at 1298.

74. *1302 ff.:* As is often the case, identification of speakers is uncertain.
These lines may be sung either by half the chorus or by Electra, or both.

who caused so many Greeks to die
by the spear, beside the river,
where tears fell upon more tears
from the iron weapons
1310   beside the eddies of Scamander.

CHORUS:
Quiet, quiet. I hear the sound of someone
setting foot on the path near the palace.

ELECTRA:
My dear, dear women, into the midst of murder
here comes Hermione. Let's keep our voices down.
1315   She comes here only to fall into the nets' trap.
She will turn out to be a fine catch if she is caught.
Take your places once more with a calm demeanor
and complexion, giving no hint of what has been done.
I, too, shall keep the expression of my face gloomy,
1320   as if I know nothing of what has now been perpetrated.

(To the approaching Hermione.)

Oh, dear girl, have you come back from decorating
Clytemnestra's tomb and offering libations to the dead?

(Enter Hermione stage left.)

HERMIONE:
I am back after securing her good graces. But fear
has come over me—while I was on the road
1325   far from the palace, I heard a noise from inside.

ELECTRA:
It's so. What's happened to us is worth lamenting.

HERMIONE:
Oh, don't say so! What news have you to tell?

ELECTRA:
It has been decreed by the country that Orestes and I
are to be put to death.

HERMIONE:

Oh no! You are so close to me.

ELECTRA:

It is settled. We have stepped into necessity's yoke. 1330

HERMIONE:

Is it because of this that the cry came from inside?

ELECTRA:

Yes, falling at Helen's knees, as a suppliant, he cries.

HERMIONE:

Who? I know no more unless you tell me.

ELECTRA:

Poor Orestes. He pleaded for his life and mine, too.

HERMIONE:

It was with good reason the house raised a cry. 1335

ELECTRA:

What else could give anyone more to cry about?
Come in and join your friends in supplication,
falling before your mother who is blessed by heaven,
not to let Menelaus stand by to see us put to death.
You were brought up at my mother's hands. 1340
Have pity on us and relieve us of our troubles.
Come in here to our ordeal—I will lead the way:
you alone hold out the hope of survival for us.

HERMIONE:

Of course. I will hurry into the house. As far
as it depends on me, you will survive.

ELECTRA:

You in the house, 1345
my friends in arms, will you not seize the prey?

HERMIONE:

Oh dear gods! Who are these men I see?

ORESTES: *(At the palace doors.)*

                                                    Be silent!
You are here to bring safety to us, not yourself.

ELECTRA:
Grab her, grab her. Hold the sword to her throat.
1350   Keep calm. Menelaus will learn this to his cost:
he has come upon real men, not craven Phrygians,
and he should not have treated us like degenerates.

    (Hermione is seized and pulled inside;
    exit Electra into the palace.)

[Choral Strophe][75]

CHORUS:
Io, io, friends,
Raise a shout, a shout and a cry
in front of the palace, so that the murder done
1355   will not strike terrible fear into the Argive people,
to make them run to the aid of the royal palace,
until I clearly see Helen lying dead
in a pool of her blood in the house,
or we hear the story from the servants.
1360   Some of the tragic events I know, but the rest not clearly.
In the name of justice, from the gods
retribution came upon Helen.
She filled all Greece with tears
because of deadly Paris, deadly man of Ida,
1365   who brought Greece against Troy.

CHORUS LEADER:
Shh, the bolts of the royal palace make a noise.
One of the Phrygian slaves is coming outside;
from him we will learn how it goes inside.

    (Phrygian slave enters from the palace in terror,
    leaping or climbing down from the roof.)

---

75. *1353–65:* This strophe is matched by the strophe beginning at 1537.
The unusual separation of the responding strophes sets the next section
apart as a self-contained scene.

PHRYGIAN SLAVE:[76]
Argive sword, jaws of death I have escaped
in my foreign slippers   1370
over cedar beams of chambers
and triglyphs of Doric façade—
gone, gone, my country, my country is gone—
in foreign flight.
Woe, woe!   1375
Where run strangers, flying up into gray air
or sea, where Ocean, with bull's head,
circles earth in his arms.

CHORUS LEADER:
What is it, man from Ida, Helen's slave?   1380

PHRYGIAN SLAVE:
Ilium, Ilium, alas, alas,
city of Phrygians and fertile
holy mountain of Ida, I lament your loss
in high keening song
with foreign cry—it was her face,   1385
bird-born, swan-feathered beauty,
Leda's hatch, Helen,
Ill-Helen,
avenging spirit
of Apollo's fine-built towers.
Ototoi. Wailing, wailing.   1390
Wasted Dardania, for horse rider Ganymede,
bed-partner of Zeus . . .

---

76. *1369 ff.*: When the door begins to open, the audience would expect
the eccyclema to be rolled out to reveal the result of the murder (as in
Euripides' *Electra*, for example) or a messenger to tell what happened (as in
Sophocles' *Antigone* after the suicide of Creon's wife). They are surprised
by the exotic appearance of one of Helen's foreign entourage. The Phrygian
slave speaks gibberish, but sensible gibberish. To get this across, articles
have been omitted and some words transposed from the normal English
order. Some critics suggest that he enters by jumping off the roof. Though
there may be comic elements in this scene, the slave's terror is real and
justified: he has just seen many of his fellow slaves butchered in a replay
of the horrific slaughter at the fall of Troy.

CHORUS LEADER:
Tell us clearly now everything that happened in the house.
[I do not understand what you said before.]⁷⁷

PHRYGIAN SLAVE:
1395 *Ailinon, ailinon,* foreigners sing, alas,
beginning of death
in Asian voice, when kings'
blood is spilled on earth by iron
swords of Death.
1400 They came into our halls—I tell you
every detail—two twin Greek lions.
One's father was commander in chief,
other, son of Strophius, evil-scheming man
like Odysseus, deceitful in silence,
1405 loyal to friends, ferocious in battle,
skillful warrior, bloody serpent.
Damn him for his secret plotting,
doer of evil.
Up to her throne they came,
throne of the woman archer Paris took as his wife,
1410 their eyes wasted with tears,
humbly they sat,
one this side, one that,
fencing her in.
They both put their arms around
1415 Helen's knees in supplication.
Up they leapt to scurry away,
the Phrygian attendants.
One said to another, in terror,
"I hope there is no treachery."
1420 To some it seemed nothing was to fear,
but others saw that serpent
mother-killer prepared to ensnare
in tight-meshed trap
Tyndareos' daughter.

---

77. *1394:* Suspected by editors as an unnecessary explanation of the previous line.

CHORUS LEADER:
  Where were you then? Or had you long since run in terror?   1425

PHRYGIAN SLAVE:
  In Phrygian style,
  it happened, beside Helen
  by Helen's head of curls, I was fanning,
  fanning with feathered circle
  fixed on long handle beside her face
  in exotic fashion.   1430
  She was twisting in her fingers
  flax on her distaff[78]
  and dropped thread down to floor
  desiring to make from Phrygian spoils
  robe of purple, adornment for her sister's tomb,   1435
  gift for Clytemnestra.
  Orestes spoke
  to our Spartan woman,
  "Daughter of Zeus, set your foot
  down here on ground, rising from your chair   1440
  and come to ancient hearth
  of Pelops our forefather,
  and hear what I have to say."
  He directs her. She follows
  not foreknowing what was about to happen.   1445
  His accomplice, evil Phocian,
  took care of all else.
  "Out of my way, Phrygian cowards!"
  He shut us out in different parts
  all over house: some
  in horse stables, others
  in outer buildings, others here and there,   1450
  keeping us far apart from our mistress.

CHORUS LEADER:
  What happened next after this?

---

78. *1431*: In Homer, *Odyssey* 4.130–35, when Helen makes her
appearance to greet Telemachus, she has with her a golden distaff along
with a silver basket on wheels and violet wool to work.

PHRYGIAN SLAVE:
Mighty Idaean mother,
mighty mother.
Woe for blood-soaked sufferings,
1455   lawless evils that I saw—I saw them
in kings' palace.
From hidden place under their purple-banded robes
drawing their swords in their hands
they turn their eyes this way, that way
to see if anyone is there.
Like wild mountain boars
1460   planting themselves in the woman's face
they address her, "You will die,
yes, you, die,
it is your coward of a husband who kills you,
betraying his brother's son
to die in Argos."
1465   She cried out,
cried, "Oh my god."
Casting her white arm against her breast,
she beat her poor head
with a blow. In attempt to run
she presses her gold-sandaled foot onto ground,
but Orestes stepping in front in his Mycenaean boot,
1470   shooting his fingers into her hair
forcing back her neck on her left shoulder
was ready to thrust black sword
deep into her throat.

CHORUS LEADER:
Where were you to help, all you Phrygians in the house?

PHRYGIAN SLAVE:
With a shout
through whole house, with bars we cast down
stable doors where we were kept back
1475   and run to her aid this way and that,
one took stones, another a bow,[79]

---

79. *1476:* "Bow" or "slings" (West 1987, p. 325).

another sword drawn in hand.
Pylades came against us,
unstoppable, he was like Hector
of Phrygia, like him or like Ajax with triple plume. 1480
I saw him, I saw him at Priam's gates.
Our sword points touched.
Then it was clear to see how much
inferior we Phrygians were
in Ares' might
to spears of Greece, 1485
one gone in flight, another already dead,
another wounded, a fourth begging
to ward off death.
In darkness we fled.
Bodies falling, others toppling, others lying dead.
Then came poor Hermione inside house 1490
at murder of her mother lying on ground,
poor woman who gave her life.
Like Bacchants running at her
but without sacred wands
they seize her in their arms
like a mountain cub. Back to Zeus' daughter
they reach to slaughter her.
But she is vanished from room
straight through their hands, 1495
Helen vanished—O Zeus and Earth
and light and night,
whether by spells
or witchcraft or the gods' spiriting away.
I know nothing that happened after this:
I took to my heels like thief from that house.
Troubles, toils and troubles 1500
Menelaus withstood, before he brought back
Helen from Troy, his wife, all in vain.

CHORUS LEADER:
Here is one more strange thing after all the rest:
and now I see Orestes coming out of the house
with hurried step, the sword still in his hand. 1505

(Enter Orestes.)

ORESTES:
Where is that man who escaped from the house and my sword?

PHRYGIAN SLAVE:
I prostrate myself, master, falling down to you in foreign
  fashion.

ORESTES:
You are not in Troy anymore, we are in Argive territory.

PHRYGIAN SLAVE:
Everywhere for sane men it's sweeter to live than to die.

ORESTES:
1510   Didn't you make an outcry to Menelaus to come help?

PHRYGIAN SLAVE:
I am here to help you since you are more worthy.

ORESTES:
Did Tyndareos' daughter die with justice then?

PHRYGIAN SLAVE:
With most justice—if she had three throats for slitting.

ORESTES:
Your coward's tongue flatters, but you don't feel it in your
  heart.

PHRYGIAN SLAVE:
1515   You're wrong—who else ruined Greece and Phrygians too?

ORESTES:
Swear it—or I'll kill you—that you are not saying it to flatter
  me.

PHRYGIAN SLAVE:
I swear on my very life, on which my oath is most true.

ORESTES:
Was the sword so terrifying to all you Phrygians in Troy, too?

PHRYGIAN SLAVE:
Move your sword. So close, it flashes bloody murder in my
eyes.

ORESTES:
You are afraid you will turn to stone as if you faced the
Gorgon. 1520

PHRYGIAN SLAVE:
Not stone, but corpse. I don't know your Gorgon's face.

ORESTES:
Even as a slave you fear death that would free you from woes?

PHRYGIAN SLAVE:
Every man, even if he is slave, enjoys being alive.

ORESTES:
Well spoken. Your intelligence saves you. Go inside now.

PHRYGIAN SLAVE:
You will not kill me?

ORESTES:
You are free to go.

PHRYGIAN SLAVE:
That is well spoken, too. 1525

ORESTES:
We might change our plans.

PHRYGIAN SLAVE:
That is not so well spoken.

(Exit Phrygian slave into the palace.)

ORESTES:
  Fool, if you think I could stand to bloody your neck:
  you are not a natural woman and you don't count as a man.[80]
  I came out of the house to keep you from raising the alarm—
1530 because Argos is quickly aroused when it hears a cry.
  I have no fear of Menelaus taking up his sword again;
  bring him on, parading his golden locks down to his shoulders;
  and if he recruits Argives and brings them to the palace,
  to prosecute Helen's murder, and is not willing to rescue
1535 me and my sister and Pylades, my accomplice in all we did,
  he will have two corpses to look at, his daughter and his wife.

      (Exit Orestes into the palace.)

           [Choral Antistrophe][81]

CHORUS:
  Oh, oh, bad luck,
  the house falls into another fearsome
  struggle, another clash around the sons of Atreus.

HALF CHORUS:
  What should we do? Report these doings to the city?
1540 Or keep quiet? That is safer, friends.

HALF CHORUS:
  Look, in front of the palace, this smoke
  billowing up into the air portends . . .

HALF CHORUS:
  They are lighting torches to set fire
  to Tantalus' house, and do not turn away from murder.

---

80. *1528:* Many readers believe that this means that the Phrygian is a
eunuch and, therefore, all the more unworthy of Orestes' manly act of
murder. Others take it as Orestes' gratuitous slur on the slave's supposed
cowardice.

81. *1537–48:* These lines are the metrical match to 1353–65, here the
chorus sings in two groups.

HALF CHORUS:
Divine power brings the outcome,   1545
whatever outcome it wants.

HALF CHORUS:
A mighty power of revenge has fallen,
fallen on these halls through blood,
all because of Myrtilus' plunge from the chariot.

Exodos

CHORUS LEADER:
Look, I see Menelaus hurrying along toward
the house. Somehow he found out what is going on.   1550
Waste no time fastening the locks with bolts,
children of Atreus inside. A prosperous man is hard
on those in trouble, as you are now, Orestes.

(Enter Menelaus stage right with his entourage.)

MENELAUS:
I heard of outrage done by that pair of wildcats—[82]
I cannot call them human—and here I am.   1555
I heard that my wife is not dead
but has disappeared into thin air—
someone, addled by fright, reported that to me,
an empty rumor and utter nonsense—
these are the deeds of the mother-killers.   1560
Someone open these doors! I'm telling
you servants to push open the doors so that
at least I can rescue my daughter from
the hands of murderers and take away
my poor dear wife's body for whose death   1565
these killers will soon die by my hand.

*(Orestes and Pylades, with Hermione
between them, appear on the rooftop.)*

---

82. 1554–59: Menelaus has been informed by the Phrygian or another of
his wife's attendants.

ORESTES:

    Hey, you there, do not touch those bolts—
    Menelaus, I mean you, swelling up in pride,
    or I will smash your head with this stone,
1570   tearing it off the parapet, the builders' work.
    The locks are fixed with bolts, which will keep
    you out of the house, however eager you are.

MENELAUS:

    What is going on? I see the gleam of torches,
    and these people holding siege on the palace towers,
1575   and a sword pressed against my daughter's neck.

ORESTES:

    Do you want to ask me anything or hear me out?

MENELAUS:

    Neither, but it looks like I will have to listen.

ORESTES:

    If you care to know, I am going to kill your daughter.

MENELAUS:

    You killed Helen. You want to add more and more killing?

ORESTES:

1580   If only I had managed it, not had it stolen by the gods.

MENELAUS:

    You deny you killed her and insult me with this?

ORESTES:

    The denial pains me. I wish I had succeeded.

MENELAUS:

    In doing what? You make my blood turn cold.

ORESTES:

    In casting Greece's pollution down into Hades.

MENELAUS:

1585   Let me have my wife's body so I can bury it.

ORESTES:
Demand this of the gods. But I *will* kill your child.

MENELAUS:
The mother-killer will add more killings to that one?

ORESTES:
Avenger of his father, whom you betrayed to his death.

MENELAUS:
Isn't it enough, your mother's blood on your hands?

ORESTES:
I could never get tired of killing bad women, never!   1590

MENELAUS:
And you, Pylades, did you take part in this killing?

ORESTES:
He says yes, though he doesn't speak. I speak for him.[83]

MENELAUS:
You will not get away with this unless you are able to fly.

ORESTES:
We will not fly away. We will set the house on fire.

MENELAUS:
Will you really destroy your ancestral home?   1595

ORESTES:
Yes. You'll never get it, and I'll sacrifice her on the pyre.

MENELAUS:
Keep killing—kill and you'll pay the price for your killing.

ORESTES:
It will be exactly as I've said.

---

83. *1592:* Pylades is now played by a nonspeaking extra.

MENELAUS:

                              Ah, no. Do not do this!

ORESTES:
    Be silent now. Endure your just deserts.

MENELAUS:
    Is it right for you to live?

ORESTES:

1600   Yes, and to rule the country.

MENELAUS:
    What country?

ORESTES:
                Here in Argos, my ancestral land.

MENELAUS:
    Would you touch the purifying waters?

ORESTES:
                            Yes, why not?

MENELAUS:
    Would you strike the victims before battle?

ORESTES:
                           —And would you?

MENELAUS:
    My hands are clean.

ORESTES:
                  But not your heart.

MENELAUS:
    Who would speak to you?

ORESTES:

1605   Anyone who loves his father.

MENELAUS:
And anyone who respects his mother?

ORESTES:
Is a lucky man.

MENELAUS:
Not you for sure.

ORESTES:
I do not like bad women.

MENELAUS:
Take the sword from my daughter's neck.

ORESTES:
Useless words.

MENELAUS:
You really will kill my daughter?

ORESTES:
That's the truth.

MENELAUS:
Ah me. What shall I do?

ORESTES:
Go to the Argives and convince them . . .   1610

MENELAUS:
Convince them of what?

ORESTES:
Not to put us to death. Entreat the city.

MENELAUS:
Or else you will murder my child?

ORESTES:
That's how it is.

MENELAUS:
   Wretched Helen . . .

ORESTES:

                    Aren't my affairs wretched, too?

MENELAUS:
   I brought you home from Troy to be a victim.

ORESTES:

                                   If only it were so.

MENELAUS:
   After undergoing ten thousand troubles.

ORESTES:

1615   Except on my behalf.

MENELAUS:
   I have suffered terribly.

ORESTES:

                        Because you wouldn't help me then.

MENELAUS:
   You have me.

ORESTES:
                    You have trapped yourself.
   Go ahead, Electra, set fire to the palace from below,
   and you, Pylades, most trusted of my friends,
1620   start the fire on the roof over the walls.

MENELAUS:
   Land of Danaans, citizens of Argos, home of horses,
   arm yourselves and come quickly to my aid.
   This man has foully shed the blood of his mother
   and to save his life, would bring down the whole city.

(Apollo flies in on the machine.)[84]

APOLLO:

Menelaus, stop sharpening your temper's edge.   1625
It is I, Phoebus, son of Leto, drawing near to call you.
And you, Orestes, with sword in hand to assault
this girl, hear what message I have come to bring.
You were eager to eliminate Helen, in your desire
to infuriate Menelaus, but you have lost her.   1630
[Here she is—you see her in the folds of the air,
rescued and not dying at your hands.][85]
I rescued her from your sword, as you can see,
at my father's command, and stole her away to safety.
She is Zeus' daughter and is fated to live on[86]   1635
forever in heaven's folds. She will be seated beside
Castor and Polydeuces, a patron to seafaring men.
Take another bride to keep in your home,
since through her beauty the gods brought
together the Greeks and Trojans and caused   1640
deaths, so they might drain from earth
the offense of men's boundless hordes.[87]
That is Helen's status. Orestes, now, you must
travel beyond the borders of this country
and live on the Parrhasian plain for a year's cycle.   1645

---

84. *1625:* "On the machine"—It is possible that Apollo appears on the *theologeion* (god platform) on the rooftop. In that case Helen would follow him onstage and he would point to her at 1633. The rooftop might be getting a bit crowded with Orestes, Hermione, and Pylades already there. If the *mēchanē* is used, the figure of Helen would appear behind Apollo. This is a truly spectacular scene, using all the levels of the playing space.

85. *1631–32:* Suspect because these lines do not mesh well with what follows. See Willink 1986, pp. 351–52.

86. *1635:* There is a play on words here: "of Zeus," in Greek *Zēnos,* is related in a fanciful etymology to "to live" (*zēn*).

87. *1639–42:* Euripides exculpates Helen more thoroughly in a brief reference in his *Electra* (1280–81) and in *Helen*. According to this story she was marooned in Egypt, remaining faithful to Menelaus throughout the Trojan War, while the Greeks and the Trojans fought the ten-years' war over her *eidolon* (phantom fashioned in her image). Helen was rescued by Menelaus when he arrived in Egypt after the war.

It will be called by the Azanes and Arcadians
Oresteion, named after your year of exile.[88]
From there set out for the city of the Athenians
to undergo a trial for your murdered mother's blood
1650   by the three Eumenides. The gods, judges of the trial,[89]
will each give a most sacred vote on Ares' Hill:
it is preordained that you will be acquitted.
It is destined, Orestes, that you are to marry her,
Hermione, at whose neck you are holding your sword.
1655   Neoptolemus thinks he will marry her but he never will.
His fate is to die by the sword of Delphi's citizens
as he demands justice from me for the death,
of his father Achilles.[90] Give your sister, as arranged,
to Pylades to be his bride: a happy life awaits him.
1660   Menelaus, allow Orestes to rule over Argos,
and you, go be king of the land of Sparta,
your wife's dowry gift to you. Though she put you
through ten thousand toils, this was always the goal.
For him I will set things right in the city since
1665   it was I who compelled him to kill his mother.

ORESTES:
Prophetic Loxias, you were not a false prophet
then, in your oracles, but true. And yet a fear
went through my mind that I seemed to hear
your voice, but really heard some demon out of hell.
1670   Still there will be a happy ending and I will obey.
Look, I release Hermione from slaughter and I accept
her in marriage, if her father gives me her hand.

---

88. *1644–47:* In Euripides' *Electra*, Orestes is exiled from Argos to live in a city "by the streams of Alpheus near the sacred Lycian precinct" (1274), which will be named after him, that is, in Arcadia on the Parrhasian plain. In *Electra* he never sets foot in his native city (1250–51, 1273–75). "Parrhasian plain"—a play on the word *parrhesia*, Greek for "freedom of speech," or in its negative sense, "license of tongue," Tantalus' crime (10), and is used of the speaker who advocates the death sentence (905).

89. *1650:* In Aeschylus' *Furies (Eumenides)* the judges were Athenian citizens. The older tragedian pointedly made the outcome of the trial the result of humans and gods working together.

90. *1655–58:* See Euripides, *Andromache* 1085 ff.

MENELAUS:
Helen, daughter of Zeus, farewell. I bless you
for dwelling in the happy home of the gods.
Orestes, to you I betroth my daughter,   1675
since Phoebus commands it. Well-born with
a well-born bride, be as happy as I am who give her.

APOLLO:
Go, each, where I have directed you
and end your quarrels.

MENELAUS:
                    I must obey.

ORESTES:
And I the same. Menelaus, I make my peace   1680
with events, and with your oracles, Loxias.

APOLLO:
Go now on your way, paying honor
to Peace, fairest of gods. And I
shall escort Helen to Zeus' halls
passing beyond the vault of shining stars   1685
where she will be enthroned beside Hera
and Hebe, Heracles' wife. She will be a goddess, forever
honored with libations poured by all mankind,
along with the Tyndaridae, twin sons of Zeus,
a goddess queen of the sea for sailors.   1690

CHORUS:
O great Victory, awesome goddess,[91]
sustain my life and never
withhold your crown.

—END—

---

91. *1690–93:* The same choral tag is used at the end of Euripides' *Iphigenia among the Tauri* and *Phoenician Women.*

Select Bibliography

Burkert, Walter. *Greek Religion.* Translated by John Raffan. Cambridge, MA: Harvard University Press, 1985.

Burnett, Anne Pippin. *Catastrophe Survived: Euripides' Plays of Mixed Reversal.* Oxford: Clarendon Press, 1971.

Cropp, Martin J. *Euripides:* Electra. *With Translation and Commentary.* Warminster, UK: Aris & Phillips, 1988.

———. *Euripides:* Iphigenia in Tauris. *With Translation and Commentary.* Warminster, UK: Aris & Phillips, 2000.

Cropp, Martin J., Kevin H. Lee, and David Sansone. *Euripides and Tragic Theatre in the Late Fifth Century. (Illinois Classical Studies* 24–25). Champaign, IL: Stipes, 2000.

Damen, Mark. "Electra's Monody and the Role of the Chorus in Euripides' *Orestes* 960–1012." *Transactions of the American Philological Association* 120 (1990): 133–45.

Denniston, J. D. *Euripides:* Electra. *With Introduction and Commentary.* Oxford: Oxford University Press, 1939.

Diggle, James *Euripidis Fabulae* Vols. 2, 3. Oxford: Clarendon Press, 1981, 1994.

Dunn, Francis M. "Comic and Tragic License in Euripides' *Orestes.*" *Classical Antiquity* 8 (1989): 238–51.

Egan, Rory B. "Electra and the Sword at Euripides' *Orestes* 1041." *Hermes* 127 (1999): 382–83.

Euben, J. Peter. "Political Corruption in Euripides' *Orestes.*" In *Greek Tragedy and Political Theory,* 222–51. Berkeley: University of California Press, 1986.

Falkner, Thomas M. "Coming of Age in Argos: Physis and Paideia in Euripides' *Orestes.*" *Classical Journal* 78 (1983): 289–300.

Gellie, George. "Tragedy and Euripides' *Electra.*" *Bulletin of the Institute of Classical Studies* 28 (1981): 1–12.

Goff, Barbara. "The Violence of Community: Ritual in the *Iphigenia in Tauris.*" *Bucknell Review* 43: 109–28. Reprinted in *Rites of Passage in Ancient Greece,* edited by Mark Padilla. Lewisburg, PA: Bucknell University Press, 1999.

Gregory, Justina. "Comic Elements in Euripides." In Cropp et al., *Euripides and Tragic Theatre in the Late Fifth Century,* 2000, 59–74.

———. Introduction to Meineck et al., *The Electra Plays* (2009), vi–xxxii.

Hall, Edith. "The Geography of Euripides' *Iphigeneia among the Taurians.*" *American Journal of Philology* 108 (1987): 427–33.

Halleran, Michael R. *Stagecraft in Euripides.* Totowa, NJ: Barnes and Noble Books, 1984.

Hammond, N. G. L. "Spectacle and Parody in Euripides' *Electra.*" *Greek, Roman, and Byzantine Studies* 25 (1984): 373–87.

Hartigan, Karelisa V. *Ambiguity and Self-Deception: The Apollo and Artemis Plays of Euripides.* Frankfurt am Main: Peter Lang, 1991.

———. *(Re)Making Tragedy: Charles Mee and Greek Drama.* CreateSpace: an Amazon.com company, 2011.

Jones, John. *On Aristotle and Greek Tragedy.* Oxford: Oxford University Press, 1962.

de Jong, I. J. F. "Three Off-Stage Characters in Euripides." *Mnemosyne,* 4th ser., 43 (1990): 1–21.

Knox, B. M. W. "Euripidean Comedy." In *Word and Action: Essays on the Ancient Theater,* 250–74. Baltimore: Johns Hopkins University Press, 1979.

Kubo, M. "The Norm of Myth: Euripides' *Electra.*" *Harvard Studies in Classical Philology* 71 (1966): 15–31.

Kyriakou, Poulheria. *A Commentary on Euripides'* Iphigenia in Tauris. Berlin: De Gruyter, 2006.

Lloyd, Michael. *The* Agon *in Euripides.* Oxford: Clarendon Press, 1992.

Lombardo, Stanley, tr. *Homer,* Odyssey. Indianapolis: Hackett, 2000.

Loraux, Nicole. *Tragic Ways of Killing a Woman.* Translated by Anthony Forster. Cambridge, MA: Harvard University Press, 1987.

Luschnig, C. A. E. *The Gorgon's Severed Head: Studies of* Alcestis, Electra, *and* Phoenissae. Leiden: Brill, 1995.

Luschnig, Cecelia Eaton, and Paul Woodruff, tr. *Euripides:* Electra, Phoenician Women, Bacchae, Iphigenia at Aulis. *Introduction by Cecelia Eaton Luschnig.* Indianapolis: Hackett, 2011.

Marshall, C. W. "Theatrical Reference in Euripides' *Electra.*" In Cropp et al., *Euripides and Tragic Theatre* (2000), 325–41.

———. "*Iphigenia in Tauris* 1391–7." *Classical Quarterly* 57 (2007): 749–52.

Mastronarde, Donald J. "Actors on High: The Skene Roof, the Crane, and the Gods in Attic Drama." *Classical Antiquity* 9 (1990): 247–94.

Mee, Charles, L. *Orestes 2.0*. Available at http://www.charlesmee.org/ html/orestes.html, 1992.

Meineck, Peter, tr. *Aeschylus:* Oresteia. Indianapolis: Hackett, 1998.

Meineck, Peter, and Paul Woodruff, tr. *Sophocles: The Theban Plays*. Indianapolis: Hackett, 2003.

Meineck, Peter, Cecelia Eaton Luschnig, and Paul Woodruff, tr. *Aeschylus, Euripides, Sophocles: The Electra Plays*. Introduction by Justina Gregory. Indianapolis: Hackett, 2009.

Michelini, Ann Norris. *Euripides and the Tragic Tradition*. Madison: University of Wisconsin Press, 1987.

Mossman, Judith, ed. *Euripides*. Oxford Readings in Classical Studies. Oxford: Oxford University Press, 2003.

Murray, Gilbert. *Euripidis Fabulae*, Vols. 2, 3. Oxford: Clarendon Press, 1913.

O'Brien, M. J. "Pelopid History and the Plot of *Iphigenia in Tauris*." *Classical Quarterly* 38 (1988): 98–115.

Page, Denys. *Actors' Interpolations in Greek Tragedy*. Oxford: Clarendon Press, 1934.

Platnauer, Maurice *Euripides:* Iphigenia in Tauris. Oxford: Clarendon Press, 1938.

Porter, John R. *Studies in Euripides'* Orestes. Leiden: Brill, 1994.

Prag, A. J. N. W. *The* Oresteia: *Iconographic and Narrative Tradition*. Chicago: Bolchazy Carducci, 1985.

Pucci, Pietro. "Euripides Heautontimoroumenos." *Transactions of the American Philological Association* 98 (1967): 365–71.

Reid, Jane Davidson, with Chris Rohmann. *The Oxford Guide to Classical Mythology in the Arts, 1300–1990s*. Oxford: Oxford University Press, 1993.

Reinhardt, Karl. "The Intellectual Crisis in Euripides" (1960). In Mossman (2003), 16–46.

Roisman, H. M., and C. A. E. Luschnig. *Euripides'* Electra: *A Commentary*. Norman, OK: University of Oklahoma Press, 2011.

Sansone, D. "The Sacrifice-Motif in Euripides' *Iphigenia in Tauris*." *Transactions and Proceedings of the American Philological Association* 105 (1975): 283–95.

Smith, J. A., and C. Kelly. "Stylistic Constancy and Change across Literary Corpora: Using Measures of Lexical Richness to Date Works." *Computers and the Humanities* 36 (2002): 411–30.

Smith, Wesley D. "Disease in Euripides' *Orestes*." *Hermes* 95 (1967): 291–307.

Schwartz, Eduard. *Scholia in Euripidem*. Berlin: Reimer, 1887. Reprinted Berlin: Walter de Gruyter, 1966.

Trieschnigg, Caroline P. "Iphigenia's Dream in Euripides' *Iphigenia Taurica*." *Classical Quarterly* 58 (2008): 461–78.

Tzanetou, Angeliki. "Almost Dying, Dying Twice: Ritual and Audience in Euripides' *Iphigenia in Tauris*." In Cropp et al., *Euripides and Tragic Theater in the Late Fifth Century*, 2000, 119–216.

Verrall, A. W. *Essays on Four Plays of Euripides*. Cambridge: Cambridge University Press, 1905.

West, Martin L *Euripides:* Orestes. *With Translation and Commentary*. Warminster, UK: Aris and Phillips, 1987.

Whitman, Cedric H. *Euripides and the Full Circle of Myth*. Cambridge, MA: Harvard University Press, 1974.

Willink, C. W. *Euripides:* Orestes. *With Introduction and Commentary*. Oxford: Clarendon Press, 1986.

Wolff, C. "Euripides' *Iphigeneia among the Taurians*: Aetiology, Ritual, and Myth." *Classical Antiquity* 11 (1992): 308–34.

Wright, Matthew. *Euripides' Escape-Tragedies: A Study of* Helen, Andromeda *and* Iphigenia among the Taurians. Oxford: Oxford University Press, 2005.

———. *Euripides:* Orestes. Duckworth Companions to Greek and Roman Tragedy. London: Duckworth, 2008.

Zeitlin, Froma I. "The Argive Festival of Hera and Euripides' *Electra*." *Transactions and Proceedings of the American Philological Association* 101 (1970): 645–69.

———. "The Closet of Masks: Role-Playing and Myth-Making in the *Orestes* of Euripides" (1980). In Mossman 2003: 309–41.

Glossary of Theatrical Terms

agōn: A formal debate in which characters deliver speeches (often of equal length).

antistrophe: see Stasimon

chorus: A group of fifteen male non-professional actors who sang and danced between the spoken scenes of the play. The **chorus leader** speaks for the group in scenes of dialogue with other characters.

eccyclema: A device rolled out of the *skēnē* to reveal what has taken place in the house.

eisodos (plural: *eisodoi*): see Parados (2)

episode: The dialogue portion of the play, consisting of speeches and back-and-forth conversation, between the choral odes. There are usually between three and five episodes in a play.

epode: see Stasimon

exodos: The part of the play after the last choral song.

kommos: A lament or song of mourning shared by chorus and actors.

mēchanē: The flying machine, a crane, used to stage the arrival of gods who take part in the plays. The crane lifted actors above the scene building.

mesode: see Stasimon

messenger speech: A narrative delivered by a character coming from offstage to describe actions that have taken place elsewhere.

orchestra: The circular area of the theater used for choral singing, dancing, and most acting.

parodos (plural: **parodoi**): (1) parodos, the entrance song of the chorus. This is sometimes shared between the chorus and one of the actors, as happens in the three Orestes plays. (2) *parodos,* a side entrance for choral entry and exit and for actors coming from or going to offstage places. Also known as an *eisodos.*

prologue: The part of a play before the entrance of the chorus. This is usually a monologue or a monologue followed by a dialogue, as in all three Orestes plays.

skēnē: The scene building, a flat-roofed structure with double doors, used for changes of mask and costume and many exits and entrances of actors.

stasimon (plural: **stasima**): A choral song and dance. The songs are divided into *strophes* and *antistrophes,* stanzas and matching stanzas (literally, "turnings" and "opposite turnings"). An unmatched stanza is called a *mesode* if it occurs between one strophe/antistrophe pair and the next. It is called an *epode* if it comes after the last antistrophe.

stichomythia: Dialogue in which single lines are spoken in turn by two or more characters.

strophe: see Stasimon

theologeion: God-platform, the top of the scene building.